MW00571746

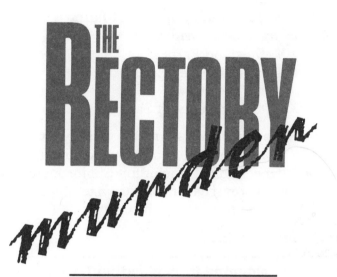

THE RECTORY murder

THE MYSTERIOUS CRIME THAT SHOCKED TURN-OF-THE-CENTURY NEW BRUNSWICK

KENNETH SAUNDERS

James Lorimer & Company, Publishers
Toronto, 1989

This book is for Linda,
and for Sara and Jenny,
without whose love and support and faith
it would not have been written;
and for my Mother and Father,
who have been waiting the longest

Cover Photos: Tom Barnes

Canadian Cataloguing in Publication Data

Saunders, Kenneth.
   The Rectory Murder

ISBN 1-55028-271-9 (bound)   -   ISBN 1-55028-273-5 (pbk).

1. McAuley, Mary Ann. 2. Collins, Tom. 3. Murder - New Brunswick - New Ireland.   4. Trials (Murder) - New Brunswick - New Ireland. 5. Crime and criminals - New Brunswick. I. Title.

HV6535.C33N48 1989   364.1'523'0924   C89-094962-X

James Lorimer & Company, Publishers
Egerton Ryerson Memorial Building
35 Britain Street
Toronto, Ontario M5A 1R7

Printed and bound in Canada

5 4 3 2 1 89 90 91 92 93

Contents

Acknowledgements

Foreword

Prologue

1	Wednesday, November 13, 1907	1
2	Gone to Dust	23
3	Monday, August 20, 1906	46
4	Tuesday, August 21, 1906	85
5	Wednesday, August 22, 1906	100
6	Thursday, August 23, 1906	124
7	Friday, August 24, 1906	145
8	Saturday, August 25, 1906	155
	Sunday, August 26, 1906	
9	September-December, 1906	176
10	The First Trial	191
	January, 1907	
11	The Second and Third Trials	236
	February-October, 1907	
12	"Not a Proper Person To Be Executed"	265
13	Thursday, November 14, 1907	286
	Friday, November 15, 1907	

Southern New Brunswick

Fredericton

Moncton

Salisbury

Petitcodiac

Hillsborough

Dorchester

Hopewell Cape

Amherst

Elgin

Riverside-Albert

New Ireland

SHEPODY BAY

Alma

CHIGNECTO BAY

Nova Scotia

Bonny River

LAKE UTOPIA

Saint John

SPRUCE LAKE

Musquash

Lepreau

St. George

Maine

BAY OF FUNDY

Moncton

to Cocagne Ferry

I. C. R.

Salisbury

S & H RAILWAY

Petitcodiac

THE PRONG

Hillsborough

St.

Dorchester Penitentiary

The Glen

William Berry

GOWLAND MOUNTAIN

Blacksmith Shop
Ruth Leaman

CALEDONIA MTN.

Hopewell Cape

THE ROCKS

to Saint John

St. Isadore
N.B.

Elgin

KENT ROAD

CHAPEL HILL

HOPEWELL HILL

SHEPODY MTN.

DUFFY HILL

Teahan's Corner

Jimmy Doyle

Sara Williamson
St. Agatha's
Rectory

PRIEST LAKE

Riverside

Albert

Harvey

Harvey Bank

Mary's Point

Grindstone Island

Harvey Mtn.

ALBERT COUNTY

N

legend
✝ Father M'Auley's Chapels
-·-·- roads
++++ railways
..·.. ferry

Acknowledgements

I wish to thank, especially, the late Iva Williamson Fullerton Kennie, for sharing her memories and for giving life back to a time that is past; and these — some of them gone now, too — for their recollections and yarns: Dudley (Tim) and Gwen Saunders, Mrs. George Keohan (Lena Campbell), Fred O'Connor, John O'Connor, Jim Rossiter, Mrs. Joe Rossiter (Clara Duffy), Mrs Theresa McKinley, Mrs. Leonard Steeves (Maimie), Bill West, Georgie McFarlane, Bennie McKinley, Sister Ellen Murphy, Mrs. Florence Newcombe, Mrs. Frances Stewart, Mrs. Millie Goddard, George Robinson, Gerald Dimock, Mr. and Mrs. Walter Milburn, Harold Terris, Mrs. Ralph Myers (for Collins' letter to her grandmother);

For their special and individual enthusiasms: good friends George Taylor, Brian Lewis, George Geldart, Tom Barnes (pictures), Linda Saunders (maps), Donna Beaton (advice), and Norbert Cunningham (sound);

For their help with the research, the staffs of the Albert County Museum at Hopewell Cape, the National Archives of Canada, the New Brunswick Museum, the Archives of Mount Allison University, the Mount Allison University Library, the University of New Brunswick Library, the Moncton Public Library, the Moncton Museum and the Saint John Public Library;

For generous financial assistance, the Canada Council; and for their help in keeping the project going: Dr. David Beatty of Mount Allison University, and David Jonah;

For his enthusiasm and sound editorial suggestions, Curtis Fahey.

I would like to acknowledge, too, Maimie (Widbur) Steeves' *Fundy Folklore*, and turn-of-the-century history students Albert W. Smith and Orland R. Atkinson, B.J. Grant's *Six for the Hangman*, Arthur T. Doyle's *Front Benches and Back rooms*, F.W. Robinson's *Hanging in Canada*, J.E. Belliveau's 1971 article in the *Atlantic Advocate*, P.M. Toner's *New Ireland Remembered* and George Taylor's *A History of Salisbury 1771-1984*.

Also useful were the third trial transcripts and preliminary hearing transcripts housed at the Albert County Museum, the New Brunswick Archives and the National Archives of Canada (where there is a 1,000-page file on the Collins' case); and the local newspapers' coverage of the story.

Foreword

When the bones of Tom Collins were disinterred from their place of rest beside the Albert County jail in the fall of 1966 (sixty years after they had been put there), they were not white. "The shovel hit something hard," recalled a county man who witnessed the exhumation, "and it was the skull. There was nothing else there but the bones, and they were sort of a reddish brown colour; they weren't white like in pictures, and they were all separated, the membranes and muscles were all gone." There was no coffin at all; or if there had been, it had long since become one with the dirt. The jumble of bones was placed into a small casket, like a baby's casket, and taken to the pauper's section of Lower Cape cemetery, a short distance down county, where it was re-interred. Sometime after that, a small stone was erected over the new plot. A misspelled inscription beneath a simple cross tells you: "THOMAS F. COLLINS IMMAGRANT FROM ENGLAND HANGED AT HOPEWELL CAPE 1907 FOR THE MURDER OF MARY ANN McAULEY AT NEW IRELAND ALBERT CO., N.B. R.I.P."

Before the remains were moved to Lower Cape — by order of the county council, in one of its last acts before it was abolished in a restructuring ordered by the provincial government — most people did not know the location of the Collins' grave in the jailyard. There are those who say that grass had never grown over it, because of a curse Collins delivered before he was hanged. (There *is* grass at Lower Cape.) Some may have been surprised there were bones in the grave at all — red or white. Tom Collins was not hanged, they will tell you; he was spirited from the jail by friends on the eve of his execution. Another story claims that he *was* hanged, but that his body was carried by friends down the hill to the Hopewell Cape dock at midnight, where it was placed aboard a vessel that took it overseas so his rich family could bury it in the land of his birth. Then again, a newspaper report which appeared a few months after the execution (with no attribution whatsoever) claimed that Collins' father had been executed in England, and his mother, who was still living, was a harlot. ("The story of Collins' confession, as briefly outlined here," the paper announced with a who-dares-question-it? air, "can be accepted by the readers of the Times as absolutely correct, as it is vouched for by the most reliable authority." What authority? No one knows.)

There was a great deal of speculation, following the execution, that Collins had admitted killing the woman, but there is no public record proving that he did, and those closest to him at the time adamantly and consistently denied it. Besides, it was not Collins at all who did in Mary Ann, some people (if you catch them in the right frame of mind) will tell you, it was really the priest (Father McAuley, for whom she worked). Why? She was pregnant with the priest's baby (even though she was fifty-two years old at the time of her death). Or she had found, by happenstance, a valuable nugget of gold in the New Ireland hills and greedily refused, to the death, to reveal where she had discovered it. Or the priest was having an affair with Collins and, somehow, she got in the way. There are other stories. Mary Ann was killed by a neighbour (or other intruder), but Collins was an unlucky and convenient scapegoat. All of the jurymen who found the young Englishman guilty at the trials came to tragic ends, it is said, like the man who bound himself with rope and threw himself into a river.

The Moncton Daily Times, in its 1908 story, beneath the headline "Thomas Collins Left a Full and Complete Confession," cited no sources at all, not even unnamed ones. "There has always been a lingering doubt in the minds of a few whether a mere youth, such as Collins, could have the hardihood to commit such a deed alone, and there has been a vast amount of curiosity on the part of the people of the province as to just how the brutal affair occurred. It has been felt that it would be a great relief and satisfaction to the public if a full confession of the crime could have been given out, but up to the present time the veil has never been lifted from the mystery in which the case was shrouded. This correspondent, however, is now in a position for the first time to give the facts of the confession entrusted by the executed boy to those who attended him at the execution." He adds that, at the time of execution, "it was believed that Collins made a confession, but those entrusted with the condemned man's confidence could not be persuaded to divulge the secret, and so far as the public had knowledge the young sailor went to his death on the scaffold protesting his innocence. But now, several months after the final act in the grim tragedy, comes the full confession."

The people, it seemed *needed* a confession, whether one was given or not. The county, it is true, was divided on the question of Collins' guilt, and there were many people who believed he should not have been hanged, even if he was guilty. At the time of the McAuley tragedy, the county had a strong religious element — Methodist, Baptist, Anglican — and while there were many people who believed in an eye for an eye, there were others who believed capital punishment, whether legal or not, was wrong. The fact, too, that Collins *seemed* to be a Protestant boy accused of a crime against a Catholic household may have further complicated feelings about the case. It has been said, too, that Mary Ann was not well-liked and there were people who would claim, however callously, that she had got no better than she deserved, whether Collins had done the deed or not.

I do not remember when I first heard of the New Ireland murder. I grew up on a small farm in the western part of the 710-square-mile county, a fair distance (in country miles) from both the site of the murder and the scene of the trials. I suppose I had heard about it many times over the years, listening in, as kids will do, on the conversations of the adults around them. I imagine, too, the prejudice in our neck of the woods was that it was the priest who had done it. But because it had not happened in our neighbourhood, so to speak, it was always rather a distant event, in place as well as time.

Many years later (but some years ago now), while I was researching an old Albert County railway line, the Collins case gratuitously reappeared. I talked to Millie Goddard at Elgin, a lady well into her eighties by then, who had been the last station agent for the railway. One of the most vivid memories of her career, she told me immediately, was of that hot August day back in 1906 when Tom Collins, the New Ireland killer, came on the run to Elgin station looking for the train. Unfortunately, Millie said, she had decided to play hookey from her part-time job at the train station that day to go swimming with her friends. As a result, she missed meeting the infamous axe murderer. It was probably just as well, she said, but then she added that she had never forgotten her playful decision to go swimming, and had always regretted it.

Millie's vivid memory, I can say now in hindsight, blew some of the dust from an old tale that was part of county lore. More years would pass before I actively began to look into the case, but I think a germ was planted then. It began to dawn on me that this was not just a legend or a folktale, it had been a real event lived by real people. When eventually I started gathering material, I was amazed to discover both how much documentation actually existed and how little was actually known about the case. I slowly began to seek out material and to interview older residents of the county, who might, I thought at the beginning, be able to shed more light on the Collins story. Most had opinions passed down by parents or other relatives or neighbours, but none had a direct connection with the 1906 events in New Ireland. None, that is, until I met Iva (Williamson) Kennie.

Iva, who has since passed on, not only had been born and raised in New Ireland, she actually had met, talked to, and gone fishing with the axe murderer. She had clear memories of the man, of the settlement, of the people, of the rectory, of the priest, and of Mary Ann, too, all long since gone to dust. And her telling me of those people gave them all life again in some sense because, though she was a child at the time, she had been one of them. So I began to see that telling the story of the New Ireland tragedy meant, also, telling as best I could about the place, the time and the people. This is what I have attempted to do with this book, and the way in which I have tried to do it requires, I think, a brief comment.

When I finally had possession of what I believed was all the material available on the murder and the trials (literally thousands of pages of transcripts, court documents, petitions, letters, and newspaper stories) I had some difficult decisions to make about the best way to tell the story. Because there were three trials with similar presentations of evidence (and a well-documented preliminary hearing), how could I give a chronological account of the events without tedious repetition? The answer was to sift through all the accounts of all the witnesses at all the trials, and put together a single narrative based on all the circumstantial evidence that eventually convicted Collins. That is the first part of the book, which details Collins' activities leading up to the killing and immediately following it. There are long sections where the participants speak in their own voices. These are constructed as accurately as possible from a number of sources: from the complete transcript of the third trial, from the transcript of the preliminary hearings, and from the extremely detailed stories of the daily newspaper journalists (especially for the first and second trials, transcripts of which have not survived). They are distinguished from direct quotations by a simple device: they are preceded by the participant's name in italics.

A newspaper of the time reported: "The Collins trials are unique in the criminal history of New Brunswick, if not in Canada. It is the first time, it is believed, that a prisoner sentenced to death in this province was granted a new trial on the ground of misdirection by the court and it is also the first time, not only in the history of the courts of New Brunswick but in the history of the courts of Canada, that a prisoner has been tried three times on the same charge of murder." That may be. No one I have spoken with has been able to affirm or deny the statements, and I confess that I did not spend a lot of time looking into it.

I was more concerned with telling a living story, even if that life was only inside my own imagination. These were real people, to whom real things happened. The oral histories, so generously given, and the other non-Collins county material I had gathered, were essential to sketch in the background against which the McAuley-Collins tragedy was played out. I sometimes think that my purpose in telling the more dramatic crime story was to create an opportunity to tell the story of the county, which is what I really wanted to do anyway. In any event, some of the county's voices are also given here. These are not the voices of specific individuals, but rather of imaginary ones. Whenever they enter the narrative, they are introduced with the italicized phrase "A Voice." They are not placed within quotation marks because their statements are not direct quotes. I have manipulated, sometimes truncated, sometimes juggled (never, I hope, distorted or falsified) their many stories in whatever way I felt was needed to have the one story told in the best way. I hope I have not done it (or them) too much damage.

Kenneth Saunders
Riverview, N.B.
October 1989

Prologue

Iva's Story, July 1982

———————————

Picture her when she was young, a beautiful eight-year-old child with a broad open face, wide dark eyes gazing out of the picture, lower lip drawn in by her teeth. No smile; photographers frowned on smiles in those days — seventy-five years ago — because the subject had to be still to make a good exposure. So she stands in a hayfield in a frilly white dress, lace on the shoulders and on the sleeves, which stop just below her elbows, embroidery on the hem, the other details lost in the antiquated light (over-exposed, after all). Her arms hang at her sides, straight and relaxed, her hands turned toward her thighs, fingers and thumbs curved gently to form of the palms tiny delicate cups. Thick hair, black in the photograph, falls behind her left shoulder, but rests in tangles on the right. Over her wide smooth forehead is the flat brim of a shallow-crowned straw hat, tilted slightly to the side, held in place by a ribbon, its bow poised like a butterfly at her right temple. Her legs are encased in black stockings. Behind her, the dim mass of the spruce forest.

Her name is Iva and, seventy-five years after the picture was made, the eyes still glow over a cup of tea and a scatter of old pictures.

Thickly-needled spruce branches stretch toward the small figure in the old photograph; one bough seems to reach like a hand for the brim of her hat. If there was menace in the murky woods, surely it's imagined now, for then she was just another child dressed in her Sunday best for the annual Catholic picnic in New Ireland. Her expression is surprisingly sombre for an eight-year-old on a festive outing; one can blame the photographer for that, too, perhaps.

More than seven decades later, Iva couldn't recall that day particularly, but she could speak wistfully and with warmth of her childhood in New Ireland. It was not an unhappy time. She remembered the solitude especially, as tangible to an only child in the country as the treeline where the darkness begins. In her memory, "It was the loneliest place in the world." At times she could speak of it as of yesterday, though she hadn't lived there since just after the murder in August, 1906. New Ireland itself ceased to be after the First World War — consigned to memory and lore at the same time as her first husband, safely home from the horror in Europe, was dying of influenza in the 1918 epidemic.

Iva did remember Mary Ann's blood on the woodshed floor at the mission house. She was eight years old. Her mother, Sarah, took her down to the rectory on that blinding August morning. Father McAuley, returning home the night before, had found his cousin's body in the wood pit, her skull riven and her throat slashed. "Poor thing, she laid in that shed in all that heat for two days before Father come back to find her," Iva remembered. "Poor Mary Ann. She was Mother's best friend, and Mother was never the same after it. She kept the last bottle of strawberry preserves Mary Ann ever gave her — unopened — until the day she died."

Iva had been told by her mother that morning to stay away from the woodshed while the body lay inside, but over the decades the picture of the dark stain, where Mary Ann's blood had soaked into the floor planks, stayed with her. "They put everything on it under the shining sun, but I think they should have painted it some dark colour, so nobody could see it. It would just send some kind of chill over you, when you would go out there and look at that wood pit. God bless us and save us, it was an awful thing."

Vivid in Iva's memory, too, was the strange young hired man, Tom Collins, who had worked at the rectory only a few days prior to the murder, and who had disappeared in its wake. "He had a broad accent. I remember one night, he was down to our house and Mother and I were alone. I don't know what I did, but he began to chase me around the kitchen table. I don't think he meant me any harm. I think he meant to play with me, but I was terrified. Then my father came in and said, 'Tom, you'd better go sit down.' He borrowed my father's razor that night, and took it with him back to the mission house."

And he came one more time, on the night of the killing, or so they believed. "I still think he came back with the intention of killing my mother and me. I don't know why; perhaps we were the last ones there. My father had gone across the road to feed the horse. After a bit, Mother went to the door to see if Father was coming back. Tom was standing there, leaning against the side of the house. He said, 'I brought you a kettle of water.' And she said, 'That's nice of you, Tom, to bring me a kettle of water.' She passed the kettle to me and I took it and set it on the kitchen table. It was one of the old cracker cans they used to have; round soda crackers came in it and it had a handle on it like a kettle. We had no water in the house — we carried it from Rice Brook — and I think he was going to use it to wash his hands with after. But then Father came back, and Tom said, 'I forgot your razor, I'll bring it next time.' Then he left."

Iva loved going to school, a tiny one-room building painted red, at Galway four miles away, where she was taught to read and write by Agnes Daley, whose motto, inscribed on a plaque over the blackboard, was, "The first law of Heaven is order." During the school week, Iva would stay with the family of her mother's brother, Michael Teahan, who lived nearby. She would pick berries with Sarah in the summer, and help prepare gooseberry preserves; they'd "do them down rich" with lots of sugar. She would watch her mother and Mary Ann, who often visited when the priest was away, quilting in the evening by the light of a paraffin lamp. Winters were cold, isolated, the house heated only by the big wood stove in the kitchen.

Iva's father, who was a lumberman, came home only on weekends, and in his absence Sarah and Iva would look after the horse and the few cows pastured on Boyle's sidehill across the road. Boyle's place was vacant and decaying, like many homesteads in the district by then, and their nearest neighbour was at Father McAuley's mission house a mile away. Iva remembered her mother frequently terrified at night. Pedlars and other transients passed by regularly; tramps would stop, looking for a handout, some not as friendly as others. Iva could recall a night she and her mother were alone at the house, and there came a knock at the door. A kettle of water boiled on the stove.

"If you don't get away, sir," Sarah called through the door, "I'll scald you to death."

The murder ended their lives in the settlement. Two months after Mary Ann's body was put into the arid gravel that passed for New Ireland earth, Iva's family left the hills and settled on the flatlands nearer the coast and its people, and the villages and the schools.

Other photographs have survived, but the one of the grave little girl standing motionless before the wall of forest, a single black-eyed susan poking from the grass at her feet, captivates. The field is gone now, returned to the woods from which a generation of labour had taken it. Gone, too, is the child in the picture, the woman that she became, and the memories that were hers. Except for those few recounted here, preserved by her and then offered like a gift.

Sarah's Story, August 1906

Our place is in New Ireland, a mile down the road from Father McAuley's home and St. Agatha's church. It's awful lonely there. My husband, William, works in the woods and he's away much of the time. We have a daughter, Iva, who's eight, but my older step-daughter, Mabel, is away a lot, too, to Albert mostly getting her schooling. We keep a few cows at the place up across the field, the old Tim Boyle place, in a barn over there — there's no one living there now — and when Mr. Williamson's away, I go over there in the forenoon and milk the cows and look after them. It's a fair distance, but I have a handy cut I use to go across.

I knew Mary Ann for thirty years. She was a good woman, always coming to my place and other places around. She was a hard worker — able to take the horse out herself and put him in. Never heard her complain, not even in the winter, when it'd get so cold sometimes, she'd have to wear mittens making the beds.

I first seen Collins the weekend he was hired by Father McAuley. It was awful warm. We was down to Albert — Mr. Williamson and myself and Iva — stopped at McAnulty's Hotel in Albert for to get a meal, and he was working on the woodpile. I come by the woodhouse and there he was, trying to saw with a bucksaw, but he didn't know much about it. Didn't know him from Adam, but he says to me he's going to Father McAuley's. He never seen me before neither, and I don't know why he said that, but I says to him, I says, I live a mile down the road from there. Said I'd probably see him there. If he's working for Father McAuley, I says, he might come down to the house for a visit.

Seen him next on Tuesday morning following. He come down to my house to have his axe ground. I was looking out the upstairs window, and I seen him talking to my husband out in the yard. Then I seen him turning the handle on the grindstone, while my husband held the axe blade on it. My husband told me he only ground one bit for him, the other bit had a hack in it. And he didn't grind it too sharp; didn't think it was much use to grind it sharp for him, he says.

The boy come back again that evening at tea-time. Asked my husband if he could strop his razor. My husband wasn't feeling well, so he said he'd loan the boy one of his own. Collins said he'd return it, but as far as I know it never come back. He stayed about twenty minutes. We talked in a friendly way. I don't remember what we talked about. You can't remember everything. A good many things slip a person's mind.

He come down again later in the week, Friday I think. My brother, Michael Teahan, was visiting and we were talking about a fishing trip to the lake back of the rectory. It was awful warm, warmer than most summers. Mary Ann had been thinking a trip to the lake might be pleasant, too. She'd asked Father McAuley about it before he left that day. Well, my brother and I were talking about it, and Collins come along riding the priest's horse. Handed me a quart kettle — you know, one of them milk cans. Said Mary Ann had sent him down for a can of blueberries. I give him the berries and he left.

We went on that fishing trip the next day. Collins and Mary Ann went along, too. They got along good, so far as I could tell. Noticed nothing out of place, no bickering or quarrelling. Seemed friendly enough. We come back to the rectory Sunday afternoon, and Mary Ann treated us to some maple sugar; dark and hard and sweet it was. There was some talk about her gold watch, which she'd had for quite awhile; it come from Boston. She wasn't wearing it, but she brought it out from her room; said it was keeping good time, or something like that.

Iva and I come home at suppertime. Mary Ann asked us to come back to visit after supper, but I said I didn't know. That was the last I seen her alive. (I seen her later — I'll never forget it — laid out on the floor of the woodshed with a spread over her.)

A couple hours after we left on that Sunday evening, Tom Collins come down to my place again. Didn't see him come, but when I stepped outside, there he was, standing on the step at the front door. Had with him a gallon can, about half full of water.

I says to him, "Is this where you are now?"

And he says, "Whose wagon is that?"

I said, "My husband come home last night."

I asked the boy to come in, and he come in and handed the little girl the can of water, and she set it on the table. He sat down at the table and says, "I have been to Pat Duffy's and paid Pat Duffy fifty cents from Mr. Gross and was up to the priest's again and now down here."

And I said, "You're a pretty smart boy."

And I said, "I think you're a nicer boy for bringing me some water."

Then he started to tell about having a good time at the lake fishing, and my husband come in. The boy spoke about

xviii THE RECTORY MURDER

the razor he'd lent him. Said he forgot to fetch it down, but him and Mary Ann was going down to Albert early in the morning, and he would fetch it when he went past. He stayed a few more minutes, then said he must go home, for Mary Ann would be lonesome.

The little girl threw the water into the pail in the kitchen, and Collins took the empty can from her and left. That was the last I seen of him. They say she was killed the next morning, but I believe she was already dead when he come to see us that night. Why else would he come down carrying that can of water, but to wash his hands with afterwards?

Chapter One

Wednesday, November 13, 1907

1.

The Intercolonial Railway's *Maritime Express* had crossed into New Brunswick and was working south through frozen burned-over timberland when John Radclive's body convulsed, jolting him once again from the brandy-induced lethargy. He silently cursed the jarring noisy roll of the chilly passenger coach, blaming it for keeping him from a restful sleep. But in his heart he knew where the real blame lay — with the vision. A green translucent bottle poked from the satchel beside him. His small delicate hand, resting on the arm of the seat, held a thin cold cigar. He sat slumped on the padded bench in the smoking lounge, thick body chilled, his neck aching.

He could hear the iron wheels racketing on the cold rails beneath his feet, and his gaze fell upon the black pot-bellied stove at the other end of the lounge. Probably needed a shovelful of coal. He would do it himself if the conductor wasn't along soon. Outside the grimy window glass was cold flowing empty darkness. Peering into it, he could see in the dim light only the distorted reflection of his face — thick black moustache and shock of hair overwhelming the pale oval shape in the glass. Inside the car the air was stale, laden with smoke from the tobacco, from the leaking stove, and from the oil lamps on low wick. He thought dawn must not be far off.

He pushed the half-empty brandy bottle into the satchel, which was cracked with age and use, jamming it against the threadbare bulk of his Prince Albert hanging-coat. The coat was folded and wrapped around two more bottles, these full, and beside it were a coil of stout coarse Manila rope, one inch thick; a pair of thin leather straps, one for the wrists, the other for the ankles; a "county kerchief," the black linen hood which adorned Radclive's subjects as they stood trembling on the trap; a spool of cotton thread, his own innovation; and a few poor personal items that he carried when he was on a job. He closed the satchel. When he was working, Radclive travelled light.

This time it would be at a place called Hopewell Cape, Albert County, New Brunswick. He knew of the area. It was across the muddy tidal river from the federal penitentiary at Dorchester, where he had worked in the past. This request had come to him from the sheriff of the county, and it had been accompanied by a plea. A young Englishman who had murdered a woman with an axe. Date of execution Friday, November 15 — two days hence. Radclive knew enough of the details to feel more than a little unease. Three trials had been required; the evidence was purely circumstantial; no confession. And all those people afterward, trying to save the Englishman's life. It was easier when a job was cut-and-dried, with no loose ends, but there weren't any uncomplicated ones anymore. The politicians, who liked to keep their distance from these things, were reluctant to grant commutations. It was virtually certain now there would not be one for the young Englishman.

The remorse which comes over me is terrible, and my nerves give out until I have not slept for days at a time. I used to say to condemned persons as I beckoned with my hand, "Come to me." Now at night when I lie down, I start up with a roar as victim after victim comes up before me. I can see them on the trap, waiting a second before they face their Maker. They taunt me and haunt me until I am nearly crazy with an unearthly fear.

That was the dream, the reason for his sleeplessness, and the excuse for the brandy.

He remembered the young man in Woodstock, New Brunswick, three years ago. George Gee. George's old man had made the trek east after the 1812 fighting and had settled on a riverbank in the woods somewhere around Woodstock. It had been isolated. Poor. Family members cohabited because they knew each other, were comfortable with each other, trusted no one else. Often, there was no one else. George had taken up with a cousin named Millie Gee. Then he had been sent away for awhile, and by the time he got out, Millie had moved in with Bennie Gee, her brother-in-law, in a one-room shack in the woods — no windows, cots in opposite corners, a rough plank table, a tin stove with a pipe through a hole in the roof.

When George came back home one day in March, 1904, he got liquored up and went looking for Millie. He carried two bottles of booze and a rifle. He found her in Bennie's shack with Bennie and another couple, she on one of the cots with Bennie. They talked, drank the burning liquor, played cards. George talked crazy, said he was going to shoot himself. Grabbing at his gun, he said, "And this is the one that'll do it." Then George asked Millie to go outside with him. Standing in the snow, he shot her through the body with the rifle. She died later from the infection. Though some blamed the doctor for letting her die, George Gee was condemned to death.

On July 20, Radclive had gone to Woodstock for the hanging. Like this one in Albert, it was the first execution in the county's history. The newspapers loved it. They sniffed at executions like dogs at their own vomit. Local girls, passing by the jail, brought George sweets and dainties. The sheriff told Radclive that he had better watch out for his job, that the sheriff had received a number of letters from locals looking to do the work themselves. One said he would do it for $2.50. Another told the sheriff to name his terms. George Gee was philosophical. He had been interviewed by a reporter, and Radclive had read his comments in that day's paper. "The sheriff should do it," George Gee had said, "but I am glad Radclive has come. He knows how to do the work, and will do it quick, where if it was left to others to do, they might make a mistake, and look at the agony I would have to suffer. I would like to talk to the man. I feel alright towards him and have nothing against him. I only think he is committing an awful sin when he takes a life for money."

After the hanging, Radclive was seen in a strangely jovial mood, charming a number of children whose curiosity had drawn them to the vicinity of the jail, where the scaffold still stood behind a barricade. He had pulled a couple of boards from the fence hiding the gallows, and invited anyone who was interested to have a look at the mechanism. By noon the gallows were gone, and large crowds turned out at Woodstock station to witness Radclive's departure by train. He had chatted amiably with them and, opening his satchel, had showed them the noose.

2.

John Robert Radclive was often mistaken for a seaman. He had the look, even though he hadn't been at sea for many years: the broad swarthy face, the expanse of shoulder and chest beneath the rough fabric of his coat. But the hue of his face now came from a bottle, not the elements; and the muscular torso from his vanity, not his trade. He sat by himself in a corner of the smoking lounge. It was his usual travelling station. He had come from Toronto, changed trains at Montreal, and would change again at Moncton. He was not an unsociable man, not unapproachable, but wary. He was an honest man and, when a travelling companion posed the inevitable question about the nature of his business, he always told the truth. He was troubled, but he was not ashamed, and he'd known ostracism for many years.

To those who lived in a world, now largely passed into history, in which the working man of the sea was as common as the mill worker, Radclive looked like the authoritative first mate of a large ship. At fifty-two years of age, he weighed 220 fleshy pounds, but the musculature of the upper torso made him look powerful. Although he was short and heavy set, the nervous fluttering personality of his small hands, particularly when he was speaking, betrayed the facade of his calm demeanour. It was just as if all the jittery energies of his high-strung nervous system were shunted down his arms to be extruded from the fidgeting fingertips.

The small brown eyes were restless, yet penetrating; behind them lay the scientific and mystical bric-a-brac that formed the lethal core of his special skill. He would brag that he could not be forced to avert his gaze. "I can look anyone in the eye for an hour at a time without winking," he had once said. "A professional hypnotist tried to put me to sleep once, and after he had tried for an hour he gave up. He couldn't look me in the eye any longer."

Radclive favoured brandy — whiskey was also acceptable — and drank it in large quantities. His speech was rapid-fire and sometimes difficult to follow. Phrases were frequently punctuated with a guttural explosion of syllables, sounding like "shapewayerform," but after some time spent in conversation, they would become recognizable as "shape, way, or form," a favourite expression. "No sir," he might say, "I don't believe that's right, sir, no shapewayerform." The absence of several front teeth beneath the well-kept moustache sometimes rendered even more indecipherable the gruff utterances of the deep voice.

He could talk knowledgeably of the discipline of *ju-jitsu* and the mysteries of the occult. He believed, he would say, in the transmigration of men's souls, and could talk upon these and similar subjects with a fluency which evidenced the amateur scholar. He showed in conversation that he was unusually well-read. His studies had carried him as far as physiology, astrology, and kindred subjects, and on one occasion while walking with a reporter, he named the stars visible in the night sky. He fancied that he could read the characteristics of individual physiology, and knew intimately the laws of mechanics that governed his work. He was a dedicated professional, who paid close attention to the details of his trade. He strongly favoured, for example, permanent scaffolds being attached to all jails to avoid the trouble and inconvenience of temporary structures which, if improperly or carelessly constructed from inferior materials, could cause a hangman (and his subject) unnecessary aggravation; a warped trapdoor built from green lumber could, and sometimes did, refuse to drop on schedule.

Radclive existed in a kind of official purgatory, neither in heaven nor in hell — at least not completely in hell. He was the public servant of last resort, a man who freelanced his singular skill not to the highest bidder, but to any bidder who bore the imprimature of local authority. He was, in Canada, *sui generis* — not on the public payroll, not holding public office. He worked for a fee. His work was sanctioned by law, but he carried no licence, except that sanctioned by his skill, his experience, and his reputation. There were few public servants in the nation who were prepared to carry out the full letter of the law. And when they came to him, he knew, it was unofficially. Executions were under the jurisdiction of the local authorities: if they were not prepared to spring the trap — and they usually weren't — they would eventually contact him, but in the most circuitous way. They would first approach the deputy minister of justice, who would tell them that executions were not under the jurisdiction of his department and that he could do nothing to help. But the name and address of John Radclive would be passed down the line, and at length he would receive a telegram.

3.

Radclive had started to drink alcohol with a kind of despairing dedication following the hanging of a man and woman, back-to-back, in Montreal in 1899. There had been great public interest in that double execution. Following the performance, which from Radclive's point of view had gone flawlessly, the mob surged toward the gallows. It was instant and dangerous pandemonium, but the police were able to contain the frenzy, until the bodies had been cut down and taken to safety. Radclive, badly unnerved by the spectacle, retreated within the prison and spent the night there with a bottle of brandy.

There had been another unfortunate spectacle, this time at St. Scholastique, Quebec. All had gone well until the victim, an elderly man, died of a heart attack on the gallows just moments before the trap was sprung. A quandary presented itself. The local sheriff stood astounded on the platform, with Radclive and the other officials. The lifeless form of the old man they had been called there to execute lay at their feet. *But he hadn't been hanged yet.* The presiding physician quickly determined that the corpse, already adorned with the black hood and the hemp noose, was indeed a corpse, if prematurely. What to do? Was there precedent for this? Under the circumstances, Radclive's view was that justice had been done and his own work finished. But the local sheriff was the legal authority at the execution. The language of the death warrant, issued under the imprimature of His Majesty the King, was unequivocal: "I do now direct you the said sheriff of the said county to cause execution of the said sentence to be done." That meant, the sheriff argued in the pre-dawn mist, that the condemned man was to be hanged by the neck until he was dead; the fact that the subject had expired inconsiderately, seconds before he was to be killed by the state, was a contingency not anticipated by the precisely worded warrant.

"Get a chair!" the sheriff commanded, as the incredulous Radclive looked on. Moments later the trap swung open with a heavy clatter, and the corpse, tied unceremoniously to a straight-backed wooden chair, fell through the hole looking as if it were part of some illusionist's bizarre trick. The lifeless neck snapped audibly, and justice was done to the letter. A distraught Radclive, deeply offended by this burlesque of his profession, hurried once more to his bottle of brandy.

4.

The *Maritime Express*, puffing smoke, steam and coal cinders into the chilly damp air, made its methodical way south through the woodlands of New Brunswick's eastern coast, stopping briefly at small lumbering and fishing communities along the way, dropping off and picking up passengers, mail and baggage. Eventually the *Express* clattered into Moncton station, noisily exhaling clouds of steam, as trainmen and passengers bustled about. Moncton, a merchant community of wood-frame buildings stretched along the northern shoulder of a bend in the Petitcodiac River, was the rail centre of the region, that honour having been taken a few years earlier, along with the regional offices of the *Inter-colonial*, from nearby coastal Shediac.

Radclive had been through Moncton before — most recently, a year ago August, to execute the murderer George Stanley in Windsor, Nova Scotia. This time, instead of continuing along the main rail line to Nova Scotia, he would change trains at Moncton, and take the western line to Salisbury village. He stepped from the second-class coach of the *Express* to the wide platform, black satchel in hand. He was spotted immediately by, among others, a trim young man named Elmer Ferguson, an enthusiastic reporter for the *Transcript*, the city's afternoon newspaper. Young Ferguson was at the head-end of what was to be a long career in Canadian journalism, which would end in affluence in Montreal seven decades later.

Radclive made his way to the second-class smoking compartment on the *St. John Express*. A curious crowd, encouraged by the delayed departure of the train, pushed into the car's rear door, necks craned, anxious to catch a glimpse of the man known far and wide as "Ratliff," a name with which to conjure, and to spook rambunctious youngsters. Radclive, puffing smoke and waiting quietly for the train to depart, took little notice of the attention he had attracted, but he did speak briefly when greeted by someone who knew him from previous visits to the area. Ferguson elbowed his way through the congestion to the hangman, who sat with his satchel and cigar, calmly peering out the steam-hazed window.

"I'm Ferguson, with the *Transcript*. Can I ask you a few questions?"

Radclive ran a small palm over the slicked-back hair and smiled slightly. Blue smoke escaped from his thin lips, and drifted in rising eddies from the narrow nostrils, as if his black moustache was smouldering. A dismissive wave of the hand.

"You may ask."

"Why are you called Ratliff?"

The hangman shrugged. "I suppose it's from hearin' the name only and not seein' it spelled." He did not add that he was also known in some areas as "Ratley." Another spelling common in the newspapers of the day was "Radcliff."

"What do you know about the Collins case?"

Radclive placed the satchel at his feet.

"Sit down a moment, Mr. Ferguson, and I will tell you what I think. The law says he's to be hanged and I'll hang him, make no mistake. It'll be a good hangin', a clean one, because that's the way I work. I don't gainsay the law or what the law says has to be done. No shapewayerform. But I don't like this Collins affair. Not a little. Didn't want it from the start, wouldn't have come at all but the sheriff kept at me and prevailed."

For the young journalist there were no shadings yet. He had covered the trials, and he harboured no doubts about Collins' guilt, nor about what the just punishment should be. (He would go to Collins' cell one last time to say goodbye, but would refuse to shake his hand. Collins' chaplain, outraged, would write a letter of complaint to Ferguson's editor, and there would be a mild admonition.) "He took an axe to a harmless old lady!" Ferguson declared in disgust. "Why shouldn't he be hanged?"

"I've kept myself well posted on the facts of the case," Radclive told the reporter, "and I've no doubt he's guilty. But I'll be frank with you; I've never been more unsettled about a pending execution. I've conducted, without hesitation or regret, more than 100 executions in this country, but the circumstantial nature of the evidence against young Collins, combined with the strong fight put up by many citizens of the area to save his life, disturbs me more than such things usually do, I can tell you. I would rather not do it, but I've been prevailed upon, so I'll do it and see that it's done properly."

The reporter wrote for that afternoon's edition of the *Transcript*: "Radcliff's face, which while not altogether brutal, is coarse and unprepossessing, and bears every mark of dissipation. He was noticeably nervous while conversing here this morning, his hands twitching constantly, while he apparently found much difficulty remaining in one position for any length of time." Ferguson, who would spend the night before Collins' execution playing cards with Radclive in his room, expanded on his description in a subsequent profile of the executioner. It began: "A student of physiology might probably find no more interesting subject then is afforded by J.R. Radclive, the Dominion hangman."

5.

Of English birth and parentage, Radclive had come to Canada with his wife and four children in 1887. Speaking of his youth, he would say with sincerity that he had at first been destined to enter the church. "But I was no hypocrite, and I gave it up." The early years of his life he spent as a sailor and a cook serving in the Royal Navy, where he became acquainted with the practice of swinging sailors from the ship's yardarm. The army claimed him for awhile, and he had much to tell of fighting in India. He could relate exuberant stories of battles with the hill tribes. Part of his earlier career was spent in the Pacific Islands of Australia and New Zealand, and in the Orient, where he claimed to have his knowledge of *ju-jitsu*. By repute a good fisherman, he would recount with enthusiasm his exploits on the lakes of Ontario with a rod and line. He was fond of "gunning" and, when at home, spent much of his time in the outdoors. He was said to be vain about his muscular development and, when younger, had worked at keeping fit.

He had learned the hangman's trade in England, but on arriving in Canada he abandoned it for a time, working instead as a steward in the Sunnyside Boating Club in Parkdale, a suburb of straight-laced Toronto. His salary from the boating club was inadequate, however, to support a family; so Radclive advertised his executioner's skills amongst the local sheriffs, and was soon plying his former trade.

Eventually, one of the boating club's more powerful members — an inspector with the Northwest Mounted Police — recognized him, and informed the owners that he did not appreciate having his drink served by the "common hangman." Radclive had never been secretive about what, until then, was a sideline; in any event, he had not thought it dishonourable. He disdained the wearing of a mask when he was on the gallows, a practice other hangmen of the time followed. He was fired from the club for his lack of discretion and, when he could find no other employment, began to practise his trade more regularly.

Mortified by his work and by his refusal to keep it hidden from public view, his family soon left him and returned to England. Just before he died in 1912, penniless and alone, from complications brought on by excessive drinking, Radclive would tell an interviewer: "My family deserted me and changed their names, but I kept right on with the job, because I argued with myself that if I was doing wrong, then the government of the country was wrong. I held that I was the minister of justice at a hanging and that if I was a murderer, then he was also a murderer."

6.

A Voice: Talked about his business a good deal, after he lit up a tad. You know, the details, how you go about it. He was proud of his work, in a way. Least he wasn't ashamed of it, though I could see he was bothered by it. Who wouldn't be? If it wasn't just the work, it could have been, too, the way people acted around him. They'd avoid him altogether when they could. And when they couldn't, they'd be polite, you know, but cool, not at all friendly. You could see it in their faces, the thinkin' that he wasn't any better than the ones he was putting to death. Even the ones who weren't opposed to the death sentence were uncomfortable around the fellow who took it upon himself to see that it got done for a fee.

Ratliff knew that, of course. And I think he was a sociable fellow, you know? Outgoing, liked to talk, but when everyone shuns you like your face is festering, you start to build up your own aversion, against yourself, or the work maybe. That's why he drank so much. No question in my mind. You'd have to have a cold heart, maybe no heart at all, to do that work in those kinds of circumstances without being affected. I think he had a heart alright. And he was lonely. That's why he talked to me, I think. Wouldn't nobody else sit with him.

He told me he'd been at sea as a young man, and that's where he saw his first hanging. They just dropped the noose over the sailor's head, and hauled him up backward over the yardarm. Even with his friends pulling on his legs to speed things up, it took the bloke a long time to die, he said. Strangulation, he said, sometimes takes up to twenty minutes. Must have got him to thinking about better ways of doing a job that the law said had to be done. Whatever the reason, when he left the sea he went back to London and got himself apprenticed to William Marwood, the official hangman. God only knows why. Famous man, this Marwood was. He come after this other fella, Calcraft, who, he said, was England's first professional executioner.

Calcraft, Ratliff told me, was an innovator. We all were, he said. Make no mistake, he said, it's kind of an art is hanging. When it's done properly, it's because it's done with skill and precision. Explained it to me this way; said the perfect execution is a kind of conjunction, a meeting of skilfully managed forces at a man's spinal column. Sounded high-falutin' to me, but he knew what he was talking about. Oh, he's a smart one alright. Said the variables in each particular case have to be measured precisely, and the calculations done carefully. Well, it don't take no genius to see that. If you want a man to die quick, you want to break his neck. But it's the knowin' how to do it is the trick. Make the drop too short, he said, and the spinal column won't break. Make it too long, and the head comes off. And it don't take no genius, nor a wagonload of imagination either, to see what that'd mean. Fella'd be dead alright, but he'd be one hell of a mess.

A bungled execution is a terrible thing, Ratliff said, and they're pretty common when an amateur's in charge. Said there's always something different to consider. The anatomy of the neck, the muscular development, the fellow's weight. Told me he had to hang a fella once had a silver tube in his throat. Had to allow for that tube when he calculated the drop. Now I can see that. Told me about this other fella, a woodchopper; always held his head the same way when he worked. Consequently his neck muscles weren't evenly developed. Had to work that into his formula, he said. Now he might have been stretchin' that one a bit, I'm not one to say, but he knows his work.

This Marwood was something of a scientist, Ratliff said. Made up a series of tables that correlated body weight with length of drop required to break the neck. See, Marwood believed that death was almost instantaneous when the neck was dislocated, and he thought that ought to be the goal of the hangman. So he got rid of Calcraft's rope, which was big — about an inch-and-a-half in diameter — and stiff as a honeymoon pecker. Calcraft's way was to make a noose from several slip-knots bunched together to make one big knot that was put behind the left ear. Then when the trap dropped and the fella fell through, the knot was supposed to hit him a good whack at the bottom of the fall, and knock him cold. Then he'd suffocate in peace, I suppose. But the rope was so heavy, the knot'd usually slip around under the fella's chin and strangle him instead.

So this Marwood decides to try something different, and goes for a softer, more pliable rope that's only about half as thick as Calcraft's. Marwood devises his own noose, too, a metal ring bound to one end of the rope. So it wouldn't slip, he used a leather washer fitted right on the rope. Well, it worked fine. Marwood first put the ring behind the left ear, but then he found that he'd get a cleaner break if he put it under the point of the chin.

This was all pretty interesting to Ratliff, who was looking for a chance to chew the fat with somebody — that somebody being me — as long as there was a bottle involved, too. Well it was fascinatin' to me, too, which is why it's stuck in my head, I guess. I always like to know how people go about doin' their work, even if their work is nothin' more civilized than snappin' a man's neck. So I'd throw in the odd question to keep him goin'.

Well he give me a bit of history, too. See, before there was traps, there was gibbets, which was just a crossbeam like an upside-down L to hang a rope from. Fella'd either be hauled into the air like a sailor, or he'd jump off a ladder or cart — more likely, he'd be pushed off it by the hangman. Then he'd slowly strangle like a sheep in a wire fence, his legs kickin' and thrashin'. They didn't tie the legs together then, because they thought it made more of a show for the public to see the poor fella jerkin' about like a fish. But they discovered, when they went to the trap door gallows, that they'd better tie the legs together. Otherwise, fella on the rope could kick a leg up and hook a heel on the opening, and pull himself up. No end of fuss and bother.

Now folks began to think a bit more dignity was in order, so they started tyin' the legs and puttin' hoods over their heads and pinioning their arms. Lot of that was Calcraft's doin', Ratliff said. But they were still short-droppin' 'em then, only four or five feet. No thought of breakin' the neck, just stranglin' them — hangman still yankin' on their legs from underneath as needed. Well, they began to experiment with the long-drop, sometimes going too far and losing a head altogether, and it was Marwood who eventually came up with a system, as I said.

Now it gets even more interesting, because Ratliff, once he'd learned all there was to learn from Marwood, began to have his own ideas. And, by god, he come up with his own gallows. Why? I don't know. Maybe he had the soul of an inventor; he certainly had the smarts. Compassion, maybe. What he told me was how agonizing it could be for the condemned person having to climb the steps, sometimes as many as sixteen, to the gallows floor. Often they'd have to drag him up. Now he come up with a contraption that not only worked slick as a wet whistle in a fog, but was also simple to take apart and haul around. I don't know what his inspiration was — kind of the old yardarm principle, maybe — but the way he described it reminded me of a guillotine. The fella's killed by a drop weight alright, but it don't slice his head off like a turnip, it breaks his neck instead. Well, Ratliff used it four times, he said, including the last time in 1896, he said, down here at Dorchester. Three of the times, he said, it worked perfect.

It had three pieces of six-by-six timber, fourteen feet long apiece. Two of them was planted in the ground seven feet apart. The third was a crosspiece on the top that stuck six feet out over one side like an overhang. Now on the outer end of that crosspiece, he had a 350-pound block of iron held up there by a pin. Hauled her up with a block and tackle, I imagine. The block — the one he used at Dorchester anyway — come from the R. F. and M. Company in Saint John. Now the rope was attached to that weight, run through a hole in the beam to a pulley, then along the top of that beam to a second pulley, then down to the neck of the poor bastard what's standing between the uprights. When everything was ready, Ratliff'd give a little yank on the cord tied to the pin, the weight'd drop, and I don't have to draw any pictures, do I?

The first two times he used this contraption was some-wheres in Upper Canada, and it worked perfect, he said. Death was instantaneous, or as near to it as it gets, leastways. Ratliff was elated, he said, and thought he had a major breakthrough in the hangin' trade, a virtually assured spinal-cord dislocation. But the third time somethin' went wrong. The neck didn't break, and the poor bastard wasn't pronounced dead for a good eighteen minutes. Now I don't know if that's what they call a bungle, but there must have been some sort of miscalculating on his part. He allowed there was some grumbling about it, but he still believed it to be the best way of goin' about it, and he got to use his contraption one more time. This was the Dorchester execu-tion back in '96.

Worked like a charm again, he told me, but word comes down that he ought to think about goin' back to the old way. Just when he'd thought he'd finished with the platform gal-lows with their green warping wood, and the traps that stuck shut like the widow's legs when they was supposed to be openin', and all of them long steps up which he'd had to drag some poor snivellin' bastard cryin' for his ma.

There was nothing he could do about it. He had to depend on the muckymucks in Ottawa to pass his name along to the locals when there was a hanging to be done, even though it was all done on the sly. There must have been some com-plaints. Figured some weak-bellied official probably had seen his new contraption at work, and decided it was too gruesome for a decent man to watch. You know, the ones that had to be there, the doctors and the preachers and the sheriffs and such. Why? Because they had to watch the poor bastard die. The whole thing was done out in the open, in full view of the officials. They'd see the guy snapped into the air like a minnow on a cable, see him kickin' and floppin' on the end of the rope. But on the platform, they'd only see the fella drop through the trapdoor. Like he'd vanished. They couldn't see what happened to him at the end of the rope.

I don't know, maybe Ratliff wasn't in his right mind. Or maybe he was, and that's why he tried to change things some. Or maybe he was, and that's why he drank so hard. Or maybe he was trying to get out of his right mind, and into whatever other state he had to be in to do the kind of work he done. I will say this. He was about the saddest son of a bitch ever I had the pleasure to drink with, but I'm glad I did. I was curious, I'll admit it. And I won't say I liked him some, though I might've if we'd had more time, maybe do a little fishin'. He was a pretty sorry specimen, I guess. Most folks thought so. Didn't want him around, wouldn't talk to him. Can't blame 'em, neither. In this part of the country, thank the powers, most people get to live their lives without having to think about such things as murders and executions, let alone having to do something about it, having to see it right in among them, in their communities, and in their homes. That's what Ratliff represents to them, seems to me. I think, when it come right down to it, Ratliff was more of a monster to them than Collins was, even though it'd been Collins who'd taken an axe to an old woman and then cut her throat. But I feel a hell of a lot sorrier for that poor bastard Ratliff, who went about the country doin' his legal work in a law abiding way all his miserable life, than I ever felt for Collins, who everybody wanted to keep alive and failed, whether he killed the old lady or not.

7.

The *St. John Express*, as chilly and lacking comfort as the express from Montreal, bore him west from Moncton toward Salisbury. Radclive spent some time thinking about the gallows he would need at Hopewell Cape. He hoped he would find lumber there that was not too green. He wanted a tidy job, no difficulties. Through the grimy glass of the train window and beyond the flashing branches of bare trees, he could see the umber banks of the mud river shining in the sunlight, as if covered in an enamel glaze. In shaded areas, lacy patterns of sienna ice had been left by the falling tide. The Petitcodiac. Strange name. They should change it to something with two or fewer syllables. It was a tidal stream, bordered by marshland that still pastured cattle and sheep. There was feed for them there yet, would be until the permanent snows came. The fields were sear and stubbled, dead until spring.

He wanted good lumber for the gallows and a good man to build it. A new one would have to be erected, because there had never been a hanging in Hopewell Cape. Sheriff Lynds had made arrangements with the authorities at Dorchester Penitentiary to have the old gallows that was in storage there ferried across the river to The Cape, but Radclive would not use it. It was the drop-weight device that he had designed many years ago; the gallows that he favoured, in fact, but that he had been forced to abandon a decade earlier.

At Salisbury, Radclive spent a pleasant few minutes watching the crew of the Salisbury & Harvey Railway rotate by hand a forty-ton steam locomotive on a turntable. He was fascinated by machines and displays of mechanical ingenuity. It seemed remarkable to him that two men could move, with their own strength, the fifty-foot wooden circular platform with the engine resting on it. He knew, of course, that the locomotive had been positioned precisely by the engineer, and that the turntable was balanced on a single fulcrum at its centre, but it was an arresting sight to see the massive steam engine slowly swing until it had been exactly reversed. The engineer then opened the throttle, released the brake shoes, and rolled the locomotive along a siding, to be recoupled to the other end of the short string of cars it had just hauled into Salisbury station from down county.

This was the beginning of the spur line that ran south forty-five miles into the centre of Albert County, emerging at Hillsborough on the west bank of the Petitcodiac River at

Mile 24, then jutting abruptly inland again to pass through Albert Mines and Cape Station at Mile 35, before turning west to follow roughly the shoreline of Shepody Bay into Riverside and Albert, the small village where the Collins-McAuley story had begun. Radclive would disembark at Hillsborough, then travel by wagon the few miles south along the river to Hopewell Cape. He boarded the small passenger car with the conductor, who began to reverse some of the seats so the few passengers could ride facing forward. No caboose on this run, just the locomotive, the tender and a couple of freight cars, hauling machine parts, mail and dry goods. On the first mile out of Salisbury, the track crossed two trestles over McNaughton Brook, then a three-span steel bridge 300 feet long over the Petitcodiac River connected to wooden trestles at either end, before travelling southeast into the interior through low-lying wet scrubland.

8.

There was no welcoming committee for John Radclive at Hopewell Cape. On the hill overlooking the river, a short distance from the new courthouse with its porch and its quartet of tall Ionian pillars, the jail was housed in a squat two-storey stone building that had, on its second floor, the living quarters of the jailer's family. The hangman climbed the stone steps with his satchel and entered unannounced. He glanced at W.E. Calhoun's work crew, which was busy putting up the drop-weight gallows in an enclosure to the right of the building, but made no comment.

Jailer Willard Porter came down from the upstairs apartment. He shook hands with the hangman, and told him that Sheriff Lynds was in the cellblock with Rev. Byron H. Thomas, Protestant chaplain of Dorchester Penitentiary. Mrs. Isaiah B. Steeves, an elderly lady who had developed a strong attachment to the prisoner over the past months and visited him frequently, was also in the cell. Collins had taken to calling her "Mother."

Porter hurried into the cellblock and returned with Sheriff Lynds and the woman. The sheriff, a big man who looked worried and weary, thanked the hangman for coming.

Though he had done his best to have the death sentence commuted to life imprisonment, and had failed, the sheriff was relieved to see the hangman. The federal justice department had notified him earlier that hangings were the responsibility of the local authorities, and if he had been unable to get an executioner to do the job, he would have to carry out the sentence himself.

Radclive shook hands with Lynds, but ignored Mrs. Steeves. She was grateful for that. She didn't like the attention she had received for befriending Collins — she had been referred to in the local weekly as "the prisoner's woman friend" — and tried to avoid the newspapermen, who had gathered for the pending execution and who were attempting to generate stories by talking to anyone remotely connected with the case. She did tell one reporter, though, that she believed the papers had not portrayed the young man's character accurately. Her opinion was that he had been greatly misrepresented when spoken of as brutal, heartless and unfeeling. "He has a very simple and child-like nature," she said, "and is generous and kind-hearted, never forgetting the least kindness that has been shown him."

When Mrs. Steeves had left the jail, Radclive, who believed that only the spiritual advisor of a condemned man should have access to him, angrily took up the matter with Sheriff Lynds. "Women have no place in a jail," he declared. "They should have nothing at all to do with the prisoner. I have made representations to Ottawa on this point before and shall do it again. What's more, there's no death watch here. There should have been a death watch on his cell immediately after he was sentenced." Sheriff Lynds said that Constable Herman Coonan could come in the morning and stay on watch until it was over.

Radclive turned his attention to the beam-and-drop gallows being erected outside, brusquely condemned it, and ordered construction of a new scaffold and trap. Lynds said he had thought the trap gallows was obsolete. "That's why I had this device brought over from Dorchester."

"That weight will throw him too far in the air," Radclive told him, "and in all probability he'll strike the beam overhead. I'm not using it anymore." He said he wanted a scaffold erected, eight feet square on posts eleven feet high. In the centre of the platform would be a double trap, four feet square, supported by a bar underneath. The bar would be connected to a lever, which would release the trap when the time came. He also wanted a boarded building — sixteen feet by eighteen feet — erected around the scaffold. He did not say whether he wanted the structure to protect Collins' last moments from the curious, or to protect himself from assassins, but it was known that he had a great fear of being shot. He claimed, in fact, to have been fired upon on three occasions.

Sheriff Lynds told Radclive that Collins had asked to see him. "Yesterday he said he'd rather not meet you until his time had come," said Lynds. "But today he changed his mind."

Radclive assented, and Jailer Porter led him into the damp dim coolness of the cellblock, where Collins waited with Rev. Thomas.

"Hello, Tom," said the hangman, extending his hand to the youth who was standing awkwardly in the small cell. "I s'pose you know who I am."

Collins was a short man, less than five-and-a-half feet tall, not slight in build, but weighing under ten stone, Radclive thought. The grey eyes were troubled under thick brows, and the face, heavily featured with a broad short nose and full lips pulled down at the corners, was of dark complexion beneath a tangle of short black hair. The high forehead was naturally creased with lines, and the ears were small and set low on the skull. The mouth pulled to the right in a weary nervous smile as Radclive greeted him.

"Yes," said Collins, taking the offered hand in his. "I expect you're the executioner."

"I'm sorry to see you in this position, my boy" said Radclive.

"I'm glad you're here," Collins replied, "so that no amateurs will bungle matters."

There was a pause as the two men peered at each other in the gloom of the cell, then Collins said in his heavy Old Country accent, "When will you come for me?"

"Two hours after midnight tomorrow."

Sheriff Lynds' muffled voice could be heard outside the thick stone walls, telling Calhoun that the work of his carpentry crew had been premature, and that Radclive would be giving them new instructions. Jailer Porter stood mute at the cell door, looking on the strange drama of a hangman chatting so amiably with his victim. They seemed to be discussing some innocuous business transaction. Porter, who had, over the past fourteen months, come to know and like — at least feel some sympathy for — the young man in his jail, was made to feel even more uneasy about the impending event. He had looked after the county's prisoners, most of them local rowdies who spent their lock-up time outside their cells doing odd jobs for the county authorities or nearby residents, for many years now, and had never witnessed anything quite so dreadfully singular.

"Not in the dark," said Rev. Thomas in his first words to the hangman. "Can't it be at dawn?"

He spoke in a quiet voice, as if in prayer, addressing Radclive as if Collins weren't standing beside them. "The boy spoke to me this afternoon, asking if it would not be possible for the execution to take place in the daylight. He feels he can meet his death more bravely then."

Radclive, with his battered satchel giving him the appearance of a down-at-the-heels country doctor, peered steadily at the prisoner, who looked at the stone floor of the cell, as if waiting for it to open beneath him.

"It was a pathetic thing," said the chaplain, "as he fell on my neck and fairly begged that I might do all I could to have this last favour granted. The fear of his going out to death with only the feeble light of lanterns and the darkness around him seemed greatly to discomfort him."

The hangman studied the prisoner for another length of time, then nodded abruptly.

"I shall come for you," he said, "at 6:30 o'clock Friday morning, then."

The short muted expiration of breath. "Thank you, sir," said Collins.

After a few words of instruction, Radclive shook hands with the prisoner again.

"Goodbye, Tom," he said.

Chapter Two

Gone to Dust

1.

A Voice: It was a long time ago. Some of it I know directly, but most of it was told to me by different folks over the years. As far as the murder and the hanging are concerned, there's documents of the trials and petitions and such around, if you can lay your hands on them, and they can tell you better about that than my poor fallible memory. As to the rest, here's what I know, or what I think I know, which comes to the same thing after enough years have passed.

The settlement of New Ireland, with all its people and farms and schools and trading posts and sawmills and lumber camps and its churches and the rectory, too, has long since gone to dust — not a sign remaining now; none, that is, but the Roman Catholic cemetery, which even itself had been lost to the wilderness for many years, until it was rediscovered and cleaned up and given its own monument, by the settlers' descendants. Consigned (or elevated) to the realm of local legend and lore and mystery, the tangible settlement has been shrunk by time's mortality and decay to the boundaries of this cemetery, with its fading stones — some tilted, others crumbling, most of them white as salt-water shells or the jawbone of some forest animal left to dry, clean as spit, in the relentless sun.

At least it has survived, this Catholic boneyard, not having suffered the fate of the Protestant place of burial down the road. When the caretakers of that cemetery departed, it was sent more quickly into oblivion than ever nature alone could do by the thoughtless members of a sportsmen's fraternity, who removed the gravestones to make a stone walkway for their clubhouse. Nothing was left behind but a cross on an old map — not even a memory (for there are none left now who knew where it was). And there are those, who claim to know of such things, who will say, despite the evidence of the cross on the map and the boot-smooth stone steps of the sportsmen's retreat, that it never was at all.

But the New Ireland Catholics still have their stones, worn and weather-battered though they are, and one is the obelisk, rising, not to a pyramidal point, this one, but to the cross of Christ's crucifixion. On the four flat faces of the mottled grey shaft, in a stone circle, is enscribed the letter "M"; and beneath the "M," on the south face of the granite column, the legend "John McAuley Died Dec. 13, 1880 Aged 92 yrs"; on the north face, "Mary A. McAuley Died Aug. 20, 1906 Aged 52 yrs"; and, toward the sunrise, the legend "Rev. J.E. McAuley Died Feb. 3, 1907 Aged 63 yrs." John Edward McAuley was a priest; he was New Ireland's priest. He was a big red-faced man, and he came out of the Richibucto area, up by the strait in Kent County, where the descendants of some of the Acadians — driven by the English out of the Petitcodiac valley — have their homes. Even now, after all these years — he died, as the stone testifies, just a few months after the murder (the second victim, the romantics will tell you, of Mary Ann's killer) — the last few old people who remember him speak wistfully of him; remembering the high, broad forehead, and the short, curly hair parted in the middle and pressed flat to his skull, so the hair curled up into short wings on either side, like the slickered waves of a dandified pedlar or a country druggist promoting his stock of new hair-oils.

Father McAuley's heart was weak, it's said, and his work arduous. "Work hard?" you scoff. "A priest? Let him stand at the base of a hemlock, with an eight-foot crosscut or a razor-sharp double bit in his hands, and bring that dammer down. Sitting in the parlour having tea with the missus ain't work, and neither is jawin' from the pulpit." There's those might say that. Father McAuley, though, was given a huge parish, and he travelled constantly to tend his scattered flock. He had secular matters to look after, such as contracting the cutting of 400,000 feet of birch and spruce and fir from the church's New Ireland property in 1905, and keeping interlopers away from the lake nestled in the hills. The locals called it "Priest Lake" and its glistening waters were a constant temptation to fishermen.

Travelling off the beaten track back then was robust work. It meant horse and wagon where the trains wasn't running, and the trains skirted Father McAuley's parish — the *Intercolonial* mainline between Moncton and Saint John across the north, the *Salisbury and Harvey* to the east, and the *Prong*, running from Petitcodiac into Elgin, on the west. They say the priest was feeling pains about his heart for ten days prior to his death, but he didn't slow down at all. That Sunday morning when he died — it was in February and you may imagine what it's like getting into the hills in winter (doctors were known to snowshoe clear over a mountain to get to a snow-bound patient on the other side) — a small congregation of his nearest parishioners had already gathered at St. Agatha's for early mass. But he had been stricken in the night, and it was too late to help him. His housekeeper, Mabel Williamson, sent a messenger for Doctor Murray in Albert, but he couldn't get there in time.

It was a large parish, and it was rugged. The parochial house was in New Ireland, and the parish church — St. Agatha's — was, too, but the priest was away from the settlement a lot of the time. He had four outlying missions to serve as well — the whole of Albert County, and missions in two neighbouring counties. He would take his own carriage or hitch a ride with the mail wagon down to Albert, then take the train up to Salisbury, and another carriage from there to the church. On the way back he'd take the *Prong* to Petitcodiac and transfer into Elgin. He had no mission in Elgin, which was a Protestant community, but there were a few "friends of the faith," as he called them, residing there. They would drive him back home into the hills, if the mail wagon wasn't due. He had his own horse and buggy at the rectory, of course, and used them when he could — that is, if the housekeeper didn't need them while he was away, or if another, more convenient, means of transport didn't offer itself.

That's a mighty lot of travelling for a middle-aged man who didn't do physical work like a woodsman or a farmer. But it was a rural parish, and he had to go to them; they couldn't all make it to St. Agatha's come mass. Wasn't as easy getting around in those days, at any time of the year, especially into and out of New Ireland. In the winter there'd be snow up there you just couldn't get through, without your horse humping through it to break single trail, or you going ahead shovelling a path, making steps up the hill for the horse, the sky so blue you think it might shatter in the cold.

Back in 1906, New Ireland was already a dying place; I don't mean boneyard dying, though that was part of it, too. It seemed like the end of the world up there for some people, and they or their children or their grandchildren, looking into the future, could see the place barren of good soil and crops and livestock and saw-logs and people. They were cut off; and the big timber had long since been cut out — the wooden ships, also long dead and gone, had carried the last of it out of the bay decades ago. Then the small timber was gone, too, and the acidic soil — never as fecund as the people who called upon it for the sustenance of themselves and their get, and their animals and their get — sifted into the holes that were left when the stones were removed to be heaped and fenced; and there was never enough of it anyways to cover the roots and the rocks of a New Ireland field.

2.

The chroniclers of the early history of the county tell of the French settlement of the marshes along Shepody Bay and the eastern shore of the Petitcodiac River, beginning in 1698. Of course, the Micmacs were there first, a nomadic people who camped along the shoreline and rivers in the summer for convenient fishing, and moved inland in the winter for shelter and game. The Petitcodiac — from the Micmac word *epetkutogoyek*, meaning "river that bends around back" — was a principal highway for their travels. Shepody is thought to have come from another Micmac word, *esedabit*, which means "turns back on itself" and refers to the winding course of the river that flows through the marshland. But there are some who argue that the word is a corruption of *Chapeau Dieu*, supposedly uttered by an awestruck French sailor gazing from his ship at the top of the mountain — the peak visible a thousand feet up, above a layer of fog over the bay.

The treeless marshland along the river, flooded in the spring and washed with saltwater during high tides, attracted the Acadian pioneers to the area. They brought with them the technical knowledge and the enduring skills to keep the salt water at bay, and to transform the marshes into fertile fields where crops could be grown. With spades, pick-axes and hoes, they dyked the river margins, then left the land idle until the rain had purified the soil for cultivation. It was hard patient toil, but easier and more familiar to the Acadians than tackling the heavily wooded uplands, where trees and their stumps had to be removed. The axe was a less essential tool for these people, although they did need wood for their homes and barns, for fuel, and for construction of *aboiteaux* (the ditch gates that released fresh water from marsh streams, but kept salt tide water out.) They followed the example of the Indians by taking to the woods to hunt and trap. Along with the game they killed, their diet included wheaten bread, peas, cabbages and pork. From France they had brought with them cattle, sheep, swine and horses.

The largest settlement west of the bay, in the early years, was at the foot of Shepody Mountain — between it and the sea, as French settlements usually were. No true Arcadia, perhaps, but it was a prosperous community, the farms successful. Part of the year was spent fishing, and the catch dried or salted. Salt, also used as a trading commodity, was obtained by ladling sea water into hollow trees and wooden vessels and allowing it to evaporate in the sun. The marshes were home, too, to many seafowl and, in season, some of their eggs were added to the diet of the pioneers.

The Micmacs and the French settlers got along well together — the Indians passing on hunting lore, their knowledge of local plant life, and the use of birchbark for containers, canoes, and for insulating shelters. The pioneers dug earth cellars to house their garden produce; they had millstones, quarried from nearby Grindstone Island, for grinding wheat and corn; and, on the eastern bank of Church Brook at Hopewell Hill, they built what was probably the first Catholic Church in Albert County — a little chapel built partly of stone, partly of logs, with a tiny cross-tipped spire. It also boasted a small bell and, as late as 1906, broken headstones could be seen, scattered among still-discernible mounds over the bones of the first tillers of the Shepody soil. Nearby was a bubbling spring of water called the "Holy Spring." The lives of the Acadians who settled in what was to become Albert County were described by an early priest, Abbe Raynal, thus: "Domestic happiness and public morality are fostered by early marriages, and homely thrift is rewarded by almost universal happiness."

They lived there, undisturbed by the politics of the old country, for half a century, until 1755 when everything changed. The English attacked the French settlements at Shepody, Hillsborough and Memramcook. The settlers were driven from their homes to the woods, and their communities burned to the ground. Those who didn't escape to other parts of the province were captured and expelled from their land to distant colonies. A large number from Shepody fled north, and there are tales of men and women wandering for months in the hills, trying to stay out of the hands of the British, who continued to scour the countryside. There was considerable loss of life, and the lives of the people of the Fundy marshes who survived were disrupted forever.

In the initial skirmish between the settlers and a force of 200 English soldiers, thirteen of the latter — (their descendants were the historians) — were said to have been killed and buried on the Shepody Marsh. (The graves were known to the English settlers and later residents recall seeing them, but their location has since been lost.) For eight years, the fertile land on the marshes lay uncultivated, unoccupied, then it was gradually resettled by people from the American colonies, from the English colonies across the bay, and from the Old Country. There were many signs of the Acadians' years at Shepody, one of them the living presence of an old Frenchman named Belliveau, who claimed to be the only survivor of the expulsion; another, the tumbled logs of the little chapel on the bank of Church Brook. The sacred bell was never found, but legend has it that before leaving, the Acadian settlers sank it, along with the sacramental vessels, deep into the bubbling waters of the Holy Spring, to save them from the desecrations of the invaders.

3.

The farms of uplands New Ireland had little in common with the tillage of the marshlands. These rock and gravel dry-dirt farmsteads had a kind of hard-won impermanence at the best of times, but the obdurate implacable mounds of stone that grew out of them, like the arrowheads and stone-chip tools and skeletal remains left in some prehistoric campsite, are there yet, and will remain there — part of the forest that grew around and over them, but furiously apart, too, like burial mounds, the inverse of the dents in the fields where the houses were. If you know where to look, you will find the rubble-filled cavity where Father McAuley's rectory was, and, in a thicket of reeds, the stone-ringed, collapsing shaft of the well. And in the dense spruce, a few rods to the east, a right-angled jigsaw puzzle of rock wall, part of the foundation of St. Agatha's church.

Still, to the Irish settlers, hounded by the pure fierce malice at large in the land of their birth, who came here in the young decades of the nineteenth century, this New Ireland must have held out more good green hope than the old; the chance, if they worked hard, to own their land, to raise their families, to create the beginning of a chain of succession; to make their mark, and leave behind a sign of their passing. They could see that the soil was thin; but it would grow crops, like potatoes and turnips and buckwheat. The fertile intervale lands down on the bay were out of their reach, their abundance long since harnessed and exploited and settled upon by the others who had come, before themselves and after the expulsion of the Acadian pioneers.

The first Irish cleared the uplands as best they could. The land was parcelled out by the government in 100-acre grants, and the homesteader was required to clear a certain amount of it, build a house and a barn, and raise crops and livestock. They planted their first seed around the trees, until they got the woods rooted out. They cut the softwood and hardwood both, burned it, burned and pulled out the stumps if they could; some they would leave to rot like molars where they stood, until they were soft enough to deal with. Then they would pull them out and plough the ground. It was a long process, six or eight years from the time the land was cleared until the last stumps came out. A team of horses could pull some like corks and, in later years, there were mechanical stump pullers; the men looped a cable around adjacent stumps, then tightened it with a winch until one of them popped. A man has the memory of his father and himself stumping and fencing four acres in one hot summer of work. And they picked the everlasting stones, their most bountiful harvest. There were so many stones that they became fences; and still there were stones, so they filled the bogs and began the mounds; and the mounds are their monuments.

The most conspicuous family in New Ireland's fleeting heyday was that sired by Bernard Duffy, who came there from Ireland in 1827. He was the patriarch of Duffy Hill, a section of hardscrabble and softwood timber with a steep pitch on its southwestern side, at the base of which two clear streams came around opposite sides of the hill and met. Their convergence whispered to Bernard of a grist mill, perhaps even a lumber mill, if the water could be harnessed and sufficiently amplified to turn the mill-wheels after spring runoff had abated. Bernard — driven out of the port city to "higher ground" by the cholera, they said — settled his family at the crest of Duffy Hill, and his sons and grandsons would farm and lumber there for the next century. The last Duffy to live and toil there — Bernard's grandson, John L. — sold his land to C.T. White's lumber company (along with eight forty-pound containers of butter to White's store in Alma), and moved out his family (the three of the six children who had survived infancy) lock, stock, and barrel in October, 1918.

As Duffys began to proliferate through the first half of the nineteenth century, the hill sprouted more homesteads and, by 1906, when the McAuley tragedy occurred just a mile down the road, there were four Duffy families on the hill, all having homes within a few hundred yards of each other. They were industrious people, with a reputation for independence. They worked hard and kept to themselves, but neighbours would come when the work was done to play fiddles and dance in Duffy homes.

At the New Ireland murder trial in 1907, there were allegations that the Duffys might have been responsible for roughing up a pedlar, who sold dry goods and trinkets from the back of his wagon to the country people of southern New Brunswick. There were two versions of the story heard by the court, both based on local gossip and neither substantiated by later testimony or evidence presented at the trials. One painted the Duffys as outraged victims of a dishonest pedlar; the other portrayed the pedlar as having fallen haplessly into a family of thieves. In both versions, neither the pedlar, who was said to have received a sound beating from the Duffys, nor his wagonload of wares, were seen in the area again. The court heard another story, pried from the reluctant lips of Father McAuley, under questioning by defence counsel. The priest said that local people believed it might have been a Duffy who, a few months before the 1906 murder there, had broken into the New Ireland mission house when no one was at home and absconded with a quantity of the church's wine and medicinal liquor. Perhaps the Duffy notoriety resulted simply from the prominence in the area of the name; perhaps, after all, they had enemies. But they had a friend, too — the stipendiary magistrate in nearby Harvey — who wrote a letter to the county's weekly paper explaining the circumstances of the "supposed robbery" of the pedlar and defending the name of an "honourable and respectable family."

The Duffys were in some ways typical of the settlers who came to New Ireland, but they were also more industrious, more prolific perhaps, maybe more far-sighted, too. When Bernard emigrated in 1827, he was either thirty-one or thirty-eight years old, or neither; the evidence provided by tombstone and census records conflicts. With him were his wife Margaret — who was aged either twenty-seven or thirty-one, or neither — and infant daughter Bridget. The couple landed with other families at Saint John and, fearing the disease and squalor they found among the new arrivals there, trekked into Albert County along the Shepody Road, one of the many immigrant trails spoking from the port.

Bernard wanted to put down permanent roots. The main road through the young settlement was part of the Shepody stage-coach trail, which coiled and cranked from Saint John through a wilderness that was slowly retreating, and it may be that New Ireland did not seem so isolated then. In 1847, twenty years after settling on his hill, Bernard, with his neighbours, petitioned the "honourable representatives of the province" for money to build a grist mill on his creek. The petition bore the signatures of forty-six residents of the community — McGinleys, McFaddens and Becks; Fentons, McArdles, McCarrons, Fitzgerald; Daughertys and Murrays and Connors and Dornans; Teahans and Barrett; Gallagher, Long and Boyle and O'Connor — many appearing to have been written by the same hand. Also attached was an individual petition from Bernard himself, signed with a heavy stroke.

The legislature agreeably voted twenty pounds for the oat mill and twenty pounds more for a grist mill. Nothing of the mills is left now, but Bernard's great-granddaughter, Clara, who spent her early years on Duffy Hill and moved out of the area with her family in 1918, has said that one of the big grinding stones is somewhere there yet, lying amidst the gravel in the bed of Duffy Brook.

That brook came from two streams, their origins even higher in the hills. The first ran southwesterly from the Kent Hills highlands, seeping out of an uninhabitable area known as Burley Bog, collecting itself into a small but respectable stream as it came down the Shepody slopes, passing from the black swampland through hardwood stands. It descended into dark cool stands of softwood, where the spongy banks were carpeted with moss and needles shed by pine and spruce, fir and hemlock, and emerged again into sunlight, where the mossy carpet abruptly became hardscrabble, sand and gravel (the effluent of glaciers). The second stream hugging the base of Bernard's hill began as a trickle of runoff, leaking northwest from a crack in the rock basin of Priest Lake, before joining with other streams and hurling itself into the deep chasm of the "Forty-Five," a violent tumble of crashing white water and soaring spray which, for more than a century of springtimes, sent millions of feet of splintered timber plummeting between high, water-slick stone canyon walls to the millponds of Alma.

Bernard and Margaret stayed and laboured and grew old and died on Duffy Hill, and so did many of their children. But the grandchildren — theirs and those of many of the other settlers — did not. Many of them left at the first opportunity. For a few, it was the natural and audacious need of the young to reach for the books and the minds and the dreams that could not then be brought to the uplands. For most, it was just to get away from the work and the weather and the weariness, to another golden place, where the work and the weariness might at least yield more tangible rewards — something to be counted and pocketed. They scattered to Pittsburgh and Maine and Rhode Island, to Saskatchewan and New Hampshire, Montreal and Minnesota. Some stayed closer to home, but they left the hill all the same, settling down below on the marshlands by the bay. One went to Albert where, until the influenza epidemic killed her in 1918, she ran the small hotel that was the site in August, 1906 of the meeting of Father McAuley and Tom Collins, the young English tramp who had been cutting wood there and looking for work.

Of those who stayed for a time on Duffy Hill, one named Kate found the cold corpse of Mary Ann McAuley in the hot summer of 1906. All of them are buried in the little cemetery with the bones of the Teahans, the Longs and the Barretts, the O'Connors, the Dornans and the Doyles. And resting with

them, too, are the bones of the priest, his father, and the
murdered Mary Ann.

4.

ALBERT MINES: John W. Steeves, 35, of Curryville
was killed when struck by a tree he was falling. When
it fell, the butt of the tree jumped 15 feet from the
stump and struck him. He was found later by his work
mates, laying under a hemlock tree with a broken leg
and a broken neck.
                        —*The Albert Journal, March 7, 1906*

A Voice: Back then, when a man was killed in the woods
while working with his axe, that axe would never be used by
another woodsman. Fellas he was working with would take
and throw it away or, sometimes, they'd take and drive it
into the trunk of a tree and leave it. No, I don't know whether
it was out of respect for the dead man or superstition about
the axe being bad luck, but that's what they'd do. Twenty-five
years after Jesse Yeomans was killed by a falling branch,
some men went back to the spot where he was killed, and
there was his axe still sticking out of the tree where one of
the men who'd found him had drove it, the wood grown all
around the iron head.

Oh, they died young then. Diphtheria and TB — the
consumption, they called it. Three Longs died in 1903. I think
they had TB. They were cousins, first cousins. Big family;
they lived right nearby. It may have been diphtheria, but I
think it was TB. Charlie Long died of it, because I can
remember him walking down to our place. He was just a
shadow. The next summer old Patrick Long — he was seventy at the time — fell over a windfall and broke his neck.

WATERSIDE: Eighty-year-old Robert Mulligan of
New Horton, who was living with Jeremiah Tingley
at The Ridge, a few miles from here, killed himself
with a shotgun. 'He had been in declining health for
some time having been afflicted with paralysis of the
tongue, which practically prevented him from talking
and almost from eating, so that recently he has be-

come very despondent, having it is understood expressed the idea that his death would be a good thing for himself and those about him.' He planned the matter carefully. 'He took his gun down in the field near where he lived and having attached a cord to the trigger, fired the gun with his foot, the weapon being pointed at his head. The charge entered near the ear, blowing out the lower part of the cranium and part of the brain.' Doctor Murray ruled an inquest unnecessary. Mulligan was a native of Ireland and a strong Orangeman, 'a man of more than ordinary intelligence being particularly well informed in the history of Orangeism and well informed on current topics.' He'd been a county resident for 50 years.

—The Albert Journal, Sept. 18, 1907

There wasn't much they could do for pneumonia. They'd put poultices on their chests to break up the congestion, and save some of them that way. They'd take mustard — the powdered mustard that they got to make pickles — and a wee bit of flour and they'd put it between two pieces of cloth — fine flannel — heat it in the oven and put it on the chest; when it started to get cold they'd put on another one. I don't know why it worked, but it loosened up the phlegm some way, so they could cough and raise up some of the stuff.

I recall the Tingley children. Happened over to what they used to call Chester; nothing there now, but it was on the sidehill road up to Caledonia Mountain. In the winter of 1906, Mrs. Beecher Tingley lost three of her children, all within just a few days, from some sort of poisoning from bad water from a cellar, the doctor thought; but it started with pneumonia that seemed to get better, then their stomachs swole up and they was dead within hours. Eight-year-old Hallie, six-year-old Fronie, and a three-year-old. There was a stone for them up in the Caledonia Cemetery. Three other of her kids never did get sick — at least not that time.

I had a brother. My dad sharpened a scythe and hung it up on a big spike in the woodhouse. And Jimmy got up and he put the scythe down, and what did he do then, but jump right on top of it. He cut his heel clean right around, right into the bone. Whatever flesh was there, he cut it all. There was a neighbour of ours living in Uncle Barney's house, a Mrs. Dolan. Mother said, "Will you go and tell Mrs. Dolan to come over." She come over and, oh, it was bleeding. She done it up, and there was never one bit of infection and it healed like everything. All they had in them days was carbolic acid, and they would dilute that in boiling water. It was about the only disinfectant they had. Buy it in a bottle, red liquid. Strong smell. There were directions on the bottle, how to use it so it wouldn't burn the flesh. Then they got creolin, horrible smelling stuff.

Jim Hayes, who was the Priest Lake clubhouse caretaker one time, was one they said could stop the blood of someone who was bleeding to death. I don't know how he did it. There was a prayer, I think he said. It was just a superstition, I'm sure. It was bad when anyone got hurt back in there, because it was so far from any doctors. Lumbering was dangerous work, and it wasn't unusual for a man to get a foot cut in the woods, especially in the winter.

We lived on the Forty-Five. Dad generally had twenty men working for him — two lumber camps. Have to keep two cooks. Buy flour by the big barrel and sugar by the hundred-weight. In the summertime, the blackflies were something awful. The men working in the woods had to put grease on their skin. And the horses would go wild; sometimes they'd run away. They couldn't stand those flies. Dad would cut lumber up until Christmas time. Twitch the logs with "dogs" (dog hooks on twitching chains) and horses to the riverbank, where it was browed on the bank. If the cut was too far from the river, you'd have to put them in big yards. Then after Christmas, shovel the snow off the yards and haul the logs to the riverbank with teams of horses. There were brows all along the river, usually 50,000 feet or so in a brow. Get them ready in the latter part of March, then drive them downstream in April after the ice broke up, to the Alma pond where there was a mill.

POINT WOLFE: Harry Strayhorn, 24, was killed by a flying slab at the mill. He was running the rotary saw, sawing birch lumber, when a piece of slab got jammed. When Strayhorn attempted to remove the slab, the saw caught it, carrying it around. As it came up through the sawpit, it was hurled with terrific force against his face, the pointed end entering the left eye to the depth of an inch and one half, penetrating the skull at the back of the eye. Muscles and optic nerve were destroyed. The eye was removed and a dozen stitches taken in gashes above and below the socket. Mr. Strayhorn, who has a family, regained consciousness, but later died.

—from The Albert Journal, Aug. 16, 1905

My dad used to work at stream-driving on the Forty-Five. It was dangerous work, and logjams especially were. They'd have to pry them loose with peaveys and, if manpower didn't work, they'd use dynamite. Those men were wet all day long, and that water in April was cold; snows twenty feet deep would be melting and running down those streams out of the uplands. Some of the men would jump in the river first thing in the morning, though, just to get themselves wet. Get it over with all at once, they'd say, can't stay dry anyhow. We used to worry about my dad, but he must have been good; he worked there every year.

I've heard stories about men working on log brows. Some of them would be high as a four-storey house. Sometimes a man would slip, get caught under them. Once they started rolling down to the river, there was no stopping them. I heard about one of the men — don't just remember his name now — somehow got caught below the brow when the logs started. Somebody yelled and down that hill he run and into the river, frozen spruce logs tumbling and thumping after him — they make a hollow sound when they're frozen. There was no time for the poor fellow to jump aside, I guess, or maybe running downhill was his first instinct. Anyway, he was figured to be a goner. When the other men got down there, though, they found him in the river alright, but the logs had teepeed around him pretty as you please, like some giant'd been weaving a timber basket. He was wet, and he was scared, but he wasn't hurt. Got religion after that, I'm guessing, if he didn't already have it.

And the dams. We used to go down and watch the logs all go out through the dams and into the main river. The school was right by the river, and teacher would let us all go and watch the drive, like a holiday. Dad always river-drove from the little dam up above the Forty-Five. They'd heist that dam, and the logs would go down to the Forty-Five. Then they'd go down there and heist the two together. The gates were hoisted with a log staff, twenty-five or thirty feet long. Three men on each side wearing heavy corks — that's boots with steel caulks on their soles and heels — would lift them with their shoulders, and push them out. Hurl the logs and the water and everything. The whole dam would just be shaking when the logs went. It made an awful roar, and it was dangerous. One fellow drowned in New Ireland that I can recall. Johnny Leaman. He was a stream-driver with my dad, a nice man, only twenty-seven, too. They used to claim that he wasn't very well, that he used to take dizzy spells. He was on a jam of logs and he fell in, went down when the logs went, right into the main river. He was gone for ten days. They found him way downstream in a great deep hole, right under the logs.

The dams themselves were built out of logs, some twenty feet high, corked hard on both sides. Four gates abreast on some dams, each gate about four by eight feet, and four more gates on the next tier. A rack was built around the gates to keep the branches and junk away. A good dam would last thirty or forty years, but they had to be kept in good shape. It could take up to ten hours to refill a dam, but with good water, you could get two or three heads a day.

Some of the big lumbermen of the time would cut 900,000 to a million feet of lumber a year. Every year in late spring the Petitcodiac River and Shepody Bay would assume their summer role of industry, and steamers large and small and sailing craft of all sizes would make inroads into the large lumber piles stacked on wharves (the outcome of the previous winter's operations) and into the huge pile of gypsum at Hillsborough hauled from the quarries of the Albert Manufacturing Company. Five lighters — small cargo boats — at a time would ferry deal out of the serpentine course of

Sawmill Creek, a tidal branch of the Shepody River, to the sailing ships tied up at Five Fathom Hole off Grindstone Island. Up to twenty million feet could come out of the Shepody River system some years; five or six million out of Waterside. Timothy O'Connor handled a couple of million feet a year. He hired contractors to cut the logs and deliver them to the river, and paid so much for 1,000 feet of lumber. Some of the trees then were three feet through. He was lumbering for Talbott, then for White, but he couldn't get along with White. Only drove the river three times after White took over. He had the Salmon River.

> ALMA: Leverett Snider and George Wilkins, while lumbering near Long Reach during the winter, frequently saw moose tracks. 'On Tuesday last, while cruising their winters operations, they came on a moose-yard. They soon noticed by the tracks that the herd numbered four, two old and two young ones. Having never seen a moose they decided to give chase and see these denizens of the forest. The snow being about five feet deep the moose could make headway only very slowly, while the men being on snowshoes soon overtook the game. As the moose did not show fright, Mr. Wilkins jumped on the back of the bull and seizing him by the mane and ears, had as merry a ride for a short distance through the woods as Buffalo Bill had on the prairies. Mr. Snider contented himself by getting his arm around the neck of the cow and hanging on to her for a short distance. After they had fully satisfied their curiosity as to the make up of the animals they let them go. Probably but few of the veteran hunters have had similar experience. The bull had already shed his antlers. The men will return to the yard after the snow goes off and search for the antlers.'
>
> —*The Albert Journal, March 24, 1904*

I was a registered guide for hunters. When that season was over, I'd run traplines up in New Ireland and around. Fox, wildcat, mink, beaver. Prices were low, but I had to do it to make a living. Cats were forty or fifty pounds average. There was a guy who was good at catching them. They called him the cat trapper, and me the mink trapper. I used the Victor trap, No. 1, 2, 3, 4 and 5 bear trap. Keep at it 'til the snow got too deep; sometimes there'd be six or seven feet of it in the woods. Trap muskrat in the spring. One time I caught 650 'rats, but I didn't get much sleep. People lost a lot of cattle and sheep to bears then, some as big as 800 pounds. I shot four or five in my time. They're a bad smelling thing. A man I knew got his boots torn off by a bear. Chased him up a stump, then come right up after him. Another fella heard him hollerin' and come on the tear and shot the bear. He was lucky. I've had them keep me up a tree all night. They won't let you down 'til it starts to come daylight. Then they leave. If the tree's big enough, they'll come up after you. Don't worry, you don't sleep!

> HARVEY: Mrs. Bishop killed a large hawk which had the misfortune of sticking its head through the slats of her chicken coop in search of dinner. She happened to be in the yard at the time and, attracted by the commotion, grabbed the hawk's head from the other side of the coop and held on, screaming at the house for someone to come with a knife. 'Before the hawk had full time to realize his situation, he met the fate of the political offender of the old days.'
> —*The Albert Journal, Sept. 27, 1905*

We'd keep cream and butter in the cool cellar. Didn't buy much in stores; salt, sugar, tea. Pig meat we'd pickle in big wooden barrels; put in salt, sugar and water, boil it all and pack it in crocks. Keep it so long in that, then when we thought it was cured enough, hang the hams in the basement. The beef we wouldn't kill 'til we could keep it frozen. In the summertime, you could hang meat forty or fifty feet down a well, if you had one, and keep it ten or twelve days. Otherwise, you couldn't keep it unless it was salted. We had a well, but it wasn't good water. Most often carried it from a spring down on Uncle Pat's place. Most people settled where there was a spring. Hardly had to dig a well at all. It'd take quite a chill to freeze spring water. We'd get ice from the lake in the winter, cover it with sawdust. Big blocks'd last all summer. We'd eat a lot of fish in the summer.

We'd lumber in the wintertime, farm in the summer. Grow oats, buckwheat, hay, potatoes, vegetables. A man would come with his threshing machine to do the oats. Take the buckwheat to a gristmill at Riverside to be ground into flour; make pancakes with buttermilk. You'd boil small potatoes with the buckwheat bran, and that's what you raised your pigs on. Fatten 'em up real nice. Shear the sheep, card the wool, and make yarn to knit our clothes. I used to wear underdrawers right off the sheep's back. As comfortable as could be. Cloth could be spun on a loom owned by the Dan O'Connor family. And there was a tailor in Albert who made and sold dress clothing when it was needed. If you had the money, you could mail order children's clothes out of Eaton's catalogue from Toronto.

> POINT WOLFE: Thomas Marshall, a negro musician and dancer gave an entertainment in the Orange Hall the night of the 30th. One of his specialties was the imitation of a train starting and running a journey over bridges and culverts and through tunnels, ending with a stop at a station with the hiss of the air brakes and the toot of a whistle. All this was performed on a common harmonica, and was said to be first rate.
>
> —*The Albert Journal, Nov. 6, 1903*

My dad played the violin and the Teahan boys — Jacky and Ronald — played the violin, and the girls used to play an organ. We'd walk up there in the evenings sometimes and they'd play the music. They used to have dances and parties in their own homes in those days. For the parties, everyone'd take a little food, a little whiskey. You could send to taverns in Saint John for whiskey. O'Neil's and O'Regan's shipped wines and liquors from Saint John by train to rural customers. It would be sent to the station at Penobsquis, where it would be picked up. Home-made, though, was better than the stuff you bought. Make it out of corn, barley, rye. Cook it and run it through a tube through a brook to condense it. Pour some in a spoon and light a match to it and there would be a tall blue flame.

> HOPEWELL CAPE: Doctor Murray of Albert, Doctor Carnwath of Riverside, and Doctors Randall and Lewis of Hillsboro all face charges under the Canada Temperance Act for prescribing liquor for other than medicinal purposes. Murray, Randall and Lewis were all fined. Charges against Carnwath were dismissed. The *Journal*'s editor notes there were many witnesses in court, and it was passing strange that most said to be suffering from various ailments were still able to work every day.
> —*The Albert Journal, Oct. 31, 1906*

My mother used to be nervous. When the men were away working, the women were alone a lot, many with young children. In them days, there used to be a lot of fellas come around, asking for lodging for the night, to stay overnight, or to have breakfast or dinner or supper or something like that. Transients and pedlars. You'd feed them, usually, and send them on their way. I remember one neighbour who regularly put heavy blankets over her windows at night, to keep the light in and the transients away.

There were many pedlars travelling the roads. One old fella — his name was Anthony Hatti — we used to look forward to. We loved to see him coming. He talked funny. He was dark-skinned, a little. Up from Saint John, I think. He had a horse and a wagon, with a flat trunk on the back full of watches and rings. There would be other travellers that would come with clothing. They would stay at a resident's house overnight. There were no boarding houses or hotels up there. The Syrian who had the run-in with the Duffys — I've forgotten his name, but I remember him well, coming to leave his pack at our place that night. He showed us a lump on his head, saying he had been at the Duffys and had been beaten, and they had taken some of his jewellery. He thought he was in bad shape, you know, with this head injury. He took our wagon to go to Saint John; my father gave it to him. I remember when he came back; they never thought he'd come back. Some of the neighbours said, "Well, he's gone, he'll never come back." He did, though.

5.

Bishop John Sweeney of Saint John was a man who believed in establishing local missions. He had been a rural missionary himself. In his early years he had served the people of the Memramcook Valley in Westmorland County and, it is assumed by church historians, had crossed the Petitcodiac River regularly to serve the Catholic people of Albert. When he was appointed to the see of Saint John in 1860 — the year the province was divided into two dioceses — Bishop Sweeny took note of the fact that in New Ireland, was the largest community of Catholics in Albert County —mostly of Irish extraction. Being centrally located on the coach road from Saint John, it was the geographical centre of Catholic activity in the area. He decided that a church should be built there. The site, selected perhaps because it was on the crest of the highest central point along New Ireland road, 1,100 feet above sea level, belonged to two sisters, who at that time were residents of the community of Sussex in adjacent Kings County.

On July 8, 1861, Catherine and Mary McDevitt set their marks to the instrument which consigned 200 acres of their land in New Ireland to Bishop Sweeny, for the sum of fifty pounds "lawful money of New Brunswick." The section of land had originally been granted in the name of David McDevitt, who had come to New Brunswick from Ireland in 1826, when he was sixty-four years of age, and settled on the New Ireland Road with his wife and family. The census taker described McDevitt as a "beggar:farmer:proprietor."

The legal work completed, Bishop Sweeny sent Rev. David O'Brien to serve the missions of Albert, with the added assignment of seeing that a church was built in New Ireland. By the end of 1866, it had been done, and the new church looked out across the dense forests of the Shepody Hills from the north side of the New Ireland Road.

That was also the year, however, that members of one branch of the American Fenian Society, in an ill-considered attempt to secure a Canadian base for its efforts to free Ireland from Britain, launched an ineffectual raid on the New Brunswick border at Calais. It has been described as a "comic-opera attack" that accomplished nothing, but it heightened what was already a considerable level of hostility in New Brunswick at that time toward the Irish Catholics. At the time of the raid, a rumour that a band of Fenians had set up headquarters at the tiny new chapel in New Ireland caused a great deal of anxiety in the Protestant villages of Hopewell and Harvey. "Persons who had occasion to pass through that way in the still hours of the night," a county historian has written, "declared that they saw lights moving about the church and made other similar alarming statements. The excitement rose to such a pitch that a system of defence was commenced, and the people lived in daily fear of being attacked. Whatever truth there may have been in the report, it is sufficient to say that the dreaded attack never came, and quiet soon reigned again."

One of the men ordained by Bishop Sweeney was Edward McAuley. Born in 1844 in Richibucto, a fishing and ship-building centre on New Brunswick's Northumberland Strait coast, McAuley was educated first in the local schools, then at St. Dunstans College in Charlottetown and finally at Laval University in Quebec. His first parish was Moncton, his second a mission in nearby Fox Creek. He went to Saint John for a short time and in 1868 was placed over the Grand Lake Mission in Queens County, remaining there for three years. In 1870 he was appointed to the mission in Albert County. He took up his residence in New Ireland, and was there but a short time when he ordered that the original church be torn down. A new structure was erected opposite the old site and named St. Agatha's. The site of the old church then became the burial ground.

Father McAuley saw a need for more chapels in his parish; the population of the county was increasing and, he thought, prosperity was in sight. In succession, over a number of years, came St. Aloysious Chapel at Albert Mines, the Chapel of Our Lady of Mercy at Fredericton Road, the Chapel of the Sacred Heart at Beaver Brook and the Chapel of St.

Isadore Agricola at South Branch, King's County. After being transferred to Saint John for a few years, Father McAuley came back to New Ireland in 1901 determined to build a new rectory. This he did, and remained at Chapel Hill until his death.

The church property lay behind a four-foot high white picket fence, which marched along the edge of the roadway for several hundred feet. The mission house was an elegant two-storey gabled affair with a steeply pitched roof, set well back from the road on the crest of Chapel Hill. The structure, with its arched windows, its delicate ornamental trim, and its full-length railed verandah, was a fine tribute to the long labours of Father McAuley on behalf of the Catholic people of the parish. It manifest in physical form the esteem in which the priest was held by his people.

Entrance to Father McAuley's home, with its wide stretch of lawn, its orchards of fruit trees, and its varied shrubbery, was gained through a wide, usually awry, gate set into the whitewashed fence. Attached to one end of the rectory, and arranged behind it in an L-shape, were the woodhouse and barns, where hay and grains were stored, and where horses were stabled. A few hundred feet to the east and also behind the white fence was Father McAuley's church, St. Agatha's, a structure with massive spruce timbers, (cut and hewn and set in place by Patrick Duffy), buttressing the central steeple at the front, as impressive in its own way as the house. Huge spruce and pine stretched their own steepled shapes high into the sky at the the crest of the hill.

As isolated and lonely a place as New Ireland could be, especially when winter storms heaped snow into impassable drifts, Father McAuley loved it there. A church history records: "The success and happiness of the Catholic people of Albert County, and most especially those of New Ireland, can be attributed to the love and devotion and fatherly care, both spiritually and temporally, he bore toward them. Amongst those Catholic people still living who remember Father Mc-Auley, there is evidence of the great love and affection that they held for him."

Chapter Three

Monday, August 20, 1906

1.

The heat came back with the rising sun. The single narrow window in the hired man's bedroom silvered and brightened, as the world outside came in with the morning light. Tom Collins came out of a restless sleep gradually, the rough pillow damp under his cheek. He rolled to his back. The spare furnishings and the wooden crucifix on the wall presented themselves to him once again. The tiny room shared a back corner of the rectory with a kitchen pantry. The bedroom was warm, its pall of air without motion. There was no ventilation, because someone had jammed the blade of a knife into the window frame so the lower sash couldn't be raised from the outside. Tom had left the knife alone. He had supposed that Mary Ann had put it there. He had learned quickly that the household functioned under a regime — Mary Ann's regime — and that there were prohibitions and expectations. So even though the room might have been made more comfortable by an open window, he had left the crude lock as it was. He had also left untouched a battered straight razor, which he found on the window sill the first night, the keen edge of its blade hidden in the handle.

A rough woollen blanket was at his feet. A heavy wool coat, stained and smelling of wood pitch and barns and sweat, and sweet horse-smell, hung on a bedpost. Tom pulled his clothes on, thinking of the day ahead. He thought of the bags he had shoved under the bed. He would have to try to harness the horse again. He wasn't used to such work — didn't like it. Horses made him nervous and he handled them, when he had to handle them at all, with great deference. The buckles and straps on the leather harness confused him. It seemed simple, watching someone else do it. Throw the web over the animal's back, buckle a few straps, coach the horse between the carriage poles, buckle a few more straps. Mary Ann did it with ease but, as soon as he reached for the harness, it seemed to tangle itself like eels in a bucket. He would become flustered and panicky. This morning, though, he would do it alone, take his time, get it right the first time.

The priest's horse was patient by training, gentle by nature, but Tom feared approaching it from behind to enter the stall beside it. He would flinch, watching the hooves fearfully, expecting them to lash at him as he moved in. The slight animal seemed huge, an immovable mass, when he was beside it in the narrow stall. Once while combing him down, the metal teeth of the curry scraping salt from the red hide, Tom was shoved against the wall by a casual shift of weight. The horse had merely relaxed a knee, flexing its leg and shifting balance from one hip to the other, as horses do at rest. There was no pain nor threat, just the pungent mass of the animal holding him. Still, he had felt as if he were suffocating, pinned in the stall, trapped in the humid dim space; the sudden fear as vivid as the dream remembrances of every claustrophobic crew's quarters he had ever inhabited at sea. His nose had seemed plugged by the thick air. Over the broad back of the horse, he had seen a triangular patch of sunlight upright on the barn floor like a swarming luminescent sail, as high as the open doors, myriad and vivid. Swirling dust and seeds in the brightness made more murky the interior of the stall where he had been pinned. He had tasted the thick air. The animal, of course, had moved away immediately when he pushed against it, oblivious of his panic, serenely apart, dignified in its detachment.

As it was with the horse, so it was with the household. Everything done was in Tom's best interest, but he seemed unhinged at times, his every move ungainly, awkward, performed without benefit of calm thought, in a fierce rush to get the task — whatever it was — over with. Nothing came as easily as it did at sea, and nothing came easily at sea. The priest was patient. Familiarity with the horse and with the bucksaw and the axe would evolve, the priest had believed, from a calm and steady routine. Tom had youth, if not an overwhelming enthusiasm for the work. "When he's learned, he'll be a good boy," Father McAuley would say, when asked about the abilities of his new hired man. But the housekeeper, who had spent the most of her life running Father McAuley's household with humourless and dedicated efficiency, was far less patient. She would wither him with a look, box his ears with her voice.

Dressed in his old dark clothes, a short-peaked cap on the back of his head, Tom walked through the empty kitchen, past the cold woodstove. He opened the back door, passed through it into the woodhouse. It was dark, close, the air smelling musty from the old cedar shingles, that had been ripped from the roof of the rectory that summer and thrown into the wood pit for kindling. The small windows of the woodhouse, hanging with spiderwebs, let in little light. Tom walked along the passageway by the wood pit, in front of which was a waist-high railing. There were four steps going down. He passed by. In the dim light, his eyes not yet adjusted to the shadows, the pit below the railing seemed to have no dimensions. He opened the door at the end of the passageway, and went through to the barn. The large dark eye of the horse caught the light, as the animal turned its head to look at him. The leather and brass paraphernalia of the harness was hanging from wooden pegs near the stall. Tom began to drag it down from the wall.

2.

This Monday morning, Shortland Harbell had to get back to his job at the sawmill in Albert. He had spent the weekend on Collier Mountain with his brother Bruce. The brothers left Bruce's farm at dawn, but they weren't on the road long before they felt the heat rising. It was going to be another warm dry day, alright. Not a sign of a cloud. "We're damned lucky," Bruce's neighbours were saying, "that we ain't been hit by a fire yet." New Brunswick's forests were being ravaged again that summer, but so far southern Albert County had been spared. It seemed that fires made damaging forays through the province every summer, and this one was no exception. Not as bad as the summer of 1903, mind you, when much of the southern coastal forest and many communities had been consumed by the "fire fiend" (which is what the popular press called it), but there were nasty outbreaks around Salisbury, at the north end of the rail-line out of Albert County, and across the Petitcodiac River in Westmorland.

Shortly after eight o'clock, Harbell's rig topped Chapel Hill and passed by Father McAuley's rectory. The brothers gazed idly at the serene mission house behind the white picket fence. In the front yard near the well, a white-faced horse stood, head down, hip-shot, tail waving lazily at flies. The horse was harnessed and hitched to an empty carriage. Reins were hanging from the bridle bit to the ground at the animal's feet. There was no one about.

The Harbells passed by in silence. A hundred yards further on, St. Agatha's Church with its timber steeple — the tip of the cross at its peak, the highest point in the county — gleamed bright and stark in the early light; opposite it, the little cemetery backed into the trees with its sere grass and small collection of headstones. Shortland turned on the wagon seat to look back at the mission house, and this time a figure stood, frozen in tableau by the carriage, poised as if it were about to step up into the vehicle. It was dressed in dark clothes but, at that distance, with only the shoulders and head visible, Shortland didn't recognize it. The Harbell wagon began the descent of Chapel Hill, and the figure at the mission house sank from view behind the rising hill.

3.

Tom Collins was walking now. He had left the rectory on foot, crossing Shepody Road to walk through the cemetery and into the woods behind, then returning to the road below Chapel Hill, out of sight of the church and mission house. Strolling in the morning heat, he was travelling east behind the Harbells. Dressed in dark work clothes, his jaunty cap pulled forward as a visor against the morning sun, Tom carried two large leather bags and a length of thin leather strap. A dozen miles ahead of him, on the edge of the bay, was Albert village, where just a week ago he had met Father McAuley at McAnulty's Hotel. There were work scows there, crossing the bay daily to Nova Scotia. He had come in on one himself, crossing to St. Mary's Point from Amherst.

East of Chapel Hill now, the mission house and St. Agatha's Church submerged into the forest behind him, Tom was familiar with the road. Ahead of him was the Williamson place. He had been there last night, visited Sarah and the little girl briefly; he had carried a large can of water to them. Last week he had visited them, too, coming away once with a can of blueberries for Mary Ann, and another time with Mr. Williamson's straight razor.

Road dust and dry seed husks rose around his legs as he walked. His forehead glistened with sweat. It was a good distance to Albert village. He thought of the McAnulty hotel there, where he had been sweating on the woodpile for his board when Father McAuley came by. It had been hard, unfamiliar work for a man who thought of himself as being of the sea. The two bags swung on either side as he strode, a brown Gladstone and an odd-looking contraption called a telescope — called that because one end slid over the other like an envelope and was fastened by straps. The thin leather strap he carried trailed in the gravelled road surface. Tall pale daisies, their yellow centres doted with tiny black bugs, shared the edges of the road with goldenrod and brittle brown grasses. There were new wagon tracks and the occasional ball of fresh horse manure. Pale green and white moss, dry and powdery in the summer heat, grew down to the edge of the road, marking the line where the forest growth began. A brown dustball exploded without sound under Tom's heel.

4.

At the foot of Morrissey Road, Bruce Harbell stopped the team. Shortland stepped down — "See ye." "Yup." — and began walking. A vague wave. Bruce turned the team then

— "Back! Back!" pulling on the reins. The horses stepped sideways in unison, then set out along the road again, starting back toward Chapel Hill and Collier Mountain.

Up an alder-choked sidehill above the road, the old Temp Boyle farm stood vacant, returning unhindered to the inevitable wilderness from which it had been scratched just a generation ago. Its sagging weathered buildings, partially obscured by brambles and thistles, looked over scant fields which pastured only a few poor animals belonging to the Williamsons. William and Sarah, who had lived on the Boyle place for some few years after their mid-life marriage, had since moved their young daughter, Iva, and their small household across the road to a tiny house vacated by a Teahan woman, one of Sarah's relatives. But they had left the animals to pasture and still used the Boyle barn, Sarah going up the path through the alders and the webs twice a day, morning and evening, to tend to them while William was in the woods.

As he approached the Williamson place, Bruce Harbell saw the figure on the road ahead, walking toward him. It was dressed in dark clothing, wearing a cap, carrying two valises, one in each hand, and what looked like the web of a pair of reins. The stranger stopped as Harbell's team came abreast.

"Have you seen Father McAuley?" the man asked.

He was young, probably from the old country, Harbell thought. He had an accent.

"No, I haven't seen him," said Harbell. "But I seen his horse standing in the yard when I come by a while back."

"Can you give me a ride to Duffy's?"

"Which Duffy's?"

"The Duffy that lives up on the sidehill."

There were four Duffy families on the sidehill west of Chapel Hill.

"That's the way I'm going alright," said Harbell. "I'll be by there directly. Get in."

The stranger threw his gear into the wagon box and climbed up. At the Williamson house just up the road, eight-year-old Iva, standing at the kitchen window, watched the team as it passed by. She told her mother she had just seen Tom Collins go by their gate twice, first walking east toward Albert, then a few minutes later riding west toward Chapel Hill in a wagon. "You must be mistaken" said Sarah. "Mary Ann is going for groceries in Albert this morning, and she would certainly be taking Collins with her." Even if she had decided to send Collins on the errand alone, Mary Ann surely wouldn't have sent him all the way to Albert on foot.

Collins was quiet riding in Harbell's wagon. He didn't say why he was looking for Father McAuley, nor that he was working for the priest. Harbell asked no questions. Strangers on foot carrying bags were not uncommon in New Ireland, nor in any other rural settlement of the day. The Shepody Road, known to some as the Immigrant Road, was the most travelled route by foot or by carriage from Saint John to Moncton, the province's largest cities. Tramps and pedlars used it frequently.

Harbell's wagon climbed Chapel Hill for the second time that morning, approaching the church and the rectory this time from the opposite direction. As they went past, Harbell noticed that the horse and carriage he had seen earlier were no longer in the yard. There was no sign of them, not was there anyone about. A large black dog lay on the grass in front of the house, panting in the heat, long tongue lolling from its jaw. It didn't move as Harbell's team clattered by. On the other side of Chapel Hill, out of sight of the rectory, Harbell and Collins met a second team carrying two men. Harbell knew them as Tilmon Bannister and his son, William. Shortly after they had passed, Collins asked Harbell to stop. He climbed down from the wagon and, without another word, started at a half run toward Bannister's team, just beginning the ascent of Chapel Hill.

5.

Tilmon Bannister farmed on Collier Mountain not far from Bruce Harbell's place. That morning he was going with his son, William, down to Albert to do a job for A.S. Mitton. As he hitched the team to his wagon in the barnyard, Tilmon heard the familiar metallic ringing of Aggie Daley's brass handbell. The teacher was calling her straggling students to class at her one-room school. Most of the older children of the settlement, who normally attended Galway school, were at work on their family's or neighbour's farms, but Aggie kept classes going for the young ones.

The Bannisters had been on the road for more than an hour, when they met Bruce Harbell's team at the foot of Chapel Hill. They nodded a greeting at Harbell, who had a stranger riding with him, and passed on by. As they started up the sharp incline, William Bannister looked back. Harbell's passenger was on the road behind them now, overtaking them on foot.

"The man who was with Harbell is coming back," William said to his father.

"Let him come," said Tilmon.

"Where do you suppose he's going?" said William.

Tilmon kept the team moving until Harbell's passenger came abreast and spoke to them. Then he reined the horses in and looked down at the man.

"Did you see anything of Father McAuley's horse and wagon?" the stranger asked.

"No," said Tilmon, his jaw working patiently. "Didn't see his nor no other horse."

"Can you give me a ride to Albert?"

Tilmon spat into the dirt. It was a warm day. He looked at the boy, who seemed overheated, sweat running freely down his crimson face. He gave a slight nod and wiped his chin with a rough palm.

Collins trotted back down the slope to Harbell's wagon, where he retrieved the two valises and the length of reins. He came back quickly, climbed into the box behind the Bannisters. As they passed the mission house, Tilmon asked where Father McAuley was. Collins told him that the priest had gone with the mail to Fredericton Road mission on Friday, and hadn't returned home yet.

"I harnessed the horse to go to Albert this morning," he said. "I left him standing when Mary Ann called me to go in for breakfast. He must have wandered off while I was eating, and I don't know which way he went. If we don't see the horse on the way, I'll get one from Mr. McAnulty in Albert."

Tilmon knew the priest only by sight, and didn't know Mary Ann at all, had never seen her, in fact, even though his farm was just a few miles from her home. He had never visited the rectory. Though he had passed it innumerable times, travelling back and forth over the last thirty years, he had never been inside.

There was no sign of human activity around the place now. The day was still and very warm. The iron shoes of the horses clattered and pinged on gravel stones. The wagon box swayed erratically on its rusted springs, giving off occasional piercing squeals of metal on metal. One of the high spoked wheels was loose and staggered as it rolled, leaving a wavy trail in the dust. Fat tubular deerflies on invisible wings circled and lit on the rolling haunches, and the horses switched their long tails from side to side. Short aromatic explosions rolled into the hot air, and a loaf of dark manure emerged and dropped in sections down the animal's haunches to disappear beneath the advancing wagon. The powerful sweet odour, not unpleasant, and as familiar to a farmer's smell as the handles of his tools to his touch, gave a moist substance to the warm dry air.

Collins looked back at the receding mission house. The yard in front was empty, the doors of the house closed. The massive timbered steeple of the church seemed to float in the haze. The only sounds on the hill came from the slow progress of the Bannisters' clattering livery.

Collins spoke again. "That man I was riding with said he saw the horse in the yard when he went by before."

Tilmon Bannister snorted, and spat over the swaying wheel on his left. "One thing's sure. If Bruce Harbell seen the horse in the yard when he went by, and then come back again with no sign of it, your horse ain't gone to Albert."

Collins remained silent until they reached the Kent Road intersection east of Chapel Hill.

"Where's that road go to?" he asked.

"Goes to Flint Hill," said Tilmon, "then goes on to Elgin. It ain't as well-travelled as the road on Collier Mountain, not so many places on it. It's a kind of handy cut, but they don't travel that way as much as they do the other."

He stopped the team and peered over the wheel at the ground. He could make out what looked like a fresh wagon trail going up the Kent Road. "Looks as if there had a horse gone there this morning."

Collins looked up the Kent Road which ran straight through trees and boulders and disappeared in the distant haze. He seized the handles of the bags he had been carrying.

"I'll go that way," he said.

Tilmon said nothing as the youth climbed down. When the Bannisters saw him last, he was walking smartly up the Kent Road heading north. Tilmon would say later that he had assumed the young man was working for the New Ireland priest.

"He appeared to be a little excited, but of course I had never seen him before. There was nothing extraordinary about him. I didn't ask him anything, and he didn't explain about carrying the valises. I didn't think of it at the time, but it struck me later as curious that he should be carrying two valises and a pair of lines while looking for the horse."

6.

Tom walked north on the Kent Road, the spruce and pine high on either side of him, a warm tunnel of pale green, yellows and browns. A vault of pale blue. The sun was almost directly overhead now, and there was no shade on the road through the woods. It was five miles to the nearest farm. He was thinking about Elgin. The man had said it was in this direction. How far would he have to walk? He looked at the hard surface of the road, but it told him nothing. He walked through the dusty dry weeds that fringed the pathway, a valise in either hand, the leather reins over his shoulders. He had never been to Elgin, but Father McAuley had said the train came in there.

The road climbed straight as a mast up the slope, and the scented softwood growth gave way to hardwood, with leaves that trembled slightly in the silence. There was no breeze, no movement of air at all, just Tom's boots scraping along the hard dry surface. Here and there balls of dehydrated horse manure scattered among the pebbles. The heat seemed less intense among the birch and maples, some with trunks two feet across, rooted among exposed black rock faces and mossy grey boulders. Delicate slender white birch, with their glowing skins, stood among the massive gnarls of insect-ridden yellow birch, great black scabs on their trunks, twisted branches deformed by weather and insects.

The road levelled off 1,300 feet above the Bay of Fundy. There was no water here. Tom had none with him. He had crossed dry creekbeds, but did not take the time to follow one to its source. The thought of a spring bubbling somewhere out on the forest floor was not yet powerful enough to pull him from the road. His arms were beginning to ache from the weight of the bags. Inside the cracked boot leather, his ankles felt as if they were being scrubbed raw. He stopped and set the bags down. He shoved one end of the leather reins through the handles of the two bags, then knotted the ends of the reins together. He lifted the bags by the improvised strap, slung them over his shoulders, knocking his cap askew. Straightening the cap on the back of the thatch of black hair, he set off again. He walked, stooped slightly from the weight of the bags, going steadily north on the road that ran straight as a plumb-line through the forest. He tried not to think of his feet.

7.

It was early afternoon when he emerged from the trees. The road went by a small field of yellow timothy going to seed. Ahead on the edge of the field there was a small grey-shingled house set back from the road, along with a few scattered outbuildings. A child, playing in the shade offered by a small orchard, noticed Collins approaching and stood motionless, watching. At the gate, Tom stopped and looked at the house. Brambles and weeds sprouted deliriously from its foundation. The child turned and ran through a side door into the house.

Tom, with his bags, walked up to the door, which stood open, and peered inside. A number of people were in the kitchen, at the centre of which stood a woman kneading a mound of mottled bread dough on a swaying table. He did not think it could be cooler in the kitchen. If there had been conversation, it had stopped by the time he tapped on the door frame. He could hear flies buzzing in the silence, as the occupants of the room looked him over, waiting for him to state his business. The woman working the bread dough ran the back of a flour-covered hand over her brow. Then with stiffened arms she drove the heels of her hands into the brown-flecked dough, folded it into itself and pressed it flat again.

Ruth Leaman was fifty-four years old, a recent widow with six children, the two oldest deaf and dumb. Her husband, Merrit Leaman, had been working in John C. Geldart's sawmill at Parkindale in March, when a "boxy" log of fir came up on the saw table. The huge rotary blade bit into the log, chewing along its length with high-pitched ferocity, until it began to bind in the tangled wood fibre. The slab that Merrit already had hold of in his gloved hands suddenly snapped and was flung downward with vicious force by the steel teeth, and Merrit went head first into the blade. The newspaper said he was "so cut to pieces that he was dead when he was picked up." One arm and shoulder were severed, and the blade flashed almost instantaneously through the skull and into the chest cavity to the heart. "Some of the strongest men," the paper reported, "turned faint at the sight." Nothing to be done, but put him into a box, then into the ground, not leaving even a stone behind to mark his time here. Just a widow and his children, and a paragraph of fading type.

Ruth had spent most of her life on the hill within a few rods of her present home. It was known as Garland's Corner, and she had been a Garland before she married. Her brother, John, and his people lived just down the road. Much of her family, as it happened, were assembled in the kitchen that day — bread-baking day; the heat didn't matter. There were the two deaf mutes, her oldest; Charlie, eighteen, the second oldest boy; an eleven-year-old daughter, and a married daughter, Mrs. Matthew Turner (christened Margaret Ellen, but called Nellie). Ruth was poor, but made no bones about it. Her life, always hard, was now harder still, even with the older ones to help, and she expected to die from it some day, just as Merrit had. She was not a timid woman — you need time to be timid — and she spoke directly.

(When it came time for Ruth Leaman to tell her story before the court of law, she wanted no part of the proceedings. Her home was a good twenty-eight miles of hard travel from the courthouse, and she had neither the time to waste nor the means to get there. She was adamant and fiery, but the authorities won in the end. When L.J. Tweedie, the premier himself told her at the hearing that they had dragged her to the first time, that she would be on her own recognizance to appear the second time at the trial — if and whenever they decided to call it — and that she would forfeit $200 that she didn't have if she didn't appear, and in lieu of the $200 that she didn't have, she would forfeit for a specified length of time her freedom — a possession that, given the state of her household, she could even less afford to relinquish — she was astonished, disbelieving. "I am a poor widow," she told the premier. "I am here in a strange land among strange people. I have no money, no place to go, and don't know who is going to take me home, and my children have to go back to the Deaf and Dumb School, and I have a lot of work to do. I won't say I will come. I'll come if I can — if I can't, I won't. Supposing I couldn't come — supposing I were in jail — if you were in jail you couldn't get out and then you couldn't come." She appeared at the trial as ordered — in fact, she appeared at all three trials and the hearing, too — but she was not intimidated. She snapped from the witness stand at an annoyingly persistent attorney, who wanted her to tell him whether she told her story each time in exactly the same words. "You must remember, I am not as good a lawyer as you.")

Ruth Leaman, then, was not alarmed by the appearance of a stranger at her door. Her home was isolated, but she had lived on the hill too long to be fearful of every passing tramp. Sometimes there was a good deal of traffic on the road and sometimes not. It was a direct route from Albert to Elgin. Usually the tramps wanted nothing more than a bite to eat, and she was never without food to spare. This man must be either a vagrant tramping through the hills on his way to or from somewhere where people were working, or a worker looking for a lumber camp. He looked awful warm with his bright red face with its sheen of sweat. When Collins spoke, it was with an accent so pronounced that Ruth didn't comprehend him until he had repeated himself, enunciating the words more slowly.

Ruth: I think the children first called my attention to him coming. He come right up to the door and requested his dinner before he come in. I invited him in and gave him a chair and he sat down right by the door and set his valises down. I asked him if he cared for tea and he said, no, he was in a hurry. It was one o'clock in the afternoon, near as I can tell. We'd had our dinner over. I told my daughter to put some dinner on the table for him. It took some time to get ready, as the girl had to wash off the table and put the victuals on it. He was a very short time at the table, somewhere along five or ten minutes.

I finished the kneading of bread and was talking with him. Sometimes I couldn't make out from the way he expressed himself what he said, and I had to ask him over again. I supposed he could not talk plain. I noticed almost as soon as he come in the house that he seemed very uneasy and couldn't sit still. The heat might have made him appear nervous. He was perspiring pretty freely. Monday was a very hot day. Saturday, Sunday, and Monday was about as warm, about the hottest days I felt during the summer. I suppose a man walking any distance on a hot day with the valises might be looking fagged and nervous.

He asked me if I had seen any team going down. He said the priest had gone to Elgin the Friday before in the mail and would be back on Thursday, and he was going to meet him. He said he was hired with the priest to take care of his horse. He said the priest had told him he could go to the lake fishing on Saturday, and said they went, him and Mary Ann and Mrs. Williamson and Iva, Mrs. Williamson's daughter. I didn't know any of them except Mrs. Williamson and Iva.

He said they locked everything up. When they come back this morning, he said, Mary Ann noticed the barn doors broken open. The priest's horse and carriage and best harness had been stolen away. I asked him what the horse was like, and he said he was a red horse with a sore on his hip and one on his shoulder. He said the people had bought it and given it to the priest. He said another man had gone the other way and he was coming this way in search of them. By the other way, I understood he meant the other way to Elgin by the Falls. I asked him what he was going to do with the two valises. He said they had been left in the place of the horse and wagon, and he was going to take them to Elgin and give them to the priest.

He said Mary Ann was all upset. I said who is Mary Ann? He said the woman that kept house for the priest. I asked him then who he was. He said he was a Mr. McAuley. I understood him to say his name was McAuley and to say the priest's name to be McCallum. I may have misunderstood him. He did not speak very plain. Charlie thought he had said his name was McCollum or McCallum. But he wasn't paying close attention 'cause the man was talking to me, and not to him. Charlie, he went out to the hayfield right soon. Nellie didn't hear him clear either. She thought he could have said his name was McCallum or Collins or somesuch, but she wasn't about to say for sure. We had no reason to want to remember his name then, anyway, did we?

He didn't eat much dinner and I asked him why he didn't eat his dinner. He said that he was all upset, that he didn't eat much breakfast, and said Mary Ann was all upset, too. That is all the conversation that I can recollect. Then he put on his hat and started out. He asked me how far it was to Elgin and I told him we called it ten miles. I think he said he was going to try and get someone to drive him a ways. He was carrying the two valises over his back. Then he met John Garland, my brother, at the gate and stopped and they had some conversation for several minutes.

8.

While Ruth talked to Collins, Nellie spotted her uncle, John
Garland, coming up the road with his team, heading with his
wife and son for the hayfield. Nellie hailed him at the gate
and told him that a man carrying two valises was in the
house with her mother.

"Do you know him?"

"No, I don't know him," she said.

"Maybe it's a pedlar," said John. He stood on the whiffletree at the front of the wagon, with the reins in his hand.
The wagon had been fixed with a wooden slat-rack for carrying loose hay.

"No," said Nellie, "he's hunting for a stolen horse."

(At the court trials, John Garland, just like his sister,
Ruth, would display an irascible sense of disdain for the
tricked-up questions of lawyers wanting him to utter the
words they wanted to hear. He was questioned closely on his
conversation with Collins at Mrs. Leaman's gate.

"How long did the conversation last?" he was asked.

"Not very long; just a few minutes. I couldn't exactly tell
how long we were talking. When people are talking the time
goes faster than they think for, and they don't know how long
they were there."

"How long do you think?"

"I don't think the conversation lasted more than half an
hour, it would be between fifteen and twenty minutes, I
think. I was in a hurry and he detained me fifteen or twenty
minutes. He detained me, I didn't detain him."

"What time of day was it?"

"It was after twelve, and I don't know what time it was
after. I had got my dinner and done considerable work and
harnessed my horse and put him in the wagon and started
after the hay, and met him."

"Can't you do any better than that?"

"I can't say what time it was in the afternoon. It was after
twelve o'clock, I won't say it was after two o'clock."

"What time do you think it was?"

"It was after dinner?"

"What time was it?"

"It was after dinner. That's all the answer you're going to get from me. Since you're so sharp about it, you'll find a man just as sharp as you are. You're not talking to a woman now. You can't work any gum games on me."

Garland was admonished by a short-tempered magistrate: "You're going to do things proper."

The farmer had the final word: "It was between twelve and four o'clock.")

Collins, who wanted nothing more to eat, left Ruth's kitchen and went down to the gate with his bags. He looked at Garland, standing on the wagon tongue, his family in the rack behind him.

"Did you see a horse come through this road?" he asked.

"No, I haven't," said Garland.

"I'm looking for Father McAuley's horse," said Collins. "It's been stolen. The harness and the carriage, too."

"When?"

"Between Saturday night and Sunday morning. I've been working for him, doing his chores. He went away to the Fredericton Road mission and left me to take care of things. We went to the lake fishing, and when we come back the barn was open and the horse and carriage was gone."

"Well, I don't think it come this way," said Garland. "If it had I'd've seen something of it."

"I'm going on to Elgin," said Tom. "Father McAuley is going to be there today and I want to tell him about the horse being gone."

It seemed to Garland that the young man was anxious, stepping back and forth from one foot to another as he spoke. Some men do that naturally and, when a man is a stranger, it is hard to say whether he's doing it from excitement or habit. He supposed the young man was worried what the priest would say about losing his horse. He looked at the valises slung over Tom's shoulder on a leather line that looked like a piece of reins, one bag in front, the other behind.

"These were left in the place where the horse was taken from," said Collins.

"What are you doing with them?"

"They told me to take them to Elgin and leave them to the station house, and that's what I'm goin' to do."

"Might be there's some papers in there that'll tell you who left them."

"No, there isn't."

"Well, if you was to leave them where they were, might be the parties might come back to get them," Garland suggested. "If you take them and put them in the station house, they'll never find them."

"What time does the train leave Elgin?" Collins asked.

"Comes in at eleven and goes out at one," said Garland. "But you won't get the train today. She won't be in again till tomorrow."

"How far is it to Elgin?"

"We call it about nine or ten miles."

"Where can I get a horse to drive over?"

"I don't rightly know," said Garland. "I can't let mine go as I'm hauling hay. If you go down the road further you might get one. Alec Bannister's got a smithy two miles down. Might be he'll have something."

Collins set off along the road once more, in the direction of Elgin, sore feet slipping inside the boots. He was walking into the heat of the day again, surrounded by the sweet smell of cut hay ripening in the sun.

9.

To the people living on Flint Hill, travelling in the direction of Elgin was going "out," while travelling south toward New Ireland and the Bay of Fundy was going "in." Tom Collins was going "out." At Garland's Corner the road took a sharp bend to the left, and struck off due east through more hardwood stands. At times the road pitched into gullies and jumped out again, forcing Collins to bend forward as he climbed. His ankles and calves began to ache. The road was empty of fellow travellers. A branch path disappeared into the trees to the right. Tiny white moths hovered and flitted, rocking in his wake. Birds he could hear, but he didn't know their calls.

Collins saw rocks glistening at the edge of the road, bright green grass with wide sharp-edged blades. Water leaked from below dark moss-covered stones. Green and yellow oval leaves floated on the tiny pool. Long-legged insects leaped and disappeared and reappeared. A small snake moved like mercury. Collins knelt, scooped warm water in cupped hands and drank, splashed it on his face and neck. The water tasted of minerals. A mile further on, the road came butt up against the Beaman Road. It was cooler here on the northern slope of the hill. Standing beneath the maples, he was surrounded by trees and could see nothing else, unless he threw his head back and looked straight up at the pale blue vault of cloudless sky. He stood with his gear in a great bowl of silence, except for a muted roar which might be inside himself somewhere, inside his own ears — or outside, in the myriad arms of the forest.

The road to the right climbed sharply again, while the left track dropped just as abruptly, following the lip of a deep cut into the hillside at the bottom of which was Sherman Brook. He turned left, descending the steep path through the forest. An ache in his thighs. Pebbles knocked loose by his heels rolled ahead of him down the slope. He picked up a stone the size of his fist and tossed it over the edge of the road, where it noisily ripped through dry foliage. He did not hear it reach the sliver of stream he could see below, a stream like the tiny brook in the hills behind the rectory, so narrow and choked with bushes that he had had to walk in the shallow water, the leather soles of his boots slipping on the slick stones, sending him flailing to keep his balance, water splashing around his legs. He remembered the heavy line floating downstream ahead of him, the hook snagging everything it encountered, except the fleeing trout. He had had slightly better luck when he got to the lake, where a man and his family staying at the camp gave him some help. But the few small fish he had brought back hadn't satisfied Mary Ann. She had looked at them scornfully, reminding him he had been gone all day. There was work to be done that he had been hired and was being paid and fed and given his board, as well, to do, and he would be better off, and so would the household, if he would spend some time doing it. Father McAuley had told him he could go fishing, but he had said nothing to Mary Ann, simply left the scrawny vacant-eyed fish on the table in the dusky heat of the woodshed.

When he finally hit level ground once more on the Sherman Road, Collins found himself beside an ancient spruce, its massive trunk festooned with dozens of horseshoes, square-headed nails and spikes, jagged tops of tin cans, and other rusted metallic odds and ends such as bits of harness and assorted pieces of machinery, all nailed to the furrowed bark like medallions from a tournament. Some had been there so long the bark had grown scornfully around them, so that they looked as if they had been pushed into the rough fibres by some great thumb. There were iron U-shaped horseshoes, affixed to the tree with their tips skyward, positioned purposely by superstitious country people who believed they attracted and retained good fortune. Collins had seen them nailed that way to barns and sheds. Turn them over like upside-down bowls, it was said, and the good fortune would pour to the ground like rainwater. Behind the tree, almost at the edge of the road was a small building made of slab lumber, its wide front doors agape. Just inside was a scarred iron anvil, a pair of long tongs lying on its flat face. Behind the anvil a forge with coal tumbled about. A slab lean-to was fixed to one side of the building. Beneath its shelter a horse, hip-shot, slowly masticating a jawful of hay, gazed over its shoulder at Collins.

Alex Bannister's blacksmith shop.

10.

A Voice: I knew of Alex, but I didn't really know him. Before my time. Heard people talk about him. He was there a good many years. Raised a bunch of daughters. Nothin' there now but a field and a road to a sugar place. Knew the Garlands and the Leamans up there, too. Old George Garland lived up on Flint Hill for many years — they called him Duster, but he didn't much like it — had a beard down to his belt. They never had much, but they were as honest as the sun, and every once in awhile they'd take a spell of religion, go to church faithful as you please. Then they'd kinda forget about it for awhile. One of them — during one of these religious spells — seen a deer out of season standing in a field below his house. Well, he studied it a long time, working his jaw hard, and it just stood there and stood there, so he finally went in to the house and got the rifle, and dropped that deer in its tracks. He was dressing it down when a neighbour come by. "Well, Joe," says the neighbour. "I'm surprised, a religious man like you shooting a deer out of season." "Well, sir," says Joe, "I studied it long and hard, and I finally figured God put that deer there for me to shoot."

No, I didn't know Alex Bannister, but I've known some smiths. They were good men, all of them — big, strong, hard workin'. Some were better than others, some were rougher than others. I've heard stories about the smith who could knock a stubborn horse to his knees by punchin' him in the face with his fist, but I don't place credence in it. Haven't seen it myself, nor talked to anyone who did. Maybe, if you hit him right, but most didn't have to.

Knew one in Parkindale, though. George Geldart. He was a big man. And strong? He might have knocked a horse down. He had make them mind, don't you think he wouldn't. He had use a strip of rubber tire that still had the wires in it. He'd whip them until they were standing and trembling. He'd really give them a going over. But then he'd shoe them, and they wouldn't give him much trouble after that. But he never lost his temper. I never saw him mad. Good thing, too. I was there one day waiting with my team. I saw this young fella, Bill — he used to help him some — I saw Bill take an iron bar to a horse, beating him across the ribs. And George grabbed that bar out of Bill's hands and threw it down, and he said, "If you want to beat a horse, use this tire. Don't ever use anything that'll mark it." Old George could give them a trimmin' though. No, I never heard of a blacksmith knocking a horse down to shoe him. They'd tie them up lots of times. Had to, some of them. Couldn't handle them, otherwise. But some of those blacksmiths were strong.

Billy Ireland in Elgin was. Billy was a great talker, too. Lot of stories and foolishness. People would go to his shop in

Elgin Saturday night just to listen to him talk. And sing? He had a big, big voice and he could sing by himself without music. You'd hear him at the back of the church, his voice big and loud, louder than anybody else. But he could sing. Some of them would tease him and make fun of him. But I never did.

His son, Herbie, he was kind of a dreamer. Sometimes he'd help Billy in the shop, by holdin' a lantern over a piece of work Billy was doing. He would hold the lantern so Billy could see. Billy'd be working away and talkin' and the other men would be talkin'. And Herbie would be listenin' to them, and after awhile he wouldn't be payin' attention to the lantern anymore, and he'd sort of drift away so that pretty soon, the lantern wouldn't be shining its light where Billy was workin'. After awhile Billy would look up — he talked real slow and he had a deep voice — he'd look up at Herbie, and he'd say in his slow way, "Can ye see good enough, Herbie?" he'd say and everybody'd laugh. "Can ye see good enough, Herbie?"

Knew another smith one time. He was eighty-eight years old and not smithin' much anymore. Closed his shop up, but he'd shoe a racehorse at the track now and then. He was a whiz with racehorses. Known all around the province. Racing people were always after him to do their animals. No one could touch him, even at his age. Could turn a loser into a winner, or a winner into a loser, by the way he shod 'em, he'd say. And it's true, I think. Poorly shod horse ain't gonna run well no matter how fast he is.

Smart, too, this fella. Couldn't get good metal one time, so he started making horseshoes out of potato-digger legs. Best metal there was, he said. Put 'em in the forge and pound 'em into shoes. Well this smithy, he told me one time that as long as he's still drawin' breath, nobody's getting their hands on his tools. People were after him, you know. Antique scavengers and such. "I've had them with me all my life," he said, "and when I go into the ground, I want a big hole dug and I want my Peter Wright anvils and my sledges thrown in there with me."

Some shops were two-storey affairs. Smith'd work downstairs at his forge with his eight to ten pound sledges, his 125 and 200 pound anvils, his swedge block for shaping metals, and his steel. Upstairs'd be the wheelwrights, turning out wooden wheels for carriages and wagons. Smiths were versatile. Wouldn't just be shoeing horses. They'd make and fix a whole whack of metal implements, sled-runners, wagon wheel plates, axles, whiffletree plates, wagon springs, chains, plowshares, cutting blades. And play at being dentists, too. Sometimes they'd be asked to file off an animal's tooth or pull one out. Sometimes a tooth'd break off and it'd have to come out. Well, they'd just tie the horse's head down to something and go to it.

Shoeing workhorses was their main work, though. A good man and his assistant could handle twenty horses a day. I've heard of twenty-three being done in one day. Normally you'd want a horse shod every five to six weeks, depending on his work, the kind of ground he's workin' on. Animals hauling lumber sometimes'd go in every two weeks.

Farm team like mine, not worked real hard all the time, I'd have done it maybe three times a year. In the spring and for haying, and then for winter with sharper shoes for ice and snow. I'd have to trim their hooves myself between times, though. Pull the nails with a big pair of tweezers, take the shoe off and trim the hoof. Big pair of clippers that'd snip off the edges, then rasp it smooth with a heavy file. Just like your own toenails. The hooves grow and the shoe'd grow right out with them. So you'd have to take them off and trim the hoof. Have to be careful putting the shoe back on. Sometimes the nail would go right into the foot — the quick. Horse'd jump. You'd pull the nail out and there would be blood on it.

11.

Alexander Bannister's blacksmith shop was empty. Collins stuck his head in the door and looked around, but saw no one. The horse in the lean-to continued going about his indolent business. Across the yard were fruit trees, branches spread like candlebra. Green apples among the leaves. Nearby, another small narrow house with grey wooden shingles. A porch. Collins dropped his bags there and walked to an open door. A spare kitchen with a high-backed woodstove against one wall. Seated at a table in the centre of the room were a man and a woman. Two young women with dishes at the sink. A girl on the floor amusing a small boy, who looked up as Collins spoke. Collins excused himself and asked could he have a drink. One of the young women took a dull grey dipper from a hook at the sink and dipped water from a bucket into an enamel cup. She handed the cup to Collins. No one spoke as he drank.

The water was warm and tasted like metal, like the can of cream he had taken from a basement shelf at the rectory. It had been cool in the basement, and he had been sweating carrying the furnace wood down from the yard. He didn't like the drinking water there and had said so, but Mary Ann had told him that was all there was; the well had gone dry as it usually did in August and they were carrying water from a spring in the woods. He had noticed the can of cream right away, and picked it up from the shelf, and it had felt cool in his palm. But he had put the can back on the shelf the first time. Later in the day he had taken it again, and this time punctured its top twice with a nail, then drained it. Mary Ann had discovered that he had taken it, of course, and had upbraided him. She had called him a thief. He had seen nothing wrong in it.

Collins drank half of the contents of the cup and handed it to the girl. Looking at the man and woman still seated at the table, he said he would like to hire a horse. He said he had to meet Father McAuley at Elgin. The man at the table was Aylesford Mitton, a lumberman and government surveyor, who also operated a farm in Coverdale, the northern parish of Albert County, bordering the Petitcodiac River. Mitton was in Flint Hill that day, looking for men for his woods crew. He had stopped at Alex Bannister's to rest and feed his horse, and Mrs. Bannister had given him his dinner. The smith was widely known and liked in the county — he served farmers and woodsmen in Meadow, Prosser Brook, Pleasant Vale, Hillside and Flint Hill — and Mitton, even though his home was more than twenty-five miles away, was a long-time friend of the Bannister family. He made a point to visit each spring, too, during sugar-making season.

Mitton looked closely at the red-faced young man. He said he couldn't take him into Elgin; it was out of his way and he was in a rush himself. Collins said that he had to meet the priest there. "I've been working for him, and his horse has took lame back on the road."

"I seen that horse last winter," said Mitton, "and he was lame then, too."

Collins reached into a pocket and pulled out two wrinkled one dollar bills, one American currency, the other what was known then as a Province bill.

He said, "I'll give two dollars to anyone to drive me to the station."

"If I do drive you out," said Mitton, "I can't fetch Father McAuley in. I'm coming a different road, and I want to see some men."

"I don't care as long as I get to the station."

Tom handed the money to Mitton.

"Do you pay the money, or does Father McAuley?" asked Mitton.

"Father McAuley left the money with the housekeeper to pay for hiring the horse," said Tom.

Mitton heaved himself from the table, thanked Mrs. Bannister for his meal and went outside. He took his horse from the lean-to, and hitched it to a carriage that sat near the shop, its bowed shafts resting on the ground.

"You got dunnage?" he asked Collins.

"They're in the wagon," said Tom.

The two bags were in the back of the carriage already. As the two men set out on the Sherman Road driving north, they were slightly more than an hour away from Elgin. The road wound like an engine crank to a flat plain. There were farmhouses and outbuildings visible in all directions. Distant figures forked hay from the field, their forms blurred and seemingly floating in a haze of hay dust — one, in a single motion, pitched it up to other figures balanced atop the swaying wagon. Mitton's carriage clattered over the floorboards of the small wooden bridge spanning Little River, passed through a crossroad, and began the ascent of Gowland Mountain. To the left and far below the road was another small stream; to the right Zackie Jonah Mountain. On the steepest inclines, Mitton and his passenger got out of the carriage and walked beside it, leather soles slipping on the stones.

At the top of Gowland Mountain, a green, blue and yellow panorama far below and behind them. Another crossroads and a church. Mitton's carriage went past it and began the descent of the northern slope. A huge vista opened in front of them, the clustered buildings of Elgin village at its centre far below. A patchwork of farms in rectangles. The dark hues of forest all around. To the right, like a miniature valley, a string of farms through Mapleton. The rail line of the *Prong* followed the incline of the slope far across the valley, from this distance looking like a dark thread dropped on a green and yellow carpet. The whole prospect was seen through a haze of summer heat, the colours muted.

Mitton's horse, rested from its climb, now picked its way cautiously down those parts of the road that pitched abruptly. Collins' arms gripped the back of the carriage seat, his feet braced against the dashboard. He said nothing. The sun, though lower in the sky, still sent heat into their shoulders. They passed by another farmer getting in his crop. Stephen Garland, who was working a small crew in the hayfield of his Gowland Mountain farm, owned and operated the hotel at Elgin Corner, purchased after fire destroyed his farmhouse. Garland saw the team go by, and recognized Aylesford Mitton, but not his passenger.

Sometime before four o'clock they reached the village centre, after passing through an echoing covered bridge over the Pollett River gorge, kids splashing in the shallow water below. Buildings stretched along both sides of the four roads spoking at right angles from the crossroads, the largest being Garland's Hotel at the corner on the left, a long three-storied building with a verandah full-length across its front. They passed that, too, going straight through the corner, down and across another small bridge over Barchard Brook, then up the incline opposite toward the Elgin station of the *Prong*.

Mitton turned his horse into the lumber yard in front of the station. The *Prong's* track curved around the hill to the village like a geometric design inside a green bowl, and ended at a wide turntable, like a huge round platter in front of the station.

Collins pulled the two valises, still joined by the length of reins, from the back of Mitton's carriage, crossed the tracks, and went into the small station house. Mitton returned to Elgin Corner and turned right to Goddard's Store, just up the street from Garland's Hotel. He led the horse into a barn adjoining the store, took the harness off and hung it on wooden wall pegs. He took some time to brush the dried sweat, salt and dust from the animal's back, flanks and shoulders with a curry comb, gave it a pail of water and half a pail of oats, then forked some green hay into the manger in front if it.

12.

Station master Sarah Daley saw from the window of her apartment the arrival of Mitton's carriage in the lumber yard. She saw the man with the bags, and was in the small office-waiting room of the station with fourteen-year-old Fred, when Collins came in.

"How long before a train is due?"

"We have a daily train," said Sarah, "and it comes in at half past eleven and goes out at half past twelve."

It was past four o'clock.

Sarah thought from his accent, the man must be a traveller. The news that there were no more trains that day seemed to disturb him. He paced the rough plank floor of the small room. Then, looking out the doorway at the empty track, he asked, "Can you tell me where I might stay tonight?"

"There's Bishop's Hotel up by the corner," she said. "They'll have a room if you have the money."

Collins glanced at the valises which stood on the floor by the door, the reins lying across them, and asked Sarah whether he could leave them with her until he could call for them. Sarah studied him before answering, but then he picked up the bags and threw them over his shoulder. "I guess I'll take them with me," he said.

"Yes," she said, "I might not be in when you call."

Aylesford Mitton had finished tending to his horse and, after making his arrangements with Goddard's proprietor, headed for the harness shop. He had just stepped onto the main road, when the stranger who called himself Connors came around the corner at Garland's Hotel.

"Well," Mitton said, "Where is your man? Has he come yet?"

"No, he won't be here till tomorrow."

"Mr. Garland keeps a hotel here, and you better go over there and stop over night."

13.

It was 4:30 in the afternoon. Emma Garland, proprietor, chief-cook-and bottle-washer of Garland's Hotel, was preparing supper for her guests and regulars, when a man came to the side door. He carried a long telescope valise in one hand. She went to the door and looked through the screen. Emma thought of herself as a nervous woman, and she made a point of studying strangers who came to her establishment, especially when she was alone. Her husband, Stephen, who was up on Gowland Mountain getting in the hay, hadn't yet come for his supper. This stranger was perspiring as if he had had a long walk; it was a hot day and his clothing was wet with sweat. She thought he seemed nervous or anxious about something. The pupils of his eyes seemed unusually huge, but otherwise he appeared harmless. Just tired and hot.

"I am stopping with you tonight," he informed her.

"Oh?" she said. "Do you wish a room?"

He said he did. He asked how much she would charge to keep him until the next day at noon. He wanted meals and a bed. Emma said she would keep him for $1.50 in advance. He said that was alright, and handed her one fifty-cent coin and four twenty-five-cent pieces. She led him into the dark still interior of the building. A glimpse of a long wide table, chairs pushed against it, pale tableware upside down in their settings, serving bowls. He followed her up a flight of stairs.

The wainscotting was dark, grained, polished. The narrow room she took him to contained a chest of drawers, a small commode with an enamel basin and a large jug of water, a single bed with elaborately curved cast-iron headboard. The room was not quite ready for a new guest, Emma told him, but she would leave him there to wash up. She would prepare his supper, and then come back to finish tidying the room. He said that would be fine. Emma returned to the kitchen.

He came back downstairs carrying his cap. His hair was pushed back from his forehead and appeared damp. He sat at the long dining table with other men, some in work clothes and smelling of hard work, wood pitch, horses — others with jackets and collars, their faces scrubbed, hair slicked back. There was a hubbub of talk, local gossip, remarks about the spell of hot weather and the dry forests and the fires burning in other parts of the province. Collins was silent, eating his meal quickly and leaving the table. He picked up a book from a sideboard in the hallway and went to the verandah at the front of the hotel, overlooking the village's main street. He sat in a chair facing the road, tipped the cap to shield his right eye against the sun, and opened the book.

14.

Father McAuley had changed his plans. It was because of the heat. He was a big man, heavyset, sixty-three years old, with a heart that was telling him more and more to take it easy; and his clerical garb was not designed for temperatures in the high nineties. When he had left the rectory in New Ireland last Friday, he told Mary Ann that he would return the following Thursday, after visiting parishioners at South Branch in rural Kings. He was feeling better about extended absences from his mission house, because Tom Collins, the young Englishman he had hired, would be good company for Mary Ann, who, in the many years she had been with him, had never got used to being left alone at the rectory. But now the priest decided the visit to South Branch could wait for cooler days, and he would return home a day earlier.

He stepped from the passenger coach of The *Prong* to the Elgin station platform Monday morning at 11:30. He had spent the weekend at the small chapel he had built a few years before on the Fredericton Road, eight miles north of Salisbury. He had held service there Sunday morning and, after spending the night at the home of Daniel Sullivan, celebrated early mass on Monday. On the way to the *Intercolonial* station at Salisbury, his driver, Stephen Keohan, asked whether he had anyone at the rectory to help him and Mary Ann prepare for winter. Father McAuley said he had a fellow by the name of Collins.

"Is he going to be a pretty smart boy?" Keohan asked.

"Yes, I think he will. He doesn't seem to know how to do anything, but after he learns he'll be quite a smart boy."

By the time he got to Elgin, even though it was still before noon, the priest was exhausted from the heat. The usual flush on his broad face was deeper. He walked immediately to the home of David and Ellen Moore, parishioners and friends with whom he usually stayed when in Elgin. Moore, who had been transferred there by a Sussex firm, managed one of its branch stores. The priest had known Ellen Moore since she was a child of eleven or twelve. He had his noon meal with the Moores, and they discussed the purchase of some lumber that was needed for the upcoming picnic. After a brief rest, and recuperated somewhat from his exhaustion, Father McAuley spent the remainder of the afternoon visiting other parishioners. Elgin was predominantly a Baptist district, but the priest was well known there and had many friends. He made arrangements with Thomas Carty, a Mapleton farmer, to drive him to New Ireland the next day.

At five o'clock, the priest was on his way to visit Mrs. Horace Goddard, an elderly resident of the village who was ill. She had left word with the Moores that she wanted to see him, but he had decided to wait until the most intense heat of the day had passed before making the call. He set out from David Moore's on foot and, at the crossroad, turned to pass in front of Garland's Hotel. A number of patrons sat on the long front verandah, their feet up, digesting their suppers. One was reading a book, with his cap tipped against the sun. The priest came to an abrupt halt in the street.

"Hello," he called. "Is this you?"

Collins, startled, looked up from the book to see his employer standing in the street. He got up and walked to the road, saying nothing, but stopped beside the priest and stared down at the dirt. A layer of fine red dust on the surface of the road. Irregular narrow tracks of carriage wheels — they rarely rolled in a straight line — and plate-sized imprints of hooves. Clops of road earth and manure tossed about. Boot prints overlaying everything else.

"When did you get here?" Father McAuley asked his hired man.

"Father," said Tom, "I am not long here."

The priest, standing with his hands clasped behind him, gazed past the young man and down the street.

"Is the horse here?" he asked.

"No."

"Is the housekeeper here then?"

"No," said Tom.

"Well then, how did you get here?"

"I walked."

"What did you leave the house for? Didn't you know I was away?"

Tom continued to look at his feet.

"Mary Ann said something to me about the day I was out fishing at the lake."

"Well," said Father McAuley, "didn't I tell you about that myself? If the housekeeper had said anything to you about that day at the lake, it was only for your own good, to let you know you shouldn't stop so long when you were sent any place when you had work to do."

He was thinking that his housekeeper had been left alone at the rectory again. She would probably go to one of the neighbours, as was her habit; still he was glad he had decided to cut his travels short and return to New Ireland tomorrow. She was probably upset that Collins had run off, especially if an argument had been the cause.

"I've paid the lady for my supper," said Tom.

"Where did you get the money?"

Tom said he had been given a dollar by Mr. Gross for looking after his horse, fifty cents of which he had paid to

Mr. Duffy for boarding the horse. The other fifty cents he had kept.

"Will you go back again?" the priest asked him.

"Yes, Father," Tom replied, "I will go back."

A team approached, pulling a wagon with a load of hay stacked in defiance of gravity. Turning at the sound of jangling harness, they could see, between the horses, the teamster standing on the wagon tongue, leaning against the hay rack, reins held loosely in one hand. Floating above his head, the animated faces of three children lying on their stomachs on the mound of hay, looking out over the team from their perch, laughing and talking, waving at the men on the verandah. The horses plodded patiently, tossing their heads as if trying to see beyond the blinders on their bridles, switching their tales, farting in lazy drawn-out burps. The warm ripe smell. Collins and the priest moved to the side of the road. The teamster nodded as he passed, hay seeds showering in the oblique light about his head and shoulders.

"How will you get back then, Tom?" Father McAuley asked.

"Walk back."

"When will you go?"

"I'll go tomorrow morning."

"Well then," said the priest. "Come along with me to Mrs. Martin's, and you can remain there the night."

15.

The third house from Garland's Hotel was the home of John Martin, whose family had been living there for the past four years. They were well acquainted with Father McAuley and Mary Ann. Elizabeth Martin had never been to the New Ireland rectory, but Mary Ann had visited at her home many times. Elizabeth knew the McAuley household well enough to know that the priest would be lost without his cousin keeping house for him. He was not a man who could do anything for himself, either build a fire or get himself a meal. In that way he was totally dependent on his housekeeper. Mrs. Martin met him at her door, and invited him to the sitting-room just off the front hall. But the man who came

with him seemed nervous somehow, uncomfortable. He took
a chair near the door. Sitting on the opposite side of the room
near a raised window, Father McAuley inquired whether
Tom could spend the night there.

The young man seemed unusually warm and short of
breath to Elizabeth. She did not want to remark on it at first,
but as the conversation continued, his condition seemed to
worsen and finally she said to him: "Are you too warm?"

"Yes," he said.

"Well, get up and go outdoors, go out to the barn."

"Yes," Father McAuley added, "go out and get the fresh
air. Get yourself a good drink of cold water from the well."

A few minutes later, still sitting by the raised window,
the priest saw Collins in the yard, walking around a corner
of the house.

"He is going wrong," he said to Mrs. Martin.

Collins looked toward the window and noticed the priest
looking back at him. After pausing a few seconds, he retraced
his steps. He returned to the sitting room and said, "I will go
down to the hotel for my bundle."

"Alright," said Father McAuley.

After ten minutes of talk about the coming church picnic,
Father McAuley said he should go to visit the sick woman.
Mrs. Martin waited for Collins to return for his supper, but
he never did.

16.

Emma Garland, after having prepared supper for "my men,"
returned to Collins' empty room to finish tidying. The telescope valise the young man had carried in with him was
sitting on the floor by the bed, the top lying beside it. The
clothing inside the bag was very white and clean-looking, and
appeared to Emma to be of a very fine texture, of good
quality. On top was a clean white bath towel. Emma
reminded herself that she had a right to be looking at these
private items, though she didn't remove them, because she
was a careful, if not a curious, woman. She wanted to satisfy
herself that the stranger was not a tramp, that he was "alright." There was another bag, a small hand-satchel, un-

opened beside the extension valise. She ran her hand down the inside to see if there might be a weapon, but found nothing.

But she noticed a smell like perspiration — kind of a sweaty smell, she would say later — and looking under the bed she saw at the foot, just under the edge, a small bundle of clothing. She supposed he had taken them off while she was preparing dinner. There were an outside shirt, a black sateen shirt, and a cotton lender, or a gentleman's under-shirt, that seemed to have been taken off together and dropped on the floor in a heap. With them were a tie, a belt and a pair of fleece-lined leather gloves, gentlemen's gloves, the right one badly-worn, the other not so badly. Taking note of these items, Emma left them were they lay and returned to her kitchen.

At about five-thirty, the young man came in once more. This time he told her he would not be staying the night at the hotel.

"Father McAuley is here," he told her, "and I am going back with him."

Emma returned his coins to him, all but a quarter, which was the price of his supper. Collins went to the bed chamber and returned with his luggage, carrying it on a strap over his shoulder.

17.

Sarah Daley was rather surprised to see the young stranger go by the station for a second time that afternoon. She had seen him walking out the tracks toward The Glen not much more than an hour before, but had not seem him come back. Now here he was again, walking down the same tracks in the same direction, still carrying his luggage on a strap. Perhaps he didn't have the money for a hotel room. Three hours later, Sarah's son Fred, walking the railbed half a mile from the station, discovered a pair of leather reins discarded in a culvert by the tracks. He left them where they lay, but seeing them still there the next day, he would pick them up and take them home.

Collins continued following the tracks, away from Elgin directly north toward Petitcodiac, rested now and with a meal in his stomach, but on feet that were increasingly sore. He followed the trackbed into the warm twilight. On his right, occasional splashes of river water shone through the trees. He stopped to have a closer look. The water in the Pollett was extremely low and slow moving — long gravel bars along its banks. A dark shape slipped soundlessly into the stream from the opposite shore. A widening trail of ripples. There was a hint of breeze off the river, and the heat of the day had subsided somewhat. He had no immediate plan, other than to continue following the rail line. After awhile the tracks curved away from the river, and he was walking through forest again.

Forest Glen, also known as Pollett River, was a small collection of houses and a store, built around C.T. White's sawmill on the bank of the Pollett, one of Albert County's busiest lumbering streams. A timber dam spanned the wide riverbed to create a holding pool for softwood logs, mostly pine and spruce, carried to the millpond by spring drives from holding dams far upstream in the high country. The mill was a large employer and generator of income, not only for the men who worked there, but for many others working in the lumber industry in the northern part of the county.

Dusk was deepening and night preparing to settle in, when Collins emerged from the woods at The Glen. The rails passed through a broad chip-littered yard, where the lumber was stacked before being shipped out on the *Prong*. When it came out of the mill, which had been built on the east bank of the river, the lumber was piled onto wagons and hauled by team across the covered bridge to the lumber yard on the west bank, where the rail line was laid. Collins could see the river again, cigar-shaped insects with wide rapid wings darting above the water, the flowing liquid seeming to gather and briefly hold within it the diminishing daylight. He could hear the water curling in the eddies, a steady rippling and plopping, myriad bubbles as the river breathed. To his left, between the outer dark and the familiar rail line, box-shaped stacks of graded still green lumber, higher than a man's head, waiting to be sold.

18.

A Voice: Horses? That's all they talked about in those days. I used to get tired of listening to them. Especially the older ones. Whenever they got together they'd talk about their horses. Good ones they'd had. Bad ones. It was like youngsters talking about their cars now. Horses was all they knew, all they cared about. Most of those fellas had never been past Moncton all their lives. Never been anywhere. Didn't know anything but horses and farming and lumbering. Had nothing else to talk about.

And my dad was the worst for horses. He wouldn't stand around gabbing about them, but he'd sell one out from under you as quick as he'd look at you. Damn, he'd make me mad! He wasn't much of a farmer. Us boys did the work. He could work with his head, but not with his hands. But he was quite a horse trader. Cattle, too. Jews'd come out from Moncton or up from Saint John, sometimes selling, sometimes buying. If Dad thought he could make a dollar or two off an animal, he'd buy it and we'd have to work it until someone come along to take it off our hands. Never had a team worth a damn, because the horses were coming and going like Maisie's suitors.

I remember one time, I had the team down on the intervale, mowing. I look up and here comes Dad down over the hill with another fella humping along behind. Waits at the crossway over the ditch till I come around to them on the mower, then he reaches and grabs the mare's bridle and I have to stop. And damn if he don't sell that mare right off that mower. Fella says he'll take her, and Dad unhitches her and away they go with the mare, leaving me with the other horse still hitched to the mower. I was so mad I could spit! Never could keep a decent team.

Teams? They'd brag about their teams, too. Meant a lot to them. If you were a good teamster then, you had it made. Lots of work, good pay. You know, they used to have to shovel snow on to the bridge at Pollett River in the winter, so they could haul their loads of logs across. Sometimes a load would get hung up anyway, because there wasn't enough snow down on the floor of the bridge. Sled runners'd seize on the planks. The teamster would have to go looking for help. Course there were always lots of teams around the mill, hauling logs and lumber, waiting to be loaded and unloaded. And he'd have to go, cursing and muttering to himself, and find another teamster to help get his load across.

He had no choice. Couldn't leave it sitting there, stuck to the middle of the bridge like a frozen turd. Oh, they'd hate that when it happened. Teamster didn't want to admit, see, that his team couldn't pull the load. So he'd hunt somebody up, and if he was lucky he'd find somebody who wouldn't make too big a deal out of it. But if he picked the wrong guy, he wouldn't hear the end of it. He'd tell it every chance he got. "Well sir," I says to him, "Unhitch that team' a yours and I'll hitch mine to her. And, by god, we did and I want you to know that team' a mine hauled that load off slick as a whistle." Lots of those stories weren't true, of course, but they'd tell it that way. Make their team better than the other fellas. Kinnear Hoar, down to Point Wolfe, once bragged he had a horse twenty-eight years old that yarded a thousand logs over the winter, besides doing other work. It was in the paper. Said he'd had the animal for nineteen years.

But they really looked after their horses in those days. Just like cars now. They'd brush them down every day, especially when they were working hard. Oh they worked hard, those horses. Don't you think they didn't! Work so hard they'd be covered in sweat. It would foam between their legs. They'd be soaking wet when you put them in at night. Have to brush them down the next morning to get the salt off them. Just like powder. Used to make me sneeze. But they worked hard. You know, in the fall when they were logging, they'd yard logs out to the pile with the horse. That was easy work. Horse thought he had it pretty good then. He'd get nice and fat. Then they'd go back after the snow came with the teams and sleds to haul those piles of logs out to the river for the spring drive. I've seen teams hauling loads as big as a truck would haul. They'd really load them up. Then those horses worked! They'd lose their fat then. In no time they'd drop a couple of hundred pounds.

19.

James Young was a teamster. He had been working as one for eight years for White's Pollet River Lumbering Company at The Glen, hauling lumber from the mill to the yard of The *Prong*. It was monotonous work, covering the same short stretch of ground back and forth day after day, but he liked being a teamster. It was a respected and envied job, a large cut above the station of the other workers. He had the responsibility for the care and grooming of the animals that he worked with every day. He boarded at Michael Joyce's, and was in the kitchen with Mrs. Joyce, when Tom Collins came in Monday night.

Young: He came in the back way about dark with Alex McAllister. Asked for a place to stay. Mrs. Joyce asked him if he would sleep in a place where other people slept. "Yes," he says, "all I want is a bed." She asked me to take him up and show him where to sleep, in the same room where I did. I lit the lamp and took him up.

We talked some before going to bed. I asked him what he done. He said he went to sea, said he was up here coasting around the shore and he was going down to Saint John then for to get a vessel. He said his father had lived in Saint John for seven years, and he was going down there to take charge of a vessel that his father had bought for him. He asked me what time the train went on the main line to Saint John from Petitcodiac. Petitcodiac is five miles by road and seven miles by rail from Forest Glen. I told him the *No. 9* went at four o'clock and the *Maritime* at half-past eight or nine, I thought. He said that was the train he would take.

He asked me what I worked at. I told him I drove team, and he said to wake him up when I got up. Then he undid his valise and took out some clothing. He laid a pair of drawers on the bed. It looked like a suit of Stanfield's, heavy winter underclothing. The clothes he had on were wet with perspiration. He said he had been doing his own washing the last six weeks, but he wasn't going to do it any longer. Said he was going down home. He said he had come from St. Mary's Point. I asked him if he had walked all the way. No, he said, he got a man to drive him for seven or eight miles and gave him two dollars.

He had some silver money in his vest pocket, pulled that out, and counted it. He had two bills of some kind; I don't know what it was. He took them out and looked at them, counted them in his hand, put them together and put them back. He put the silver in the pocket book, too. I think it was quarters. It was a dark leather pocket book about four-and-a-half inches long, with a strap around it. It was new looking, red leather. He put the wallet in his pocket. I don't know how much money he had, but he paid for his night's lodging and breakfast — thirty-five cents.

A man named Rowley Brewing from Sussex, who was in Forest Glen doing some painting and also staying at the Joyce's, opened the bedroom door about then and asked the time. Collins, who was sitting on the bed, pulled a little gold watch from his vest pocket. The vest was hanging on the end of the bed with his coat. He opened the watch, looked at it, and said it was a quarter of nine. It was a small-sized watch, looked like gold. Saw no lettering on it, it was about six feet away from me.

But it looked to me like a lady's watch.

Chapter Four

Tuesday, August 21, 1906

1.

Five o'clock Tuesday morning. The bedroom window in silver rectangles, dark whorls like tiny whirlpools in the glass. A wan light surrounding the three beds where one man still slept. Two were awake. Tom Collins lay on his back squinting at an object in his hand, turning it this way and that so as to catch the light. James Young, sitting on the edge of his own bed, began to dress in the dawn light. He paid no attention to Collins and dressed quickly, simply pulling on the same rank work clothes that he had dropped on the floor the night before. His first job of the day was to look after his team, which he had left in Michael Joyce's barn. Outside it was warm already, and he paused for a moment to gaze into the deep brush-and-thistle-filled gully that cut in front of the house. Tiny white moths hovered above it in the dawn light, as if they had come out to warm their wings. A narrow wooden walking-bridge with high railings on either side had been built over the ravine. Beneath it, the wild growth.

Joseph Joyce, sleeping in the third bed in the room, had stirred while Young was dressing. Rolling to his side away from the light that was beginning to stream through the window, he noticed the stranger Collins peering at a lady's gold hunting-case watch. A sawmill worker at The Glen, Joe was used to fellow mill workers and passing travellers renting his room, usually by the week or the month, so the presence of a stranger in one of the beds didn't surprise him.

At breakfast, there was little conversation beyond the usual chat about the hot, dry weather. Eating breakfast, at a boarding house for working men, was a business-like affair. Forearms and elbows were planted firmly on the table on either side of the plates, as the men hunched over and dug in. Remarks were cryptic, responses held to grunts around mouthfuls of food, or simply implied by slight head nods or winks or sudden guffaws. Dry spells were hard on mill towns, especially in the spring, when lowered river levels could cut off the supply of logs. That's what had happened three years earlier, when much of southern New Brunswick had gone up in flames after forty days of drought. The woods on both sides of the Pollett River, all the way from Elgin on out, were ablaze, and the rail lines and streams swarmed with forest animals trying to escape the flames. People blamed the spark-spitting engines of the railway, but sometimes — as in the case of the conflagration that devastated Hopewell Cape that summer — it was a farmer carelessly scorching a field.

But this was August, and the mill at The Glen was idle. That's why Joe Joyce, usually alerted by the whistle at 6:00 a.m., overslept. Breakfast was nearly over when he got to the table, but the stranger Collins was still there, just finishing his tea. Joe pulled a chair up and sat down, feeling a little sheepish for having slept in.

"What's the right time?" he said to his mother.

"I'm not sure," she said, "the clock's a little fast, I think."

Collins pulled a watch from his pocket and looked at it. It was an open-faced silver timepiece, not like the one Joe had seen him with earlier in the bedroom. Joe thought little of it at the time — some people were in the habit of carrying two timepieces about, that is, if they could afford two timepieces — but it was an event the lawyers would want him to recall with precision at the trials.

Sometime after nine o'clock that morning, W.B. Simpson, Intercolonial station agent at Petitcodiac, sold a $1.40 second-class ticket for Saint John to a man wearing a rough suit of clothes with no colour, a handkerchief about his neck, and a cap. He looked to Simpson like a foreign sailor in need of a shave.

2.

Tommy Mellen was virtually deaf. He was well-known throughout the lumbering districts of New Ireland and the Shepody Hills and the southern New Brunswick communities of Albert and Alma, where many men earned their livelihoods in the sawmills. Tommy had come to New Ireland as a child, when he was ten or twelve years old. He had been taken from the almshouse in Saint John, where he was sent as an orphan boy. By 1906, it was said, he had been working in the area for twenty-five years or more. A bachelor until he died, in the 1930s in the home of one of the New Ireland Duffys, he was a transient labourer, who ate and slept with the people who gave him work. When asked where he lived, he'd say, "My home is wherever I work."

Early Tuesday morning, Tommy, walking east to west, passed by the New Ireland mission house. He had not visited Father McAuley's home since the day last April, when he had left for the stream drive after doing some chores for Mary Ann. She had made him promise to return later to cut her wood, and he did, leaving behind an axe, which he had put in the oat bin in the barn, and an overcoat, with a straight razor and a shaving brush in its pocket. The coat had been left in the hired man's bedroom off the kitchen, where Tommy slept while working at the rectory.

Tommy's hand was hurting. He had injured it while working at Prescott's mill in Albert and, now that he was back in New Ireland, he had it in mind to stop at Michael Teahan's place to have the hand tended to by Teahan's woman. A short distance past the rectory, he spotted Father McAuley's horse wandering loose along the edge of the road.

Tommy: I come up to the horse. I knowed the horse. One trace was dragging in the dust, and I knotted it up; there was no trace on the other side. I takes the horse by the head, and leads him up, and puts him in the barn, locking him up in the box stall. Found this stage-barn door half open. Takes and puts the horse in the stand. Took no bridle nor nothing off the horse; didn't unharness him, didn't take the bit out of his mouth. Touched nothing that was on the horse, for I was laid up with the hand. Couldn't.

Spied this door, leading from the stage barn into the woodhouse, that was wide open; passageway was wide enough to roll a barrel of flour down. Went in. As I walked by this wood pit, as they call it, I seen it was filled with shingles; nothing else there only shingles. Didn't take notice to nothing, unless this pile of shingles; she was full up with shingles. They were all piled up high, most to the top of the pit. Walked on by this pit, spied this other back door of the woodhouse partly open, with an old mat and spade up ag'in it. Spade was bottom-side-up against the door. Noticed a broken chair lyin' on the floor. Lookin' around, I found the kitchen door leading from the woodhouse was wide open, too. The whole house was open for anyone to go through.

Went to summon the housekeeper, to assist me in unharnessing the horse. Called the housekeeper by name, if she was in, for to come out and see to this horse, that I wasn't able, that I was laid up with a sore hand. There come no one for the call. Called repeatedly, but got no answer.

Didn't stay over ten minutes at the furthest around the place. I walked out the same door that I came in. Opened no doors, left everything as I seen it. Didn't see the priest's dog anywheres about. Went down to John Duffy's place, told John Duffy's about it; asked them was Mary Ann McAuley there. She wasn't there. I stayed long enough to find that out, for she was not there to be seen around. Stayed at John Duffy's till nine o'clock in the day. Went then, and started for Michael Teahan's place. Went into Mrs. Kent's. I told Mrs. Kent about this horse, and about finding these doors all open; told the same at Mrs. Duffy's. Went on to Michael Teahan's place; stopped at Michael Teahan's place for to get this hand seen to; told Michael Teahan and his woman about findin' this horse and findin' the doors all open. There went no one in my time to see about the horse.

3.

At ten minutes past two in the warm afternoon, Father McAuley, satisfied that Tom Collins was no longer at Elgin village, set out for home with Thomas Carty, the farmer who had agreed the day before to drive him to David Doyle's place up at Galway. The priest was beginning to feel uneasy about Mary Ann being alone at the rectory. He didn't know why Collins had disappeared from Elgin, nor what to make of reports that he had been seen carrying two bags of luggage; he had been carrying nothing but a knapsack when he came to the rectory.

Carty's team took the river road out of the village, following the winding boulder-strewn bed of the Pollett River from Elgin south to Church's Corner. Timber-covered hills were all around — Boyd Mountain and Church Hill to the right, the southwest end of Gowland Mountain to the left, Collier Mountain pitched abruptly in front of them. They passed through Church's Corner, and began the steep ascent of Coleman Road. That took them to the farm-cleared top of Collier, hard won from the forest by the settlers, who had established Galway and Kerry and, further south, Teahan's Corner just two generations before.

It was blazing hot, the two men sweating heavily, as they rode the open wagon seat under the pale blue sky. The hides of the horses gleamed with sweat under the harness straps. It was an ordinary dry summer's day in rural Albert County. The countryside seemed to the weary priest perfectly normal, ordered, filled with tranquillity. He loved it there, especially during the summer months, and these must be among the reasons. There were those who said that anyone with a sharp eye and a clear mind could see plain as day that the district was dying a slow death; that more and more young people were leaving their homes and families behind as the years passed; that the lumber was gone and the homesteads would follow; that there were no new people coming in, except the tramps looking for handouts or, if worse came to worse, a day's menial work, and the pedlars looking for sales of their trinkets and gewgaws; and that he had been perverse, if not a fool, to have established his mission house and church in such a remote, godforsaken and dying district. Nothing to be gainsaid in any of that, really; still, Chapel Hill, if not precisely the geographic centre of Father McAuley's scattered flock, was the point of land nearest to God's good Heaven.

Father McAuley: Tom Carty took me as far as David Doyle's, which would be all of seven miles — I think a little more perhaps — a little more than halfway home at least. We got there about quarter to five, I think. I remember passing some school children on the way — school was out at four o'clock — and looking at my watch when we got there, and it was a quarter to something. I was stopped at Doyle's about twenty or twenty-five minutes. It was another five or six miles to the rectory from there. Jimmy, Mr. Doyle's son, was driving me, but he had to go to the pasture to catch the horse. I tried to hasten him along. I said: "Now that the boy is away, if we don't get there before dark she will likely be out."

Jimmy Doyle: We drove at a fair gait covering the distance in about an hour, arriving at Father McAuley's about half-past five. As we were going out, Father McAuley told me to drive along quite lively as he was afraid Miss McAuley would go away. He didn't think she would stay at night because the hired man had gone. He said he had seen the hired man in Elgin that afternoon, before he came through. It was the first I'd heard of Collins. When we drove into the yard at the mission house, the dog was the only sign of life.

Father McAuley: I went into the house by the kitchen way, and immediately noticed the dishes all every way on the table there. I took my valise to the hall, took out what little things I had in it, and left them beside the table. Immediately then, I went to the barn; there seemed no one in the house, and I wanted to see whether the horse was gone. The kitchen door was open, and I went out that way.

In the barn, I saw right away my carriage was gone. But I found the horse, standing in the box stall, with the harness on. Some of it was broken. I think the check-line was off, too. My new bridle was lying by the right forward foot of the horse. I thought it was ruined, but when I took it up, it was alright. The new harness was still out in the barn. Mary Ann and Collins were to have taken the old harness, when they went out to Albert for groceries on Monday morning; at least, that had been my orders.

Jimmy Doyle: I didn't notice anything in particular, except that there was no fire in the kitchen stove, and the house looked lonely. Then Father McAuley called me down to the barn, to see the horse and the way the harness was on him. The horse was in the box stall, and the upper half of the door to the stall was closed. The horse was wearing the old harness, with a collar and hames and back saddle; and the bridle and reins of the new harness were under his feet. There were no reins on the old bridle that he was wearing. One trace was broken, and the britching was gone. I took the old harness off the horse, and hung them up. The new harness was lying partly on a bundle of hay on the barn floor. It was customarily hung on hooks. The collars and hames and traces were all in one piece, but there is a kind of steel frame in the collar, and it was bent.

Father McAuley pointed out that the carriage was missing, and we discussed the matter. He said he had called to Mary Ann, and had looked through the kitchen and dining room, and he didn't think she was around. He asked me to go down to Mrs. Williamson's, to see if she was there. I went down, but Mrs. Williamson hadn't seen her since Sunday night. It was a two-mile trip to Williamson's and back. I drove along quite lively, and it took about thirty minutes. When I returned to Father McAuley's, I met him in front of the house. When I told him she wasn't there, he said to go down to Duffy's and inquire for her there. He told me if Miss McAuley wasn't there, bring up Kate Duffy to get his supper.

Father McAuley: When Jimmy left, I went back to the house. I noticed two valises seemed to be missing; they weren't at the place where I left them. I looked around and couldn't see them in the house. The telescope valise, a drab-coloured valise, and a leather valise, what they call a Gladstone; it had been a very good one, and leather inside and out. The Gladstone valise I had bought in Portland, Maine, I think in the year 1893 or 1894 — somewhere about that. I had left it standing empty in the hall.

I went upstairs. I saw that Mary Ann's bed appeared to have been slept in; that is, the bed-clothes were strewn around the bed, and things around on the floor, and so on. I went into my own bedroom, and immediately saw that the panel of the closet door where I kept the tin money-box was broken. The whole panel was fractured down as far as the framework in the middle, a crack about three inches wide. Some pieces of the shattered panel were on the inside of the closet, and some on the outside. The door was kept locked all the time, and the very first thing I did was try to open it. It was still locked. I went and got the key and opened it, but nothing seemed to be missing; there was nothing touched at all. The box was still on the closet floor where I had left it, with $140 still in it.

Then I walked up and down on the verandah, thinking and thinking quite a while, and then I walked out on the main road. I was anxious for Jimmy to return to see if she was at Wiliamson's. He came along, and said she wasn't there. I asked him to go straight to Mr. Duffy's — the next nearest neighbour to the west — and see if she was there. If she wasn't there, I said, he was to ask one of the girls to come down and get our supper.

Jimmy Doyle: I went on to Duffy's and found that Mary Ann was not there, having inquired at Captain Patrick Duffy's and then at John Duffy's. By this time I had begun to be a little alarmed. I returned with Kate Duffy, and a little girl named Lena Martin. It took about forty-five minutes to go up there and back, and it was about 7:30 or 7:45 when we returned, and it wasn't yet dark. Father McAuley came out on the road again, and the four of us went into the house.

Kate Duffy: I have known Mary Ann and Father McAuley for as long as I remember, about fifteen or sixteen years, but I had never met Tom Collins. The last time I had seen Mary Ann was Saturday night, a week before. Father McAuley was out at Albert, and she came down and stayed all night. They had no man there then. She always stopped at a neighbour's when Father was away and there was no man about the mission house.

The four of us went down the drive to the rectory together. We entered the side door of the woodhouse facing the church, and went through the woodhouse and into the kitchen. It was not quite dark yet. I stopped in the kitchen. There were dishes on the table that had been eaten out of: two plates, two cups and saucers, knives, forks, a sugar bowl, and a teaspoon holder with spoons in it. There were tea grounds in the cups; one was at the side of the table and the other was at the end. There was some potato peelings by the side of one plate. There was a couple of potatoes in the oven, evidently placed there to be warmed over, as they had been boiled. There was a frying pan and a teapot on the stove.

The dishes had not been washed, but it had been Mary Ann's habit to wash up the dishes right away after the meal. She never let them stand any time. I washed them up myself later. The frying pan had been used. I would judge these things had been used for breakfast. I have never known them to have potatoes for tea.

We went into Father McAuley's bedroom. We saw where the closet door had been broken in. The bed wasn't made. Mary Ann never made up that bed, excepting he was coming back that day or the next day. When he was away three or four days, she never made up the bed until he was coming home, that day or the day before. She had the clothes thrown across the foot of the bed, and some on a large Morris chair that was there. I noticed the commode, because Father Mc-Auley picked up the holy-oil box that was on it, and said, "This is tampered with, too." He took the key off the top of the box, and he said it wasn't locked. He locked it and put it on the shelf above the commode, where it had always been.

Jimmy Doyle: Father McAuley then asked us to go and see the way his desk was tossed up. We went through the hall to the office. It was getting dark, and we lit a lamp. We found the desk badly littered, and it appeared as if the drawers had been searched. It was a roller-top desk with the top rolled up. It was all tossed up, a lot of papers, and the little drawers or tills in the desk were all open, or nearly all open, There was a lot of papers, thrown on the floor and over the top of the desk. The priest said a pipe and a box with some postage stamps were missing from there.

Kate Duffy: I went to put on a fire to get the priest some supper, and there wasn't any kindling wood. Father McAuley told James to go and get the wood. So he started out, and I went to light the lamp. I had two lights lit, and I left one on the table. James went out to get the wood, and I took the other in my hand.

Jimmy Doyle: I went into the woodshed and over to the wood pit, with Miss Duffy behind me carrying the lamp. The pit was about three feet deep, and there was quite a bit of wood in it. It was three or four steps below the floor, and formed part of the woodshed, which was only partially floored. There was a railing all around the open space where there was no flooring, to prevent anyone from falling down.

I started down the steps. Miss Duffy was right hard by and the light shone over the rail. I went to step into the pit, and I saw a woman laying at the foot of the steps. First I saw her feet, and then the form. One of her slippers was lying on the shingles beside her. It dawned on me, taking into consideration the state of the house, that there was something wrong. I didn't go all the way down.

I turned around and said, "Father come here." He asked me what was the trouble.

I told him, "There's a woman there and she must be dead."

Father McAuley and I went down together with the light. As we went down, I thought she might have fainted. I put my hand on her arm, which was bare, and found that it was cold. I stooped to pick her up, but as I did I smelt the deathly smell and desisted. Father McAuley held the light in front of her face, and we caught a glimpse of her throat. He put his hand on her face. Then he put his hand under her chin and raised it up.

"Poor girl," he said, "her throat's been cut; she's been murdered."

Father McAuley: Jimmy went down into the wood pit in the woodshed, and he immediately saw. He said to me:

"Father, there is a dead woman down here." I went down and I found my housekeeper, dead. I gently put my hand under her chin and lifted it up, and I saw her throat was cut, and I said nothing more than these words: "Let me out of this." There were bags on her head, but I didn't look at that at all — a bag or bags. I was so overcome by what I had seen, that I had to go away from there.

Jimmy Doyle: There was a salt or meal sack partly over her, partially over her face. There was some blood on the sack, but whether it had come through the sack being placed on the blood, or through the blood running down, I could not say. I could not see any pool of blood, but I saw little spots of it. The body was lying feet to the steps, as if it had been dragged by the head or arms along and down the steps. The head was towards the east, and the face towards the kitchen, lying on the right side.

Kate Duffy: Just as I was going over the steps of the kitchen door, I heard James tell Father McAuley he had found a dead woman laying by the bottom of the stairs. I went towards James with the light in my hand, and I looked down and saw it was Mary Ann. She was lying at the bottom of the stairs. Her feet was kind of resting on one step, and her head was down further. She was laying angle-ways, not straight, lying on her right side. Her face was towards the kitchen. There was a salt sack kind of resting across her breast and face. I could see her face, not quite all of it, but I could see one eye.

I didn't go into the pit. I could see she just had her house clothing on. I don't think she was dressed to go out. She had a black sateen shirt waist and a dark skirt. One slipper was on; the other I saw the next day under the old table in the woodshed. I noticed a mat lying on the shed floor, near a door held shut by a spade propped against it. The door was open just enough to let the dog in. I saw him come in just after we found Mary Ann, and go out again.

Father McAuley: We had our supper, and I sat down after that to write a letter to David Moore, the man with whom I'd stopped the day previous in Elgin. I had to try twice —

couldn't get my mind controlled sufficiently at all. I gave a description as near as I could of Collins. Then I dispatched Jimmy Doyle to Elgin with the letter, and to Petitcodiac to send a telegram. Jimmy left the house somewhere, I think, about ten o'clock.

Jimmy Doyle: I harnessed up Father McAuley's horse to our wagon, and headed for Petitcodiac. I stopped and told the neighbours about it as I went along the road. Father had given me a letter for Mr. Moore at Elgin. I delivered the letter, and stopped and fed the horse at Garland's Hotel there. I got a description of the prisoner from Mr. and Mrs. Garland, then went on to the telegraph station at Petitcodiac. I gave the operator some messages which contained a description of the man, to alert the police at Saint John, Sussex and Moncton.

Kate Duffy: Later that night, Father McAuley asked me to go to the woodshed to close the doors, and I did. I went to put the mat down with my heel where it was wrinkled, and couldn't get it down. I lifted the mat then and saw the stain underneath.

Some time after, we went to Mary Ann's room. Father McAuley missed her watch and some other jewellery, rings and things like that. The watch case was on the table in her room. It was a small ladies gold watch. I had last seen it about two weeks before; she drove down to my home, and she was wearing it then. A handkerchief or handkerchiefs were missing. I remembered a silk one that had her name on it, and Father said it didn't appear to be around.

The bed wasn't made. It looked as if she was airing it. She had all the clothes thrown over the foot of the bed. There was some clothes — some waists and things — on the floor. There were three or four pieces on the floor by the chair. They seemed to be scattered about. She was a neat woman, and it wasn't her habit to keep her clothes like that.

We went into the bedroom off the kitchen where Collins had slept. Father McAuley had missed a looking glass, and he said that Collins wanted a looking glass in his room. I went in and saw one on a chair, and picked it up and took it out. I saw a razor case on the window and brought it out, and Father McAuley said to put it back, because it wasn't his. I took it back and left it on the window. We later found out it had been left there by Tommy Mellen, who had used the room before Collins came. Otherwise, there was only the bed and the chair in the room, and Tommy Mellen's coat hanging on the foot of the bed.

I found two clothes baskets. The large high one, that is used for soiled clothing, I found in Mary Ann's room. It had some socks in it. The smaller one, for clean clothing, was on top of a barrel in the woodshed near the kitchen door. I think it was usually kept in one of the spare rooms. It was empty.

We searched for the two dollars that Father McAuley said he had given Mary Ann before leaving, but couldn't find it.

Father McAuley: Kate Duffy and the little girl stayed with me that night at the rectory. Later Kate Duffy's brother came along, to see what was keeping her and to take her home. I said: "John, you'd better keep on to Albert and notify Doctor Murray." So he did. The remains were left where they had been found, until Doctor Murray came the next morning. Some neighbours, when they heard of it, came around during the night; gradually women came in and men came in and so on. A good many people came, for a fact. Of course, Mr. Doyle gave them word as he went along and, of course, they gathered.

4.

As Father McAuley was on his way back to New Ireland Tuesday afternoon, Tom Collins, still on foot, was a hundred miles away. He had debarked from the *Express* at Saint John station at two o'clock, and continued going west. By half-past four he had reached Spruce Lake, a long narrow loch eight miles from the city. John O'Regan's farm there, one of the largest in the area, was run by Daniel Buckley, who was in the barn that afternoon, working on a wagon, when Collins came by.

Buckley: He stopped at my door, wanted to know which way was John the Greek's place, which is about a quarter mile down the road.

"Are you going down there to work?" I ask him.

"No," he says. Says he was directed there, was told he could find a night's lodging there. Well, I put down my oil rag — I was oiling the wagon in the barn — and looked at him. I'd never seen him before, but he looked like he had been travelling some. Had kind of a crooked grin and was wearing a cap on the back of his head. It was a warm day, I remember that; it'd been warm all week, but he was wearing a coat, and toting a valise along.

"Well," I says, "if you're a stranger here, then John will give you a night's lodging alright.

"But," I says, "there's a couple of fellows that stay around here — David and Joe Guthro — well, they don't bear a very good name; so far as I understand, they're a little light-fingered."

I told him if he had much money on him — and being a stranger — to look out for himself, or they might get it from him. I thought the fellow was a stranger in a strange place, and I would give him a bit of advice.

Well, he told me he hadn't much money. Said he had nothing but a gold watch that belonged to his sister, that she gave him at the time he was coming away from England. And he showed me the money he had, took it out of his pocket, and he had possibly thirty-five or forty cents — somewhere along there. I think it was a twenty-five cent piece and a five- or ten-cent piece, something like that. I know one piece he had was a nickel. He didn't show me the watch, but he said he wouldn't like to lose it.

I was looking to hire some men about then, so I ask him if he's looking for work. He said he was.

I said, "Have you worked on a farm?"

He said, "A little."

I asked him if he could milk, and he said he couldn't.

"Well," I says, "I've got quite a lot of cows here, and a man who can't milk wouldn't be much good to me."

I think he told me where he came from, but I can't say for sure. He had been footing it for a time, though. I remember he told me his name was Thomas F. Collins.

Well, when he left, he went on down the road toward John Martin's place, carrying his valise.

I did see him again the next day, Wednesday, at about four in the afternoon. I was going to Fairville, which is towards the city, with my team, and when I got about half a mile from Fairville, I saw him walking. He was going in the same direction I was, but he was a little ways ahead of me. By the time I got up to where he was, he was talking to this young Willie Dean from Musquash. Willie Dean had a load of lumber on and he was going towards Musquash. I passed and left them there. I was in a hurry.

Chapter Five

Wednesday, August 22, 1906

1.

Wednesday morning. This was a different kind of landscape; not like the country Collins had left behind in New Ireland. All the green things here seemed to be growing out of the grey rock and shale. Heavy moist air came in off the Bay of Fundy. His clothes were sodden from a chilly night spent wormed beneath some alder bushes at the roadside. The girl at John the Greek's had told him there was no room for him there last night, so he had continued on his way, but had found no shelter. He shivered as he crawled from under the bushes, his body stiff from the night of lying on pebbles and roots. But the chill was only a mild discomfort for a man who had spent much of his young life at sea, where he had sometimes thought he would never feel warm again. But the August sun rose quickly and heated his back, as he resumed his journey along the road hugging the southern shore of Spruce Lake. He looked around at the tumble of rock and forest and the still, empty surface of the lake to his right. Nothing to do, but keep going.

His head bowed as he walked, Tom absently watched the cracked leather of the boots come and go, one after the other, into and out of his field of vision, dislodging the occasional gravel stone or ball of black horse-dropping. He wore no socks, and his feet inside the old boots were raw and blistered now. The single bag he carried, a rough pillow in the night, flopped on his shoulder. The feel of the morning air, heavy with moisture, reminded him that he wasn't far from salt water. The bay was out of sight, though, beyond the hills on his left. There was dull pale grass, heavy with dew, scattered among spiky weeds along the roadside. Golden rod and thistle gone to seed, dusty violet burdock. It was quiet, except for the occasional squawk of a roaming gull. Tom had come a long way from the priest's house. He thought he had not walked such a distance so steadily for weeks, not since tramping east from Montreal in June, but he would stay on this road until there was reason to leave it. Perhaps there'd be a sawmill with a job.

He heard the team before he saw it, the jingle of harness and brittle clatter of horseshoes sliding toward him on the slick air, bubbles of sound splashing around him. He stopped, wondering before actually seeing it yet, whether to hail the approaching team. He had caught a number of rides in New Ireland, changed direction a couple of times. This team was coming toward him and, if he joined it, would carry him back toward Saint John. He considered, but in the end, stepped to the side of the road as the wagon approached, and waited for it to pass. The horses, their bellies full and spirits high, went by at a relaxed start-of-the-day trot, their heads up, shoulder muscles working under smooth, already sweat-slicked hides. A clod of dirt spun from a platter-sized hoof and spattered near the man standing by the edge of the road. The teamster, riding the high seat of an empty wagon, was a young man about his own age. He sat hunched over, his jacket collar up and his cap tilted forward. His elbows rested on his knees and the leather reins, held loosely in both hands, dangled carelessly between them. Four axe-trimmed hardwood stakes stuck up from the bed of the wagon behind him, their tops loosely connected from side to side by drooping clattering steel chains.

William Dean Jr. lived in Musquash, a coastal village which, in the days of the tall ships, had been a busy seaport. It had declined with the shipbuilding industry in recent years, along with many other small coastal ports in southern New Brunswick, but still shipped timber and fish by rail. Dean's father, William Sr., was a councillor of Musquash, proprietor of its only hotel and general store, and one of the few men whose property had escaped the devastating fires of 1903. He had decided to take his son out of the hayfield this day, and send him to Fairville for a load of saw boards.

"I remember Collins," Dean Jr. recalled. "The day I saw him first was early in the morning, about seven-thirty or eight. It was haying time, but I had to go in to Fairville to pick up a load of lumber for my father. That's about a sixteen mile trip from Musquash, so I had to get an early start. I'd gone about two-and-a-half mile from home, when I met this man. He was walking along the road going the opposite way from me, and carrying a small grip. I thought nothing of it, lots of men on the roads these days. Went on into Fairville and got my load."

Collins also went on. He would say later that he had tried that day to find work at mills and farms in the Spruce Lake area. There is no evidence that he did or that he didn't. But, whatever happened, at some point he found a reason to change direction. Or, perhaps, there was no reason. Perhaps he was simply worn out and hungry and, with no clear idea of what lay ahead of him to the west, he decided to turn around and walk back toward Saint John. At least there was food and shelter in that direction. But his decision, and his second encounter with young Dean later in the afternoon, would seriously impair his bid to remain free.

2.

In New Ireland, Mary Ann McAuley's body still lay on a pallet of shingles in the wood pit at the rectory, her face partially shrouded by the rough flour sack. The uncovered eye that had caught, unseeing, the light from Kate Duffy's lamp the night before, was still open, without lustre, smeared by a dull film. If it could see, it would look into the rough-hewn shadowed angles beneath the woodshed's sloped roof. The shiny points of shingle nails, driven from the outside that summer, poked through roof-boards in ragged lines. What might have been a mouse scurried somewhere nearby; beneath the eaves, looking like a growth of fungus, bulged the crusted homes of swallows. Pale morning light, slanting through dusty translucent window glass, pooled on the plank floor of the shed, but did not yet reach the body three feet lower in the wood pit.

The smell in the shed, not yet pervasive, not yet seeping, was still unstinting, unlike any other. But there was nothing to be done with Mary Ann until Doctor Murray arrived. The coroner, who lived down the long, steep hill at Albert, had sent word that he would come up in the morning as soon as he could make it. The air where Mary Ann lay, sheltered from the sun's direct heat, was sibilant with silence. The big Newfoundland dog had stayed by the shed through the night, keeping company with the remains of his mistress. Some of the neighbours wondered where he had been while the killing was being done. It was thought he had not detected the danger, perhaps because the assailant had been familiar to him, until it was too late and he had already been shut out of the shed.

"There's no trace of blood in the kitchen," Father McAuley pointed out to his neighbours, "but there's a pool of it in the shed, covered by a mat. There's a small spade there in the shed that's barring the door from the inside. When I came in, the spade was at an angle against the door, and the door was partly open." Had Mary Ann, pursued by the killer, jammed the spade against the door to keep him out? Or had the killer used it to secure the room against the dog while he finished his work?

Friends and parishioners continued to arrive through the night. Word spread rapidly as neighbours were alerted by Jimmy Doyle. Some drove down to Chapel Hill immediately; others waited for dawn and the completion of farm chores.

(One, then a child, remembers: "It was awful warm. Oh dear dear. I'll never forget it. I was too young, and my brother was too young, to get up when Jimmy came that night and announced what had happened. He and Father McAuley had stopped at our place earlier in the evening. They nearly always stopped at our place on the way by. Jimmy looked after him and took him places on the mission. Jimmy was a nice little man with light hair, and Father was fat with a round face, nice looking, a big man. But they wouldn't stay for lunch. The priest was awful anxious to get home, because Mary Ann was there alone.

"Then that night Jimmy came back alone to our gate — we all had gates then — and they all went down to the road to see what was going on, all but Fred and I. Shocked to death! Oh yes. Momma came back from the road, and she barred every window and the door. I thought we were going to suffocate with the heat. There was an awful heat wave, I'll never forget that. The house seemed to be sealed. Everybody was frightened. I didn't know anything about it until the next morning. When I got up, they were getting ready to go out to the rectory. I remember my oldest sister kept house. And the neighbours were all so frightened. We were handy, and they all came down and stayed with us, and we didn't dare go into the house to eat! We just ate out of the garden — cucumbers and stuff.")

As the neighbours continued to gather through the night, Father McAuley, straining to cope with the sudden destruction of his household, went to his room, with its smashed closet door, to try to rest. It became accepted in the community, in the months that followed, that the priest, whose frame was husky but whose health was frail, never recovered from the terrific strain of that day and its aftermath. Some parishioners brought food with them, and Kate Duffy kept kettles of water warming on the stove for tea.

The women maintained a pretense of busy activity in the kitchen, talking quietly among themselves, preparing food, taking down plates and cups and saucers, serving food, washing dishes, putting them back in cupboards and shelves, later starting the process over. They speculated in subdued voices about the cause of the event, and conjectured where this Collins, whom most of them did not know, might be now and might be headed. The men tried to keep busy by feeding and watering the horses, and carrying wood into the kitchen from the outside pile. The woodshed was unapproached — unapproachable.

So they waited and watched and talked through the night, the men with the men, the women with the women, profoundly bewildered, outraged, and saddened; waiting for the dawn and for the doctor, so that the men's work with their shovels, and the women's work on the remains of what was still Mary Ann McAuley, could begin. As the light began to come back high in the night sky, some of the men returned to their own homes to look after their stock. Those who remained went solemnly to the little cemetery across the road, to hack at the stark stubborn dirt with picks and spades, to begin excavating her place among the stones and roots and moss, in the dry dust and shale, beside the grave of John McAuley (her uncle and Edward's father) buried there in December, 1880, aged ninety-two.

And others remembered: The priest should never have taken him in. He made a mistake. Poor housekeeper. She was such a nice person. She was up to our place just the weekend before the murder. Oh, she was lovely looking. She had red hair. She was mild, and just a lady. She put up a fight, too, I think. One shoe was off and the carpet was all turned up. She was a spinster lady. She was one of those very strict spinsters. She always was very prim, but she would talk, too. She used to come down and visit my grandmother and my aunt Clara quite a bit. She was a nice housekeeper, she kept everything nice. She was quite plump. She had a wig, you know?

I never seen her express any temper. Some say, I don't know, they said she was hard. You know in them days, maybe the unmarried ones was all like that. I don't know. They said she was old-maidish, awful hard to get along with, hard to suit, you know? She wanted everything done just so. I heard quite a few of the boys who used to work there say she was awful hard to suit. No matter what they'd do for her, it wouldn't suit her. I don't know. I think she and the priest got along alright, because I don't think he paid much attention to her.

And this: I've heard mother tell this so many times. There was a poor old fellow that came along. I don't know where he come from. I don't think he was a tramp. I think he was probably out of work, and just didn't have any money. But anyway, he went in there to the rectory and wanted to get something to eat. Father McAuley was away. Mary Ann was alright when he was there, but this time he wasn't.

Well, the old fellow just asked for a piece of bread and a cup of tea, and Mary Ann refused to give it to him. "Well," he said, "if you're afraid of me," he said, "you just pass it out to me, and I'll sit out here on the steps and eat it, and I'll be on my way." But Mary Ann didn't give it to him, just told him to go on, kind of sarcastic-like.

Well, he came down to our place — the rectory would be about a mile from where my home was — and he told Mother about it. And he said, "All I asked for was a cup of tea and a piece of bread." So Mother went to work and she gave him a lunch, and she packed a lunch for him and he went away. But before he left, he said to Mother, "When I hear tell of her death, I'll pray for her." That's what he told her. And Mother said there was just no reason whatsoever that Mary Ann couldn't have given him a piece of bread and a cup of tea. But she was just that kind, I suppose.

3.

Kate Duffy, who had stayed the night on Chapel Hill, saw the dawn light bleed silently across the hills and into the kitchen. More parishioners began to arrive, knowing no more what to say to their priest than had their neighbours who had come through the night. Some of these also brought food. It was an offering, an empty gesture, meant to be neither empty nor simply a gesture, an admission of helplessness and a declaration (perhaps just a recognition) of solidarity in the face of what must be borne, so that what was left could go on. The women made ready to prepare their friend's body for the earth.

Michael Teahan, one of the last of Mary Ann's friends to have seen her still alive Sunday afternoon, got word at sunrise and drove to Chapel Hill immediately. He was there by seven o'clock. Michael was a farmer and a woodsman, a strong-looking man with a thick neck, big hands, and deep-set piercing eyes above huge moustaches that completely hid his upper lip. There were deep lines on either side of his mouth, and his hair, at least while posing for a photographer, was parted in the middle and combed like wings across his forehead. He was one of the few residents of the district who had met the fugitive Collins.

Michael and his son, Everett, at Father McAuley's behest, had tried last Friday to teach the new hired man to cut and split hardwood, but Tom had had no talent nor taste for it at all. He had seemed distracted at times, and one of his hands, injured earlier, had bothered him when he attempted to grip and swing the axe. The lesson had ended with Michael and Everett doing most of the cutting, and Collins carrying the sticks to the basement of the rectory and stacking them there. Michael had thought it unlikely the priest would ever get a good day of hard work out of this rather ineffectual and vague young fellow. He couldn't even handle the horse.

Collins had told Teahan of an argument he had had with Mary Ann over a can of condensed cream, but Teahan couldn't believe that such a minor dispute could have led to this atrocity. And there had been the fishing trip on Saturday. Michael and his family, with Mary Ann and Collins, and Michael's sister, Sarah Williamson, and Sarah's young daughter, Iva, had gone to the lake behind the rectory, and had stayed at the camp overnight. Everyone had been friendly, relaxed. A lot of fish were caught, and there had been no disagreements. He had observed no animosity between Miss McAuley and the hired man. Still, where was Collins? If he wasn't guilty, why had he run off?

Another Teahan (John), who had come down to the rectory the night before, went at daybreak to fetch Kate a bucket of water from the spring in the woods. The well in the front yard was dry for the summer months, but there were two springs on the slope at the rear of the property. The one to the west, said Kate, was the one used most frequently by Mary Ann. She had not liked going to the east spring in the dense woods behind the church; it made her nervous. John set out for the west spring. He circled the barn, crossing dew-slick grass in the pasture behind the mission house, the sun warm on his back. The forestland birds, darting, fitful and oblivious, whistled and chattered in the woods all around.

Teahan: I found the missing buggy that morning on the path that goes from the back of the barn to the spring. We knew it was missing, because Father McAuley had told us about finding the horse in the barn with the broken harness. No one had looked for it much the night before, because of the dark. Still I was surprised to come across it like that on the way to the spring. There's a cleared field of pastureland behind the rectory, then a fence that runs along the edge of the woods. There are supposed to be bars where the path to the spring passes through the fence, but they were down or missing that morning. I walked right through and down the path and there it was, just a few rods in, fetched up against a tree. It was facing toward the spring. The top was up, and one trace was attached to the whiffletree; the other one was broken away. There were no other straps or pieces of harness laying around, that I noticed. Where it was fetched up, it couldn't be seen either from the road or from the priest's house. I knew it was Father McAuley's buggy right away, I'd seen it many times before.

4.

In Albert village, fourteen miles from the scene of the tragedy that he had learned about just a few hours earlier, coroner Doctor Suther Murray had his usual early breakfast of a bowl of oatmeal, two boiled eggs, two slices of toast, and a cup of tea. He had harnessed his horse and hitched it to the buggy while breakfast was being prepared. He ate quickly, said goodbye to his wife, picked up the black leather bag with its instruments, and set out for New Ireland. He knew what he would find at the rectory — John Duffy had given him the details — but it was incomprehensible that anyone would kill Mary Ann McAuley, a fine woman whom he had known well for thirty years.

A large, red-haired, jovial man, Suther Murray, though he was not a parishioner, had been a good friend of Father McAuley for the same period. A Colchester County Presbyterian of Scottish and Irish descent, Doctor Murray had graduated from Harvard Medical School and married his wife, another doctor's daughter, in 1871, then moved across the Bay of Fundy to Albert County two years later, where he had remained. He was one of the county's best known and — despite an occasional fine levied under the prohibitionist Scott Act (an amused fate suffered by other county doctors whenever they were caught issuing certain prescriptions for less than life-threatening ailments) — one of its most respected citizens.

As his horse picked its way up the steep road into New Ireland, the doctor pondered the news. He knew Mary Ann as an active, energetic woman, quite intelligent, and a very capable housekeeper. Father McAuley, in fact, had been fortunate to have had her with him all these years. It could have been a lonely life for her, because the priest was away from the mission house so frequently, but Mary Ann had friends among her neighbours and spent as much time with them — when the priest was away — as she did at the rectory. "I have my friends here, doctor," she had once told him. "And when Father's away at mission, I visit them. Besides who would look after him if not for me? Why, he couldn't make a cup of tea for himself." Mary Ann knew her responsibilities, and carried them out as capably as two people. When there was no man about, she could handle those duties as well, caring for the horse and doing the barn chores, carrying water and wood.

In two hours of hard driving, Doctor Murray reached the rectory. He left the horse and buggy standing in the front yard, and beat the dust from his trousers and jacket with his hat. It was mid-morning by then, but very warm and dry. He was thirsty and so was his horse. A group of people stood on the front lawn outside the mission house, awaiting his arrival, talking quietly among themselves in a kind of shocked and amazed incomprehension. Doctor Murray knew many of them. Most were women; he had passed by some of the men a few minutes earlier, determinedly at work in the cemetery, the dull clank and scrape of iron on stone violating the thin serene air. A young man in the group on the front lawn took the bridle of the doctor's horse, released him from the carriage and led him to water and a pail of oats. The severe faces of the women passed before the doctor as he made his way to the wide verandah of the mission house. Children gamboled among the trees, the sobriety of their morning having evaporated with the dew. The woodshed, butted to the end of the length of the rectory, was closed in mute testimony to what lay within, even to the big Newfoundland dog, prone and panting still in its weedy shadow.

On the verandah, Doctor Murray greeted Father McAuley, who had just come from the dusky warmth of the house. The two men shook hands. The coroner removed his hat and stood, slightly stooped, his hands clasped behind his back, gazing into the face of the priest.

"Father," he said, "what is this terrible news?"

"She's lying in the wood pit, poor girl. She's been murdered, I fear. Her throat's cut. I told them to leave her there untouched 'til you examined her. And there she's lain, poor girl, all night."

Doctor Murray said he would go in straight away, and would ask the jury to view the body as well. He asked John Duffy to assemble a half dozen men to act as a jury of inquisition.

To the priest, he said, "Young Duffy last night mentioned a hired man you'd had here. He's still missing?"

"Tom Collins, yes. He's disappeared. I had Jimmy Doyle take word to Mr. Moore in Elgin last night. I saw Tom there on Monday, but I haven't seen him since."

"I sent word to Sheriff Lynds at Hopewell," said Doctor Murray, "and a message to your niece, Mrs. Morris, in Harvey. I expect you'll hear from them today. Now I'll look at the body."

The doctor crossed the verandah, entered the wide front door of the rectory, then turned left down a hallway, and passed through the dining room to the empty kitchen. Mary Ann's room, he thought. He paused at the door that led to the woodshed, then pushed it open. It was dim on the other side, and he had to wait a moment for his eyes to adjust to the gloom, so that he could see the shape of the table that he knew was near the kitchen door, and the waist-high wooden railing that ran the length of the wood pit. His other senses seemed to adjust with his vision. The smell of death was part

of the dusky buzzing air, still faint, yet almost with substance. He could hear the clatter of flying insects, drawn to
the place of death, their busy sounds magnified in the
charged interior of the woodhouse.

As he approached the steps to the pit, Doctor Murray
passed the side door where the spade had been leaning earlier, and pushed it open, letting the August light crash into
the gloom. The black dog bounded in and stopped, whining,
poking his snout into the still form on the shingles. Doctor
Murray called for someone to get the dog out. When he was
alone again, he went down the steps to where Mary Ann lay.
She was on her side on the shingles, as if indulging herself
in a mid-morning nap. Even in the dim light in the pit, he
could see the black mass clinging over her left ear like a
parasite. His fingertips moved gently over the crust of blood
and hair.

Looking up and away from the woman's body, he saw
dust motes swirling in the wide slash of sunlight bristling
through the open door. Weaker rays seeped like pale stains,
through hanging dirt and cobwebs clinging to a small window
frame beside the door. Stooping over the form in the pit,
registering the attitude of limbs and thorax, Doctor Murray
was suddenly aware again of the humming silence. It was as
if all the people gathered outside had melted into the trees,
leaving him alone on this mountain with the dead woman.

On his knees beside the corpse, Doctor Murray breathed
harshly through his mouth. He lifted the sack from the slack
face. The left eye, flat, glazed, was like a dark hole. On her
throat was something that made him think of a black velvet
choker. His mind continued to register the details, as he
swatted the back of his hand at a persistent fly. The body
appeared to have been dragged into the pit head first, the
feet resting at the foot of the steps and the head further
away. She had been dead about forty-eight hours, he
thought, not more and maybe less. Decomposition had begun,
but rigidity had not completely passed from the limbs. Rigor
mortis gradually sets in about six hours after death and
takes from twenty-four to thirty-six hours. As it passssed,
putrefaction and decomposition would slowly begin, the

speed with which it worked depending also on external conditions.

The throat had been cut with a haggled incision extending from left to right. The windpipe was severed almost entirely, as well as the principal blood vessels on one side. The jugular vein and carotid artery also were cut. Those wounds alone, Doctor Murray thought, were sufficient to cause death. The skull, just above the right ear, had a pronounced deep incision severing the cranium bone, so that the soft, pulpy matter of the brain was exposed. That wound of itself was also fatal, and would have meant death in from eight to sixteen minutes. The doctor's first thought was that a fairly sharp axe had struck the blow. There was very little blood around the wound, except in the hair, but the hard blow of an axe could have compressed the small blood vessels and prevented blood from spurting from the wound. The clothes seemed not to have been disordered, and he concluded there had been no sexual assault. There were a few small abrasions, the skin off one finger on the back of the hand, and a swelling on the face caused, he thought, by the blood gravitating to that side as she lay in death. Doctor Murray covered the swollen face with the sack, and went up the steps. In the pool of light splayed through the open door, he could see a jumble of material on the woodshed floor. It looked out of place, and he bent to examine it. He found a large stain of what seemed to be dried blood, covered with an old mat and a pair of black-and-white-striped overalls that were also stained. There were smaller traces from there to the steps.

5.

By noon the jury had been empanelled, and the inquest was under way in Father McAuley's disordered office. The members, besides John Duffy, were Herbert Doyle, Michael and James Teahan, James Long, Thomas Campbell, and Arthur Huckins, all residents of New Ireland settlement and neighbours of the dead woman. Doctor Murray told them he was of the opinion that Mary Ann McAuley's death "from violence, criminal or unfair means or culpable or negligent conduct of others" required investigation by a coroner's inquest.

The jurymen stood about the priest's house, some on whatever chairs were available, others leaning on walls, hipshot, ankles crossed, worrying soft-billed caps with big hands more accustomed to gripping reins or axes or peaveys. They were farmers, woodsmen, millworkers, awkward in the role they had been given by the coroner, but attentive, patient, curious, still uncomprehending.

Sarah Williamson heard of her friend's death early Wednesday morning. By the time she and Iva, in a shocked and dulled pantomime of work, had finished up the morning chores on their small farm — William was working in the woods at West River, twelve miles away — and walked the mile to Chapel Hill, it was already mid-morning. The inquest was just under way in the priest's office. Sarah stood at the doorway briefly, looking in on the solemn doctor and the taciturn men of the settlement, most of whom she had grown up with. As he began to describe the wounds, she turned away to Mary Ann's kitchen, thinking crazily of a bottle of strawberry preserves. Mary Ann's chair stood by the table near the kitchen window; from there, with a cup of tea on the table in front of her folded arms, Mary Ann, seated on her chair, straight-backed, severe (with some, but not Sarah), had watched the front yard for visitors, not all of them welcome or made to feel welcome. Across the kitchen, behind the cast-iron range and beside the narrow pantry, was the small bedroom where the hired man was put up. Sarah crossed the kitchen, wide floor planks giving slightly under her weight, and looked into the bedroom — Collins' bedroom. The room was neat, spotless, the bed made, woollen blanket lumpy over the pallet mattress. An empty wicker clothes basket stood on the bed, out of place but familiar.

On the window sill, within arm's length of the bed, was a straight razor, its blade folded into the handle. Sarah remembered that the boy had borrowed a straight razor from her husband the week before, but she didn't touch this one. She lifted the cast-iron lid of the wood-stove, and stirred the embers in the fire-box with the poker she found hanging from the back of the warming oven. This done, she lowered the lid and turned to face the back door, its narrow crosspieces nailed over the wide rough boards in the shape of stacked letters 'Z'. The nails that had been driven through from the opposite side had their points bent over into the soft wood, hammered flat by the carpenter. The door and the nails were covered with cream-coloured paint. Behind it was the wood-shed that Mary Ann called the "outer kitchen." Sarah lifted the latch.

"When I saw her first that morning," Sarah later told the jury, "she was lying on the floor of the woodhouse. I just opened the kitchen door and looked out and shut it again. There was a spread over her. She wasn't in the pit at all. There was no one else there when I looked; they were all in the office having the inquest. When they took her out of the pit, they just laid her down on the floor and left her. I just looked out and saw her and shut the door. I couldn't bear to look more. Afterwards they put her up on the table to wash, and I went out and looked at her, but I couldn't touch her. She was so pale and bruised."

6.

Tom Collins, still on foot in the Spruce Lake area, even more hungry, weary, footsore, perhaps even more confused, suddenly turned back toward Saint John. Walking away from the afternoon sun, he had almost reached Fairville again when, for the second time that day, he met the team of William Dean Jr. Dean's horses were less frisky than they had been on the way out in the morning. The wagon they toiled in front of was no longer empty, laden instead with newly sawn, reeking boards. The horses humped along, their heads bobbing in ever decreasing parabolas, their ears revolving and shortened tails flicking with diminishing enthusiasm, but still ponderously satisfied and uncomplaining as long as the oat pail and the water dish and the stall lay ahead of them. Dean himself dazedly reclined against the lumber, his cap tipped down, the reins loosely wrapped around a wrist, not even bothering to affect a pretense of teamstering. He might have been — probably was — napping.

Dean: I was on my way back home with the load of lumber when I met this Collins fellow again, about four-thirty or five in the afternoon. It was just a short ways out of Fairville, and this time he was walking in the other direction, opposite to the way he was walking in the morning, and he was still carrying the valise. I stopped the team this time and asked whether he had a job.

He said, "No."

"Do you want one, then?"

"Yes."

"Well," I said, "can you tend cows or chop wood?"

"A little," he said.

I said, "Well, come on down and I'll see if my father can't get you a job." I sometimes hire men for my father.

He jumped up on the wagon behind me and we continued on our way. I didn't ask him his name, I just called him Jack. I don't know that he ever told me where he was from, but I do believe he told me he was a sailor.

Then about three or four miles west of Fairville, I stopped at a grocery run by William Abel and bought a piece of cake. Then, as we were driving along, me with the reins and him riding behind me on the lumber, he hauled out this watch and showed it to me — opened it up. I don't know why, don't know whether it was running either. I didn't say anything, but he tells me he had a girl and he bought it for her and she died suddenly and he got it back. There was an initial or something like it on the back of the front cover, but I didn't see what it was. I was in kind of a hurry to get home that night, and I didn't notice. He held it out, I glanced at it and that was all.

7.

Three women of New Ireland district, who had had no role (nor expected one either) in the legalities of the inquest, took charge of the corpse of Mary Ann McAuley. They asked the men to place it on the work table in the outer kitchen, to be washed and dressed for burial. Three men picked up the body gently, one at the shoulders, one at the waist, one at the knees, the broken head cradled so it would not fall back to expose the destroyed throat. They laid it on the worn, work-stained table.

Martha Teahan, the postmistress at Teahan's Corner, and Jane Connor, the goose woman from the Lang Road, went to work with Kate Duffy, stripping the body of its clothing and washing it with delicate precision in a solution of soapy water and carbolic acid. The hair around the head wound was matted and crusted with dried blood. Martha had known the dead woman for many years. She and Jane did what they had to do, washing the body with soap and water after the acid. Kate Duffy helped remove the soiled clothing, then dressed the body in fresh burial garb.

Kate: The body was lying on the table in the outer kitchen. It smelt very bad, as if it was decomposing. Mrs. Teahan washed her and I helped to undress and dress her. There was a little blood around the neck of her shirtwaist and inside clothing; just a little on the inside garment around the neck. She was clothed in house costume. She had on a black shirtwaist and some kind of a cotton skirt. It was very dark in colour. I think it was black or brown with a white strip. She was wearing no shoes or slippers. She was not dressed as she would be if she were preparing to go somewhere. I removed the outside clothes. She had no collar on, only just the collar belonging to her waist. Mrs. Connor put the clothes in a box, and later on they were put out back of this outer kitchen.

The wound was on the back of the head, a little nearer the left side and running up and down. Her hair was all clotted with blood — hard. It was a very light head of hair, all her own. She did wear artificial hair, but didn't have it on then. She was never without the artificial hair when she went out, but I don't think she'd bother putting it on working about the house. It didn't appear as if her hair had been done up that morning; there were no signs of it. It was down and there were no hairpins in it. It was solid caked in around her head with blood. I washed her hair. It was completely saturated in blood.

There were no wounds on the fore-part of her head, but there was an abrasion on the right side. It looked as though she had been struck with something. Like a blow from some hard substance. It didn't leave a cut, but it left a bruise. It was all swollen there, and the hair was completely off it. I couldn't compare it with nothing but a piece of fat pork. Her face was all black when I saw her. There might have been a wound on the forehead, I couldn't tell, her head was so swollen, but where the axe went in on the left side there didn't seem to be much swelling. There were two wounds on the throat. They began like a "V" on one side, and extended into one cut on the other side. There was a little skin off one of her fingers.

And this (much later), the memory of an aged one, having seen with the eyes of a child: "I seen her when she was laid out. Couple of the neighbour women did it. Jane Connor was one. They laid her out. She had a white ... you know her throat was cut from ear to ear, and they had a white cloth all around her throat. I can remember that. And I guess she had a big gash on the back of her head, but that wasn't noticeable then. Carbolic acid they used for a disinfectant. See they wasn't embalmed in them days. There was no undertaker parlours in them days. And that was August, you know? It was awful.

"I can remember going to funerals in them days. I've seen quite a few of them. There was such an odour, you could hardly go in the room. They really shouldn't have been kept at all, because they wasn't embalmed or anything. And her casket ... you'd come in the front door and then the priest's office (he had his office there, there was a big desk), and there was a little conservatory they used to have for her plants and flowers and things. That's where her body was laid out in the casket."

8.

By mid-afternoon Father McAuley's niece, Mary Morris, who had been his housekeeper decades earlier before Mary Ann came from Boston to live with him, arrived at the rectory from her home in Harvey. Mary was an authoritative, precise, well-spoken woman, who took charge of the household immediately. Her husband, Charles, was a police magistrate and a customs officer.

Mary: Father McAuley was my uncle, my mother's brother. I'd known Mary Ann for thirty-four years. She was fifty-two at the time of her death. It was when I was living there, that she came as housekeeper. Father McAuley had been there two years at the time of my coming. His father, John, lived with him then, but he was an old man, and Father McAuley was very anxious to have some of his own relatives there to help take care of him, in preference to a stranger. Grandfather came down to my mother's house, and asked her to let one of her girls go. I was the second oldest, but my older sister was in poor health, so I was sent. I was there for four years previous to Mary Ann coming in 1876.

She was a smart, active, capable woman. And a good housekeeper, both indoors and outdoors, I should say. She was highly thought of in the community and more than highly regarded by Father McAuley. She had full charge inside and out. If anyone was there, she never went to bed without that horse was properly taken care of and watered and fed. Her very particular care was the horse, he was a great pet. She wasn't only a housekeeper, but the same thing as a sister or a mother to Father McAuley. She was a capable woman. She studied his comfort and took charge of everything. His business called him from home a good deal, and he had to have a person who could look after everything.

I hadn't seen Mary Ann since June. We got word at home about noon that she had been found murdered. I set out right away, and arrived at the rectory about three or half-past three in the afternoon. The inquest was going on. I had the opportunity to see the wounds, but I couldn't look at them. I saw the corpse after she was washed, though.

All the time I was in the house, we were from one room to another looking. We knew it was her custom, when she was going out, to hide money and things like that, putting them away. Her watch was the one most valuable thing missing, and that was one thing we searched for. That and the axe were the two most important things, in our estimation, to be found. There was also a gold chain bracelet — rolled gold with a locket on it — a set ring and a band ring — a plain gold ring that was carved. I don't know what kind of stone — one or two stones, I can't remember which — was in the set ring, it was a very nice one, though, considered a valuable ring.

Mrs. Williamson found thirty dollars that day. It was under the carpet in the spare room. She came to me and said: "Mary Ann told me often of hiding money under the carpet; come and we will go and look." And she found it and handed it to me. I gave it to Father McAuley. There was no money, nor anything else found in Mary Ann's clothing. Father McAuley mentioned two dollars he had left her for groceries, and we looked for that, but couldn't find it. Money like that she used to keep in a little tin box that stood on the hall table.

The washstand in Father McAuley's bedroom always stood over by the window facing the door, on the west side of the house, up against the wall. It was right handy by the window. We were looking for the axe, moved everything in the room except the commode. It had the basin and pitcher and other things — mug, brush dish — and we could look under it. Never thought of moving it. It had been in the room from the time we moved in. Never was moved, as far as I know, except at house cleaning, because you could put a broom in under. I didn't look behind it. Looked under it, could see the baseboard. Pieces of the broken closet door were lying on the floor and in the Morris chair.

9.

It was early evening. Tom Collins, William Dean Jr. and their load of lumber had reached John (the Greek) Martin's roadhouse at Spruce Lake. The two men had changed places on the wagon, and Tom now had the reins of the team, while young Dean was taking his ease on the pile of boards, a creature of leisure with a hired man to do his work. In addition to a dining room and beds for overnight guests, John the Greek's business included an entertainment bar.

Two men were standing in the Greek's yard. Joseph Mc-Cann, foreman of the nearby Union Ice Company, and Daniel Lynch, a resident of Carleton, who had been working with McCann for two months as a labourer, sometimes relaxed at the roadhouse with a cold drink, waiting for the train back to the city. They watched the approaching load of lumber, the patient plodding team in front, the stranger with the leathers in hand, young Dean in repose on the boards. Lynch mentioned to McCann that the driver looked like the young fellow they had seen on the road the night before, looking for a boarding house.

As young Dean jumped to the ground, Lynch sang out, "Are you going to do the beer?"

"Boys," said Dean, "if I had enough money on me I would treat. But I've got no money to spend on beer."

Turning to Collins, still on the wagon holding the reins, he said, "How about you, Jack?"

Tom pulled out a red pocketbook, with a strap. It looked to Lynch like it was made of morocco leather. Tom dug out some coins, about thirty cents it seemed, and handed them to Dean.

"Do you have any more in there, Jack?"

"No."

"That will do," someone said. "Let's go in."

"I'll pay it back when we get to the house," Dean said to Collins. "I've just hired him," he told the men.

McCann, a resident of West Saint John, as well as being foreman of the ice company, was also a railroad telegraph operator and yard master for the New Brunswick Southern Railway. He did not go directly into Martin's house with the other men, but held back a bit with Collins, who was chatting away, saying he was from Liverpool, England. He allowed that he could use a cup of tea.

McCann went inside to see about the tea, leaving Tom in the yard. John the Greek himself came to the door and called Collins into his kitchen.

"Are you wanting a drink?"

"I'll have a cup of tea," said Tom.

"Come here," said Martin, "and I will give you a drink."

After they had had drinks, the men went to the piano room, which was elevated four or five steps from the bar room. Davey Guthro was playing the piano. Two young women — Bertie Steadman and Grace Beecham — were listening to Guthro, laughing and clapping their hands. Collins began to tap his feet to the music, then got up and step-danced, giving his audience a few steps around the floor. When Maggie Goguen, a Moncton girl who was working at Martin's for the summer, came into the room a little later, Bertie was playing the piano and Tom Collins was singing. He tried to play a violin, too, but with little success. Young Dean, prevailed upon to dance a jig, was in the middle of his frolic when someone yelled that his team, anxious for their supper, had started away for Musquash on its own. Dean dashed out, leaving Collins behind.

Daniel Lynch: After a bit this man Collins goes over to Miss Goguen and he hauls out this small gold watch from his pocket and shows it to her. Miss Goguen is trying to open the case, and Collins takes the watch from her and opens it and shows it to her. He says, "This is a present I gave my girl, but she died sudden and they returned the watch to me, and those are her initials on the watch." Or maybe he said, "That's her name on the watch." I'm not real sure. I couldn't take my oath to it, but I believe that's what he said. I didn't pay a lot of attention; he was talking to the lady. I kind of walk over to have a look, and I could see there was an "M", or maybe it was a "W", on the outside of the case. Inside the case there was more initials carved, but I couldn't see what they were. It was a lady's gold hunting case watch, though, too small for a man's.

Miss Goguen give the watch back to him then and he put it in his vest pocket. Then he produces another watch, this one's a large open-face silver watch. I don't know why he showed it; he said nothing about it. But Miss Goguen says: "You've got lots of watches on you."

Then he tells me he's hired on with young Dean, asks me where I work. I tell him, "At the ice company over there." Then he asks can I get him a job with the ice company. "Well," I said, "no, not right now, but if it's a few days later, I might."

The watch came up this way, Maggie Goguen would recall. After the others left, Dan Lynch asked about the time. He was waiting for the train down to the ice house. Collins pulled something out of his pocket. "I didn't see what it was. But he put it in his pocket again, and then pulled out a watch — it was a gold watch. He was showing it to Dan Lynch and I said to him, 'Let me see it.' He gave it to me and I tried to open it, but it was hard to open. So he took it from me, and he opened it. It was a lady's watch; it was carved and there was an initial — I think it was an 'M,' but I wouldn't swear to it — on the back of it. It might have been a 'W.' The lettering was in an old style that's not very familiar. And I think there were three initials on the inside, but I don't know what they were. Then Collins said he had bought the watch for his girl over in Halifax and sent it to her, but they said she was dead and sent it back to him."

Tom went to the dooryard, where young Dean now had his impatient team under control. With Collins driving again, they set out for Musquash, ten miles away. It was rugged country, and the road wound and turned and rose and fell with the uneven land. Humped-backed hills and jutting rock formations gave way to marshland and shallow streams, then to timberland. As it approached Musquash, the road came out on a wide grassy marsh, crossing the mouth of the Musquash River near the railway bridge. Three years before, an unprecedented dry spell — forty days and nights without rain — had lowered the river levels so severely that they had become clogged with logs heading for the mills, and finally ignited the ruinous fires that devastated much of southern New Brunswick. In a few incendiary hours, the flames levelled entire villages and huge stretches of timberland, from the American border in the west to Nova Scotia in the east. In just two hours on June 5, the "fire fiend" (so called by the daily press, which kept a running tally of the losses) virtually wiped out the neighbouring villages of Musquash and Prince of Wales, destroying 110 buildings, railway trestles, timber bridges and culverts, and sending 200 people fleeing for their lives. Gone were houses, churches, stores, barns, a school house, a factory, lumber camps, cabins, a mill, sheds, barns, and a railway station.

"The parish of Musquash," said the *Daily Telegraph*, "has about received its final blow, and where there was once a thriving community, whose people were all employed, there is now nothing but a smoking wilderness." In Musquash village itself, only the Church of England and William Dean's hotel were left standing, and that was where the homeless had congregated. The hotel was a large three-storey structure, light-drenched by many windows, with a verandah running its length along the front and across one end. There were two barns in the yard, joined at the end in an "L" shape. It sat about 200 yards from the highway, which ran between the property and the New Brunswick Southern Railway.

Almost at their destination, Dean and Collins were overtaken by William Dean Sr. in a market wagon, returning from Saint John with a load of merchandise for his store. It was well after nine o'clock, but the old man put them to work anyway, carrying his merchandise from the freight wagon into the warehouse. When they finished, they went to the house for supper.

When the meal was finished, young Dean showed Collins to an upstairs bedroom and lighted a lamp on the bedside table. His three days of furiously resolute, curiously deviant travelling had brought him less than 200 miles from New Ireland. He sat on the edge of the bed with his valise, bent forward and alternately massaging his bone-white feet. When Dean left him, he was winding a silver watch that had a key attached by a string.

Chapter Six

Thursday, August 23, 1906

1.

New Brunswick learned about the New Ireland killing in Thursday's newspapers. The Wednesday afternoon daily in Moncton, the Transcript, carried the first report, but it was sketchy and, in some of its particulars, downright wrong. By deadline on Thursday, however, the paper had a better handle on the story. A Saint John editor thought the authorities in Albert County were extremely lax in sounding the alert, and said so in print — twice. It was a sensational story, not only because the murder had occurred in the home of a Catholic priest, but especially because the killer was still on the loose. Many residents of southern New Brunswick would be anxious in their beds this night. Children were told to stay close to home, and some were kept inside; no one knew where the killer had gone, or where he might turn up, or what he might do next.

The *Transcript*'s first announcement of the crime Wednesday was startling and graphic. It pushed news of the province's volatile forest-fire situation from the top line of page one.

**ALBERT COUNTY WOMAN FOUND WITH
THROAT CUT.**

A Horrible Murder Committed at Little Settlement of New Ireland.
**Fifty Year Old Miss MacAulay the Victim,
and German tramp named Collins Suspected of**

the Crime Has Disappeared — Inquest Being Held To-Day

In a two-column box beneath these headlines was *The Story in a Nutshell*, offering the impatient reader the pertinent details in four paragraphs of bold type. It told of a "horribly mutilated" corpse, and described the suspect: "Short and stout; about twenty years of age; complexion, dark; black eyes; full mouth; slight impediment in speech. When last seen wore black, square-cut coat and cap; generally carried two grips." The main story told of Father McAuley's return to his remote rectory Tuesday, to find the "fearfully mutilated" body of his cousin and housekeeper. "From ear to ear the throat of the unfortunate woman had been cut." All in all, it was a lip-smacking portrait of mayhem. The report speculated that "the implement had evidently been a keen-edged one, presumably a razor." Chief suspect, declared the paper, was a "German tramp" named Collins, who had been in the employ of the priest, and who had disappeared from the area after a two-week stay. The story claimed that Father McAuley, on his way home after a three-day absence, had encountered Collins at "Sussex," and had received an evasive answer when he inquired how things were at home. Collins later vanished. Motive for the killing "is largely a matter for conjecture."

New Ireland was described as a remote little settlement, some nine miles back from the village of Albert. "Located as it is, without telegraphic or telephone communications direct, it is exceedingly difficult to ascertain many particulars of the startling affair, and it is necessary to depend on such information as can be secured by telephone from points near to the settlement in which the affair took place. All through Albert and Westmorland, and throughout the province as well, a great deal of interest has been excited by the mystery surrounding the case. The *Transcript's* informant in Albert County says that there is little doubt in the minds of those living in the district that a foul murder has been committed, and the disappearance of Collins at such a time has naturally tended to cast suspicion in his direction."

2.

Albert County's sheriff, Ernest W. Lynds, was a bachelor shipping and lumber merchant who lived in the big family home at Hopewell Cape, the county seat, with spinster sisters, Belle, Lily and Margaret. At the time of the New Ireland murder, he was three months away from his fifty-first birthday. Described as a big man, heavy and chunky, but not tall, he was said to be friendly and good natured. He generally thought well of people, and he was liked in return. A photograph, which appeared at the time in a Saint John newspaper, shows a stern-looking man with a high broad forehead, thinning hair cut short, and a clean-shaven face. He seems to be glowering over the left shoulder of the photographer, and his mouth, set in a thin line, is pulled down at the corners. Perhaps he wasn't himself in front of a camera.

A Baptist by religious conviction, Lynds (pronounced to rhyme with "winds") was Liberal in his politics, and probably had the appointment because of it; his father, Silas, had been sheriff before him. Ernest "retired" in 1908 after eleven years in office, replaced by Captain Benjamin T. Carter, also of Hopewell Cape, when the Conservative party formed the provincial government. He later returned to office for a second term, "his official duties being carried out with marked ability," according to a surprisingly generous obituary in a Conservative newspaper. A life-long Liberal, he took an active interest in the policies of his party and, at his death, was described as "a man of far above the average intelligence, a lover of the best in literature, practically well-informed in politics, and well versed in the political history of the province."

Engaged in business activities from his youth, Lynds had extensive interests in shipping, being builder and managing owner of many vessels: the *Maggie Lynds*, the *Endeavour*, the *Maud Pye*, the *Victory* (which, built at Waterside in 1890 at 124 tons, burned in Dorchester Harbour in 1903, loaded with lumber bound for the American market), the *Waterside*, and the barque *W.W. McLaughlin*. He carried on a general mercantile business at the shiretown and, in company with

Capt. R.C. Bacon, operated the Hopewell Hill plaster quarries for several years.

A Voice: There were good sheriffs and there were bad sheriffs. They had a lot of functions. In those days, people got put in jail for debt. Mortgage sales were sheriff's babies then. There were some who had mercy on humanity, and some who didn't. I think Ernest was one of the former.

He had boats, ships, sailboats. He was never a captain; I think he hired captains. Down in Hopewell Cape in those times, in his vintage, sailing ships were very common. There were very few people who didn't have a ship, if they had means. They hauled cargo. In Lynds case, it was coastal trade. I don't think he had any ocean-going vessels. The big anchor on display at the Cape is off one of Lynds' boats. I don't know how many he had over the years, but I think he was the type would have only one at a time. He had an income off the boat, but the family also had extensive lumber lands in the county. I have no recollection of Lynds lumbering himself, but he sold the stumpage. I suspect that Ernest was pretty comfortable, although I don't know his finances at that time. They obviously wanted for nothing. His father's name was Silas. I don't know whether he or Ernest or someone else built the house at Hopewell Cape. As far as I know, Silas didn't have ships. I think he just probably depended on the land more — the land and the woods. Ernest's brother, Jim, went to Ann Arbour, Mich., and made his fortune.

I was five years old when Ernest died in 1929, so I don't remember a lot about him personally. He had the first car that I remember. It had snap-on windows. I remember his funeral. It was just massive for a country funeral. The hearse was drawn by horses. Many years later, when I came back from the war — the Second World War — I found it extremely interesting to talk to the two surviving sisters of Ernest Lynds. We'd talk about things that were sometimes just a slight memory, or recognition of some kind, on many, many subjects and Ernest would always come into the discussion. Jim was very successful, but I think these girls had developed a closer relationship with Ernest. Out of a family of five — three girls and two boys — only one married, so I suppose they became closer than a lot of brothers and sisters.

From what I've learned over the years from the girls — who I was pretty close to right up until the time they died — they were very kind people, and they had great respect for their brother. So he must have been much the same and, if he was, there was no way he could hang anybody. People in those days were very sincere about their duty, you had to do it whether you liked it or not. Bear in mind, I've got this in discussions with the sisters, not with Ernest, because I was too young. But it seemed — I don't think there was any question — that there was a real friendship established between Ernest and Tom Collins, while Collins was in jail there, one that probably, tore him right apart. I think it just literally tore him apart.

When Sheriff Lynds got word of the murder in New Ireland, there was no indication in which direction the culprit had fled. If he was on foot and had any knowledge of the lay of the land, the most likely and shortest escape route would be southeast from New Ireland to Shepody Bay, and then across the water into Westmorland County or further south into Nova Scotia (exactly opposite the route that Collins had actually taken). Acting on this assumption, Lynds telephoned Marshall O'Blenis in Sackville with a description of the fugitive. Lynds suggested that the man — if he had boarded a vessel at Mary's Point, Albert County, and landed at Wood Point, Westmorland County — could have on his boots the gluey, reddish tidal mud from the shore of the bay.

There was a swift arrest. Making his rounds that evening, Marshall O'Blenis spotted a stranger whose appearance tallied with the description given of the killer. The man was taken to the office of Police Magistrate Cahill for questioning, then placed in the town lockup to await identification. News of the murder, and of the arrest of the stranger, travelled rapidly throughout the Sackville area. Large numbers of townsfolk went by the jail to gawk at the rather sorry-looking prisoner.

Suspicion that the man might be the New Ireland fugitive deepened, when he decided that his name was Melbourne

Sabeans and not John Wilkins, as he had initially told Marshall O'Blenis. Sabeans had no money. When asked where
he came from, he gave more conflicting information. He told
a newspaper reporter that he had been in Apple River, Nova
Scotia, on Sunday and came with the mail wagon from there
to Joggins Mines. He then went to River Hebert, he said,
where he helped load freight on the steamer *Mildred C.*,
paying his passage to Wood Point, New Brunswick. From
there he walked the short distance into Sackville, arriving
Tuesday night. He stopped at a Sackville bakery where he
asked for lunch, but had no money to pay. He was said to
have bent the ear of proprietor James Teare with a number
of stories.

Sabeans, if that was his name, had tattooed on his arm
the letters *M.M.S.*, which may have been his initials and, on
his wrist, a star. He suffered from asthma and spoke with
difficulty, but told a reporter he had not been informed what
he was being charged with. He said he had been in Albert
County about four months earlier, but had never been to New
Ireland. He said he was thirty-four years old, had been going
to sea for eighteen years, and was addicted to drink. He
would go to sea to earn money, then return to shore to spend
it all on a spree.

Though the newspapers which reported his arrest eventually decided it was unlikely that Sabeans was the New
Ireland killer, Sheriff Lynds thought the man should be seen
by someone who had actually met the missing Tom Collins.
He asked Mrs. L.V. McAnulty, whose husband was
proprietor of McAnulty House in Albert, to accompany him
to Sackville to have a look at the prisoner. Mrs. McAnulty
told him that the man known as Tom Collins had spent three
days at McAnulty House in August, before being hired by
Father McAuley and taken to New Ireland. She said he had
behaved in the quietest manner, had volunteered little information about himself, and had shown himself quite willing
to do chores about the hotel in return for board and lodging.
Despite his quiet ways, he showed her on several occasions
that he was quick-witted and, in her opinion, quite shy. She
claimed, however, that he seemed unable to speak English

well. That statement probably gave rise to the widely published report that Collins had a speech impediment.

Mrs. McAnulty said she came across a letter he had left behind, unfinished, and with no address. It began "Dear Bertha," and contained many incorrect statements about his situation. He had written that he had been offered 100 acres of land for a trivial sum, and asked if "Joey and the children were well." Before arriving in Albert, Collins, according to Mrs McAnulty, had been staying at the house of Arthur Edgett in nearby Harvey, where he was known as Charles Fitzsimmons. Sheriff Lynds was also told that Collins, earlier that summer, had earned a bad reputation while working at Grindstone Island, just off the shore at Mary's Point, where he had been employed loading a steamer. He was reported to have drawn a knife and threatened to stab one of the men. He was ordered to leave, and did so.

Sheriff Lynds escorted Mrs. McAnulty on the ferry across the Petitcodiac River from Hopewell Cape on Thursday. After getting a look at the prisoner Sabeans in the Sackville lockup, she reported that he was not the man known to her as Tom Collins. Sabeans was released.

3.

Newspaper editors at the turn of the century were fond of the colourful, emotion-packed adjective. One they used frequently in this case was "horrible"; another was "brutal." The editor of the Moncton paper, in fact, promoted "horrible" from its subhead status on Wednesday, to the main headline for Thursday's edition. He also enlarged its type size.

MURDER MORE HORRIBLE THAN AT FIRST SUPPOSED.

Miss McAuley's Skull was Crushed in with Axe, and then Her Throat Cut.
Robbery Seems to Have Been the Motive of a Murder which will go Down in Criminal Annals of the Province as One of the Most Horrible in History.

The victim, it was reported, appeared to have been fleeing her assailant, when she was struck down from behind by a blow that split her skull. "The monster made sure work of his job. The blow on the head was sufficient to cause instant death, but he completed the horrible butchery by cutting her throat with a jacknife or razor." Another report claimed rather boldly, "There was no evidence of outrage, and the motive for the terrible crime was unmistakeably robbery." The story of the finding of the body was related. It was conjectured that the killer left the mission house Monday morning in the priest's carriage, but that he later abandoned the rig. Collins' trail was traced from Elgin to Petitcodiac where, it was thought, he had bought a ticket for Saint John and left on the 10:10 train Tuesday morning.

4.

Newspaper readers in Saint John didn't learn of the crime until Thursday, and the possibility that the fugitive had come undetected and unhindered to the port city by train, did not please either the law enforcement authorities or the editors of The *Daily Telegraph*. If the police had received word of the murder and the manhunt the day before, they apparently didn't inform the local media until after Wednesday's deadlines had passed. The scribes of the city's afternoon paper decried the delay, whatever its cause. A strong editorial rebuke appeared.

A SHOCKING CRIME

Further reports from the scene of the murder in a remote section of Albert County tend to en-hance the horror of the occurrence. Brutal murder from the most sordid motive appears to be the only explanation. Owing to several circumstances the province was not alarmed until the guilty man had had a long start and had left the neighbourhood, every avenue of escape from which might have been carefully guarded had the news been sent out earlier.

Even when the county authorities were made aware what had happened they lost much time. This is said, not because it seems probable that the murderer will get clear away, but to emphasize the wisdom of using publicity as fully and as soon as possible under such circumstances. The newspapers, had they been informed promptly of the crime and furnished with a description of the suspected man, would have converted the entire population of the province into an active detective force. Any stranger resembling the suspect would have been narrowly observed wherever he showed himself and compelled to give a satisfactory account of himself. In most of these cases the value of publicity as an aid to justice cannot be overestimated.

New Brunswick's record with respect to serious crimes is not a bad one. It is good compared with most other regions, and particularly when compared with most American states. The public hope in connection with this shocking affair will be for speedy apprehension, conviction and punishment. As we write, fortunately, the man wanted may be in custody.

The editor's last statement was wrong; Tom Collins still had a few hours of freedom left. The *Sun* had this to say:

The murder in Albert County, chronicled in the *Sun* today was as cruel and atrocious a crime as has ever blackened the records of this province. The killing in so horrible a fashion of an estimable and well-loved lady by a man whom she and her uncle had greatly befriended is almost incomprehensible to a sane mind. In the interest of justice and of the good name of New Brunswick all hope that the fiend who is guilty will speedily be apprehended and receive the extreme penalty of the law. In his terrible bereavement the sympathy of the community will go out to Father McAuley.

The Saint John newspapers worked quickly and soon had a local angle for their stories. The headline in Thursday's *Daily Telegraph*:

MURDERED WOMAN NATIVE OF ST. JOHN; CRIME MOST BRUTAL

Father MacAulay's Housekeeper at New Ireland Slain While Fleeing from Man Priest Befriended Jury Names Thomas J. Collins as Suspect But He Has Apparently Made Good His Escape ... Man Arrested at Sackville Likely to Prove Himself Innocent ... Murderer Robbed House and Drove Away With Priest's Horse ... Likely in St. John Tuesday ... Murdered Woman Has Relatives Here.

Murder, the most atrocious and most foul recorded in the annals of crime in New Brunswick, is the only fitting description of the tragedy at New Ireland, which came to light last evening. The story of the crime is hard to believe. The victim, a maiden lady, was of about fifty years, and the suspected murderer is not more than twenty years of age.

To be butchered at her home in New Ireland and almost within the shadow of the church where she had been a beloved and devout member, has been the fate of Miss Mary Ann MacAulay, house-keeper and cousin of the parish priest, Rev. Father MacAulay. The tragedy is one of the worst in the history of this section of the province. It is the one topic. Wherever men meet the ghastly details are discussed, and to Fr. MacAulay, who is almost overwhelmed with the suddenness and horror of the crime, all possible sympathy is extended.

Mary Ann was described as "a woman of estimable character," who had been born in Saint John. Her family had moved to Boston about twenty years earlier, but there were relatives still living in the city. She was the daughter of Patrick McAuley, who lived many years in a house on what was known as McAuley's Lane, running between Waterloo and Brussels, but which later became Middle Street. About twenty five-years earlier, Patrick McAuley died and his wife (née Whelan) went with the four children to Boston. "The relatives who are at present residing in the city are Mrs. Josh Ward, and Edward Hogan, proprietor of Hogan's Stables, Waterloo Street, who are second cousins of the dead woman. Mrs. Ward last night said that she had met Miss McAuley about twenty-five years ago in New Ireland, and that she was then keeping house for Rev. Father McAuley, her cousin. Mrs. Ward said that she thought the dead woman must have been somewhat over fifty years of age. Rev. Father McAuley is the uncle of Mrs. Ward and Mr. Hogan." At the time of the crime, Mrs. Ward told reporters, Father McAuley had been away from his home preparing for the church picnic scheduled for the following Sunday, August 26.

5.

Saint John city's veteran police chief, W. Walker Clark, was worried. He was afraid that, by the time he had received word of the murder and the fugitive's probable flight path, it was likely they had missed him. If Collins had come to the city on the train from Petitcodiac Tuesday morning, he could already have passed unnoticed through the chief's jurisdiction. Clark told reporters he regretted the news had not reached him earlier than Wednesday. When he did get the telegram, he had ordered close watches put on all the trains and boats coming to and leaving the city, but he believed it likely Collins was already west of Saint John and trying to reach the American border. Clark notified the authorities in Charlotte County, which bordered the state of Maine, and began a series of telephone calls to hotel keepers, warning them to be looking for the fugitive.

One such call paid off on Thursday. Early that morning, the Saint John police were contacted by a man who claimed to have met the suspect near Spruce Lake. If it had been Collins, it was the first solid indication to Clark that he had not shipped out at the port, and wasn't holed up in the city. The chief placed a call to Councillor William Dean of

Musquash, who had a hotel and general store on the road ahead of the fugitive. If Collins continued westward from Spruce Lake, he could eventually show up at Dean's. Dean told the chief he had heard nothing of the murder nor of the manhunt, but a man of Collins' description had been at his hotel that very morning. He could be there still. Excited by the news, Chief Clark warned Dean, who was speaking loudly into the telephone receiver, to keep his voice down. He told Dean to seize the man if possible, and to keep him there until Clark and his officers arrived. The chief quickly ordered that his team and carriage be prepared, and he and Dectective Patrick Killen, one of his best and most experienced officers, set out immediately for Musquash, fifteen miles west.

6.

In New Ireland Thursday morning, preparations were being made for the burial of Mary Ann McAuley. The body lay in a pine coffin in the parlour of the rectory. It was carried across the few rods of rock and dirt in the August heat to St. Agatha's Church for service, then taken across Shepody Road to be interred in the little cemetery beside the grave of her uncle, John McAuley. Rev. Father John Savage, of Moncton's St. Bernard's parish, old friend of the McAuleys, had come as requested to celebrate mass. At three o'clock the remains were laid to rest, with neighbours, friends and relatives gathered round "with sad hearts to pay the last tribute of respect to one beloved and mourned by all."

7.

Tom Collins was oblivious of the sensation his abrupt departure from New Ireland was causing in the province's media. Early Thursday morning he roused from the bed he had been given at Dean's hotel. He seemed in no hurry to leave. After his breakfast, he helped young Dean get the team ready for mowing the marsh hay. The two men had little to say. When Dean left with the team and mower, Collins struck a deal with Mrs. Dean that would pay for his board and meals. She told him he could split the firewood piled in the yard. He agreed and went about the yard trying to locate an axe. He could not find one. But he spotted a wheelbarrow and, after further instructions from the woman, began to wheel the wood to the front verandah of the hotel.

An overnight guest from Saint John, William Heffernan, standing in the shade offered by the wide verandah of the hotel, bemusedly watched the young man at work.

Heffernan: When I first seen this man Collins, he was talking about an axe. It was Thursday morning and Collins was talking to Mrs. Dean, the wife of the proprietor. He wanted to chop wood and the axe was missing. I next saw him coming from the woodyard wheeling a barrow full of wood. The woodpile was about 100 feet from where I saw him. He had to wheel the wood along the whole front of the house to where I saw him. He took an armful of wood off the barrow, came up the stairs, went along the verandah, came around to the end of the house. He was piling it on the verandah at the end of the house opposite the telephone room window. When he came back I spoke to him. That was the first I had to say to him.

I said, "There is a nearer way for you to take that wood and not cause you so much trouble." There was a pathway at the side of the house between the verandah and the flower garden. I said, "If you wheel your wheelbarrow in that pathway and bring it right up to the verandah, you can take your wood off without taking it up in your arms. It will be much easier." So he did.

Then I heard the telephone ring.

I was standing on the verandah by the front door. Even though I was over twenty feet away from that window to the telephone room, I could overhear some of the conversation Dean was having on the telephone. I would say that Collins was about seven and a half feet away from the window. The telephone was on an inside wall opposite the stack of wood. I would think that anyone standing on the verandah opposite the window could hear another on the telephone, regardless whether the window was open. I judged by Collins' actions that he was interested in the telephone conversation. All the time he was handling wood, he had his eyes fixed on the window. I heard Dean say into the phone that there was a man of that description, or something similar to that, came with his boy from Fairville last night.

Well, after he got through with that load of wood and put away the wheelbarrow, Collins says, "I must get a handkerchief."

Then he went into the the house by the side door, and came back out with a coat over his arm. He crossed the yard beside the hotel, and went into a barn door. I seen him next, about six or seven minutes later, in the centre of the field behind the barn, walking toward the main road. He had his coat on then, and was walking very fast, but not running. He climbed over a fence about 700 feet from the hotel and went on up the road. I'll say this, he took a longer route to the road than if he had gone by the usual way.

Dean Sr.: I thought nothing about him wheeling wood, supposed he was doing it on orders of Mrs. Dean to pay his board. Went about my business. About that time, Mrs. Dean called me to the telephone. It was Chief Clark from Saint John. He described a man he was looking for, but he didn't tell me about the woman being killed. As I talked to the chief I could see Collins through the window, standing at the edge of the verandah where he was piling wood. He would be about eight feet away from me, I suppose. The window was closed, and Mrs. Dean had closed the door into the telephone room so that no one could overhear the conversation.

I was guarded in my replies to the chief, so anyone hearing wouldn't understand the message he was giving me. But I had to speak louder than ordinarily, so the chief could hear me. I looked at this fellow Collins, and there was another man standing on the verandah who had arrived a little before. He had come in from the lumber woods, but I didn't know his name. I sized the both of them up. The chief described a man with dark eyes. Collins had light eyes, but the other man had dark eyes. So I said, "There are two of them here." I think those were the words.

A few minutes later, this Collins fellow went into the kitchen, and came out almost immediately, carrying his coat. Then I saw him go by the window. I left the phone and went outside and through the shed, I think, and I saw him go out the road, what I thought was him. I went out to take a look at the other man, at both of them, and I saw what I supposed was Collins going up the hill, not a quarter of a mile away, about half-a-quarter, I suppose. I next saw him walking up the highway going west, but not moving rapidly.

I suppose he could have seen me on the telephone if he had looked in from the verandah. He could've heard the bell of the phone ring, I suppose, and he could have heard the conversation if I had spoken loud enough. I don't know. But after I seen him leave like that, I went back to the telephone, called Chief Clark and told him he might be the man he wanted.

8.

Back home in Moncton, Father Savage had returned from his duties at the little New Ireland cemetery, and was talking to the newspapers. He described the scene at Mary Ann's funeral:

> The whole countryside was present, as she was greatly loved for many kind and charitable deeds. I was scarcely able, on account of the sobs of women and even strong men breaking down, to make myself heard in expressing the words of consolation. The scenes of the last few hours are the most stirring in my life, and will live in my memory as long as life lasts.
>
> Some people up there are still so terrified that I would not be surprised at their leaving the settlement. The tragedy has left a blight on New Ireland, from which it will not recover for a long time. Many residents of the place avoid the house of the tragedy, and at night not a soul stirs abroad. The whole vicinity is shocked and stupified by the awfulness of the crime, and the women especially have been rendered hysterical and nervous.

9.

By noon Thursday, Police Chief Clark and Detective Killen had reached Dean's Hotel at Musquash, but they were too late to intercept Collins. The suspect had been gone for an hour and, as far as anyone knew, was still on foot and heading west toward Lepreaux. The veteran police officers set out after him.

The two men were used to working together, having between them many years of service on the Saint John police force. In 1903, Killen had been called before a court of inquiry headed by Premier Lemuel Tweedie, to defend Chief Clark against charges of drunkenness and improper conduct in office, brought by a Saint John citizen, John McKelvey. When his turn came, Killen told the inquiry he had seen the chief under the influence within the past three weeks. Within a year-and-a-half, in fact, he had more than once seen him under the influence of liquor, he said, but never incapable of performing his duties. He said the chief was an A-1 officer, who gave too much attention to his work. There was no better man to his men, Killen added, and he was most generous to sick officers.

James Knox, ships chandler, who knew the chief for many years, said he had never seen him under the influence. He had gone fishing with him several times and never saw him drink liquor.

"There was liquor there?" he was asked.

"Well, I should think so," was the reply.

"Wouldn't be much of a fishing party without," interjected Premier Tweedie with a smile.

"No," said the witness, "but I've been fishing many times and never took a drink."

"But it's handy in case of a sickness," said Tweedie dryly, and after a pause, Knox replied, "Yes, but I've never known the chief to take sick."

McKelvey eventually admitted he held a grudge against the chief, for harsh treatment he had been dealt in an incident at the *Intercolonial* station in 1899, as the first South African contingent was departing to fight in the Boer War.

He said he had been trying to get square with him ever since. Tweedie's ruling was that, while he deemed it reprehensible that an officer should at any time appear in public in a state of intoxication, the facts adduced were not sufficiently serious to sustain the charges. Even though Chief Clark appeared to be under the influence on occasion, he said, he was capable of carrying out his duties efficiently and properly.

As Clark and Killen went after the man who had evidently fled Musquash, they couldn't know whether he would be following the Southern New Brunswick railway line, which crossed in front of Dean's Hotel, or the highway to St. George. But if he had taken either route, Killen thought, and if he stayed with it, he would eventually show up at St. George station, where the rail line and the road converged.

Killen: When Chief Clark and I had got to Dean's and found he had gone away from there, we stayed only a few minutes before setting out for Point Lepreau further west. It was nearly one o'clock when we got there. We found that a man answering our description had gone on by Lepreaux about an hour before, so we gave our horse a drink of oatmeal and water and continued on, making inquiries along the road. We came to a junction where two roads meet — the Post Road and the Shore Road going to St. George. We didn't get no trace of him, but we took the Post Road and went clean through 'til we come to Lake Utopia. We inquired there from a man by the name of Spinney if anyone had gone by there, and he said no.

We drove on from there to St. George. Got in St. George about a quarter after four that evening, and put our horse up at Mr. McGee's, who keeps the Carleton House. I went from there to the railway station, to watch for anyone that answered the description of the man we were looking for to come in there. Chief Clark had business in Saint John, so he took the train back. The railroad and the highway road goes right by the station. I stayed there with the marshall of the town, by the name of McAdam, until daylight the next morning.

Back in the city, Police Chief Clark told reporters the majority of people he and Detective Killen had met along the route that day had already known about the New Ireland murder, but only the Deans, William Heffernan and another man had seen anyone resembling the description. He said the man at Lepreaux, who claimed to have seen the fugitive about an hour before the arrival of the officers, said the man "was hastening as if under the impression that he was being pursued." There was always the possibility they were on the wrong trail, but there was also a good chance the man was Collins. Clark strongly believed that if he approached St. George or tried to pass through, he would be captured.

10.

They didn't know it yet, but somewhere along the way between Lepreaux and St. George, the two police officers had passed the man they were after. His tender feet increasingly tormenting him, Collins had continued walking west from Musquash, but by late afternoon the policemen were ahead of him, having already reached St. George. It's likely that had Collins followed the New Brunswick Southern rail-line, out of the sight of the two policemen, who had stayed on the wagon road. The tracks crossed the road, just east of Lepreaux, then dipped south a good distance toward the bay to run through Pennfield Station, before meeting up with the road again and passing north between it and Lake Utopia. At six-thirty that evening, Collins reached Lake Utopia. He turned on a road that crossed the rail line, and walked only a short distance before coming to the home of postmaster-farmer Douglas Spinney.

Spinney: Well, I'd guess it was six-thirty or thereabouts and I'd guess it was a Thursday. I don't just remember now, but that's what they tell me. He was coming down the road from the head of the lake when I first seen him. Stopped at my place and asked for something to eat. I didn't know it then, but he had come twenty-eight miles from Musquash that morning. Mister, that's a fair distance.

He come into my yard — he wasn't carrying anything that I could see — and he asked me if I'd be kind enough to give him something to eat. I told my boy to go in and get him something. The boy brought it out in a paper and give it to him. I asked him where he was coming from, and he said Saint John. I asked him where he was going, and he said St. Stephen. He made some remark about his shoes hurting his feet; they were quite muddy.

After he ate he started back the way he had come from, going north out the lake road towards the lake. So I says, "If you're going to St. Stephen, you'd do better to take the Post Road. It's the shortest way there." He listened to me, but said nothing, and then turned and headed down the Post Road toward St. George. But after he had gone about 120 rods, he takes a right turn off the road, and heads north again towards the lake. "Suit yourself," I thinks to myself, "if you're so damn determined to take the long way around." I never saw the man again, after he made that right turn and stepped into the ditch. I don't know where he was headed. Nothing north of my place but water, trees, and flies.

11.

In Moncton that evening, Father McAuley's nephew, Charles Morris, spoke to a newspaper reporter. He had been at the murder scene with his wife most of the day Wednesday, searching unsuccessfully for the murder weapon.

I can tell you what folks in Albert are saying about this man, Tom Collins. I never met him myself, but they say he ran away from the *Edna M. Smith* — that's a barque that works the Petitcodiac — at Hillsborough earlier in the summer, sometime in July, I believe. Then he worked for a time loading the *Gadsby* — that's a steamer — at Grindstone Island, before going to board at Mrs. McAnulty's at Albert. He was supposed to cut wood for them for his meals and room, but then Father McAuley came along and offered him work at the rectory in New Ireland.

It's been said around that Collins bore a bad name among the stevedores on Grindstone. They say he was put to cooking for them, but the men didn't much like his disposition. They convinced the boss to discharge him from that job, and put him to work carrying lumber. It's said that Collins threatened the boss he would square with him some day for that. I don't believe he ever did. I think Collins is out of the country by now; they say he might've got to Boston on the *Calvin Austin* on Wednesday.

It's clear to me that the murder was committed Sunday evening right after supper, because the used dishes were still on the table when Father McAuley arrived home. It's a terrible thing. The people of the whole area are awful worked up over it. It's the one thing they talk about, and the one thing they want most is to see Collins caught and punished. Poor Father McAuley, I fear he'll never be the same.

Father McAuley's emotional state was the subject of a dispatch from the correspondent for the *Sun*, who had visited the settlement Thursday.

The terrible tragedy at New Ireland continues to excite the deepest interest, and furnishes the leading topic of conversation throughout all the surrounding county. The people of the quiet settlement where the crime took place, have been shocked beyond measure by the terrible event, and coupled with their sorrow and sympathy, is the overpowering wish that the perpetrator of the awful deed be brought to justice. No further trace of the murderer is known here at the present writing.

Last evening when The *Sun* representative visited the home of Father McAuley, where the tragedy took place, the grief-stricken priest, worn out by loss of sleep, and well nigh prostrated by the terrible blow that has befallen his house, was in the seclusion of his room and unable to see anyone .... When earlier seen on Wednesday, Father McAuley showed the effects of the strain he had undergone the last few days, and with deep emotion related what he knew of the terrible occurrence. The young man, Collins, who is suspected of the crime, and who had been in the employ of the priest for a week, was apparently a harmless fellow and, the priest stated, was well educated and devout, attending mass during the short stay with regularity and apparent zeal.

12.

By late Thursday night, Saint John reporters had learned that a man thought to be the fugitive had been traced to the Lake Utopia area, and that Detective Killen and Marshall McAdam were after him. Arrest was thought to be imminent. A *Telegraph* reporter was told the suspect had been seen moving at a leisurely pace near the lake earlier in the evening by T.R. Sheraton. The area was searched, but the man was not found. Killen telephoned Chief Clark with the news at 10:00 p.m. By that time there was nothing to be done, but wait the night at St. George station in the hope that Collins, walking along the highway or the railway tracks, would stumble into their arms.

At 1:00 a.m. Friday The *Daily Telegraph* went to press. "His capture," it reported, "is expected by morning."

Chapter Seven

Friday, August 24, 1906

1.

Collins spent the night walking north through the woods along a log road east of Lake Utopia. He had been last seen Thursday by Douglas Spinney. Chief Clark and Detective Killen had stopped at Spinney's place earlier on Thursday, asking if he had seen any strangers in the area. At the time Spinney had not, but Collins came later in the day asking for a bite to eat. When he left Spinney's, he had resumed his westward direction, then abruptly turned north toward the lake. He was not seen again until Friday morning, in country north of Lake Utopia, a considerable distance from Spinney's. He must have walked in darkness along the logging road that ran the length of Lake Utopia, between it and Trout and Mill lakes, connecting eventually with the road running east-west from Red Rock Lake to Bonny River. The country, too, had been heavily burned by the fires in 1903, and there was little tall timber growth along the way, and ground berries were flourishing. Tom stopped at Patrick Kehoe's home in time for breakfast, then walked to Cornelius Sullivan's at Upper Mills, where he had dinner. After resting a short time, he continued on his way on increasingly tender feet, heading west across country.

That morning a party of lady tourists, who were staying at the Bonny River hotel, decided they would go on an outing to Sparks Lake, just south of Red Rock Lake. The excursion left the hotel in a team driven by proprietor T.A. Sullivan. Bonny River, a hunting and fishing resort and site of one of the most modern sawmills in the province (having been built two years earlier, after fire destroyed the village), was a small community on the Magaguadavic River west of Lake Utopia and a few miles north of St. George. The area was one of the hardest hit by the 1903 fires. From Magaguadavic Lake south, 100,000 acres of the province's finest timber land — 30 to 50 million feet of lumber — were destroyed. What was left standing was cut down and hauled out later to prevent an infestation of insects.

Early that afternoon, about midway between Bonny River and the lake, Sullivan, who already had been alerted about the police search, spotted a figure on the road ahead making its way into a clump of bushes. It could have been the man Killen was after, but Sullivan had no wish to put the group of lady clients travelling with him at risk. He continued along the road and, as luck would have it, they soon met Wilkes Reynolds, a guide. Leaving Reynolds in charge of the tourists, Sullivan took Reynolds' rig and turned back to Bonny River to try to reach Killen.

2.

William Craig of Back Bay, Charlotte County, a former man of the sea, was returning home alone after a fishing trip to Red Rock Lake. He was driving a team pulling a high narrow freight wagon with a rack. Balanced across the top of the rack was the canoe he had taken out on the lake. Craig knew nothing of the manhunt, and was neither surprised nor startled to come upon a stranger walking along the road toward Bonny River.

Craig: I remember the man very well. It was a comfortable day, not too hot, about three in the afternoon. I was driving my team along the road from Red Rock going southwest toward Bonny River. I'd guess I was about four miles from Bonny River, and it would be ten or eleven miles north of St. George. I come up behind this man Collins, who was trudging along the road carrying only a stick. I drew abreast of him — I was driving a truck wagon and carrying a light canoe — and bid him good day. He didn't ask for a ride, but he looked beat, so I told him to get in and I'd give him a drive along the road.

He climbed up. It was a high wagon with a rack on it and I had the canoe balanced across the top of the rack. I was standing, kind of leaning against the canoe, handling the reins. He slumped down into the cart with his feet under the canoe, resting his back against the rack. He seemed heavy with sleep, acted very tired, kind of stupid-like. We went along leisurely and talked some. Didn't tell me his name, but said his feet were sore; blistered and sore, he said. Said he had walked all the way from Saint John. I asked was he from Saint John, and he said he was and he had a brother and sister there.

I asked was he a sailor — I've been at sea myself — and he told me he was. Then he said he had run away from a ship in Saint John, and there were six more besides himself run away from this ship. I said it was queer some of the sailors hadn't come with him, and he said, no, they went in different directions. He said he had heard there was plenty of work in St. Stephen, and he was going there. Said he had been told this road we was on went to St. Stephen. I asked did he know any other work besides sailing. He said he was a candymaker and he was going to look for a job in St. Stephen.

I began to take notice that he seemed restless and uneasy; he was looking behind a good deal. He was sitting to face the front of the cart, and I saw him turn and look back several times. Finally I said, "You're not afraid of those fellows catching you now are you?"

He was sitting in the bottom of the wagon, and he kind of jumped like and looked at me and said, "What fellows?"

I said, "Those fellows, the captain and the mate of the ship you ran away from."

"Oh no," he says, "I ain't a bit afraid of that."

"Well," I says, "how're you planning to get to St. Stephen?"

He said he was going to walk. I suggested that he take the train from Bonny River, and he said he hadn't the money. I told him I would see he wouldn't have to walk to St. Stephen. Told him the train was leaving Bonny River about four o'clock, and I would see that he got on it alright, if he wanted to go to St. Stephen.

"No," he told me, "I intend to walk."

The subject of dinner come up, and he said he had had none. So I told him to come to the hotel in Bonny River and I would see that he got something to eat. He didn't answer anything to that, didn't say whether he would or he wouldn't. Then I told him there was a mill there at Bonny River he could work in, and there was no need of him walking to St. Stephen. I said he had better stop in Bonny River, he could work a couple of days and get the price of his fare. I told him it would be seventy-five cents or a dollar, I didn't know which.

"No," he says. "When I left Saint John, I made up my mind to go to St. Stephen and that's where I'm going. And I'm not going to stop 'til I get there."

Now I don't rightly know how he got to where I picked him up from Saint John. He said something about the way he come, but I wasn't much acquainted with it. Said he come across by way of the lake, come through a logging road apparently. There is a road leading north from where Douglas Spinney's is that runs into a lumber road. That might have been the way he come. He sure seemed beat, however he did it. I left him to his own thoughts, and made no more conversation as we rode along. He didn't seem to hanker much for my advice in any case. Then about two miles out of Bonny River, just before the bridge at Second Falls, he made an excuse to get out of the wagon. Said he would catch up to me in a few minutes. Told me to wait for him, and I told him I would. He went off into the bushes.

So I drove along slow and crossed the bridge, holding my horse in all I could. Possibly a hundred yards or so further on, I stopped my horse and looked back. Didn't see him at first. I waited a little while longer, and soon I saw him coming slow-like across the bridge with his hand on the railing. He was walking so slow that I thought he didn't want to overtake me, so I said to myself, "I won't wait for him any more." I whipped up my horse and went on to Bonny River.

3.

Detective Killen and Marshall McAdam had spent the night fruitlessly at the train station at St. George. Admittedly, the chance that Collins would come walking into their arms had been a long shot at best, but there was little else they could have done after dark settled in. When daylight came, Killen figured it was time to move again. He went with a railway section crew on a trolley to search the track bed, while McAdam took the road. They had heard that the fugitive had been seen at Spinney's at Lake Utopia the night before, and that Spinney had directed him along the Post Road into St. George. They searched a number of barns and vacant houses, but saw no trace of Collins.

By four o'clock in the afternoon Killen was back in St. George. He was beginning to think his man had pulled a vanishing act, but when he arrived at the Carleton House there was encouraging news. While he had been out on the Shore Road, T.A. Sullivan had called from Bonny River. He wanted to talk to Detective Killen and it was urgent. Killen hurried to the hotel's telephone and put the call through. Sullivan told him they had a man answering the description penned in the woods a little above Bonny River, and to come quick. Killen said he would be there shortly. He got the horse again and, taking the marshall with him, set out for Bonny River.

Killen and McAdam covered the twelve miles from St. George in fifty minutes, a record time, according to one newspaper account. "Up hill and down and lashing the horse as it had never been lashed before, the officers hastened across country to what looked like the certainty of a capture." By that time William Craig had arrived at Bonny River, looked after his horse, and gone to the hotel for supper, still unaware of the law's interest in his former passenger.

"About five o'clock," Craig recalled later, "along to the hotel where I'm eating, comes Detective Killen from Saint John and the marshall from St. George. Say they're looking for this man Collins. Well, I didn't know his name, but I told them about this fellow I'd just given a ride to. I climbed into their wagon, and we went back up the road to the bridge where I'd left him. There was no sign of him, so we figured if he was still on a road, he must have taken the one that goes north to Lee Settlement and then to Piskehagen. A few miles further on, we met Frank Keough's team."

4.

Frank Keough was a farmer who lived at Second Falls, a few miles north of Bonny River. News of the police search hadn't reached his place either.

Keough: I was out mowing oats in one of my fields Friday afternoon, when I saw this man pass by going north, walking along he was. Passed by about 100 yards from where I was working, but I didn't recognize him. Thought nothing about it then, but about a half-hour later, a man named Alexander Taylor stopped by with another young man named James Hill. They told me about a murder that had happened up in Albert County, and how the police thought the man responsible might be down our way; had come from Saint John and might be trying to get to the U.S. border. Said Mr. Sullivan down at Bonny River had seen a man that matched the description coming this way on the road from Red Rock, and had sent Mr. Taylor and Hill out looking for him.

Now there's a road that goes around the western side of Lake Utopia up to Red Rock, then east to Lee Settlement and south to Second Falls, Bonny River and St. George. It's possible alright to go that way to St. Stephen from Saint John, but it's certain it's the long way to go about it. My place is just about eight miles north of St. George, straight up the Magaguadavic River, on the road that runs from the Second Falls bridge up to Lee Settlement.

I told Mr. Taylor and Hill about this man who went by, and the three of us set out after him in an express wagon with my horse. We'd travelled along an hour or so, covered five miles, I'd say, when Hill nudged me and said he had just spotted him off in the bushes a way. Hill was standing in the back of the wagon, and Mr. Taylor and I were up front on the seat. I didn't see the man just then, but we told Mr.

Taylor to take the horse to a branch road just up ahead, and wait for us there. Then Hill and I got out and started into the bushes. We were in there a very short time, when we saw this man Collins coming along on the road. We had passed him — he must have stepped off the road — and now he was coming along the same way we had come with the team.

I went out on the road and asked him where he was going. He said he was going to St. Stephen.

"Well," I said, "you will have to go back to Bonny River with us."

He said, "Back to Bonny River? What for?"

I said, "They want you back there."

When I said that, he started to run, ran pretty fast. Hill, who was right behind me in the bushes, stepped out then.

"Hold on," he said, "I've got you."

He had a rifle in his hand. Collins didn't appear to mind that, and he kept on running up the road. I went after him and Hill was behind me. Then Hill fired the rifle — in the air, he told me afterwards — and Mr. Taylor came out from the branch road. Consequently he was on one side and Hill and I on the other. Collins tried to avoid Mr. Taylor, who was right in front of him, went to dodge him, and fell into the ditch. I was close behind and I had him in a minute. We'd intended to tie his hands up, but he turned pale and looked rather pitiful.

"I am tired out," he told us, "and couldn't have gone much further."

He said he would go back peacefully, so we didn't tie his hands. We put him in the wagon and started back. He sat between Mr. Taylor and me on the seat, and Hill stood in the back.

We didn't ask him his name, but at some point, Mr. Taylor said, "We're going to take you back to Bonny River, and if you have not committed any crime, it will be alright." No one mentioned anything about a murder. But when Mr. Taylor made that remark, Collins just said the word "crime" in a questioning way.

Later on Hill asked him how old he was. He said he was twenty-one. He asked him where he was from, and he said he was from Halifax.

Hill said, "I thought you said you belong to England."

He said, "Well, I do belong to England, but I came from Halifax."

Hill said, "You didn't think I was going to shoot you when I fired that gun?"

He said, "I don't know what you would shoot me for."

At some point during the ride, I remember, someone asked about the time, and Collins pulled out a watch. He looked at it and said it was twenty minutes to five. The watch might have been silver, but I'm not certain of that at all.

After a half-hour of driving, we met two teams coming from Bonny River, one with Detective Killen and Marshall McAdam of St. George, the other with T.A. Sullivan, George Williamson and William Craig.

Mr. Killen got out of his wagon at once.

He said, "Hello Tommy, come down here. What did you leave your valise at Dean's for?"

Collins said, "Dean's."

He just gasped the word. He seemed very nervous, pale. He fell back in the detective's arms and Mr. Killen had to support him.

5.

Killen, Marshall McAdam and William Craig met Sullivan's team near Frank Keough's farm. Sullivan told them that Keough and two other men had set out after the fugitive in a wagon. McAdam was wearing the uniform of a police officer, and Killen told him to change his coat and hat. The men set out up the Lee Settlement road, where they soon met the Keough party coming back. Collins sat on the seat between Alexander Taylor and Keough, his elbows on his knees, hands clasped before him, and his head hanging to his chest. He was dirty, bedraggled, exhausted. Killen stepped down from his own rig and went to the other wagon. He pushed his cap back and peered up into Collins' red face.

Killen: "Hello, Tommy," I said. "Jump out."

I reached out my hand and he jumped right into my arms. I think I asked him his name then and he answered. Then he put his hand up and fell right back into my arms, and commenced to cry. So I told him, "Now don't cry like that, you'll be alright; I will look after you and take care of you."

I took him into the wagon. I just forget the conversation I had with him — a few words in the wagon — but on the road I told him who I was and where I was from, and about this woman being murdered. He said he didn't know anything about it until then. I told him I was arresting him on a telegram received from Albert County for the murder of a woman — I didn't remember the woman's name at the time — and as I told him, he kind of grabbed himself and fell back into my arms. I think I made the remark then for him not to die here, or die with me, or something.

I got the boy into the wagon, and he appeared to be very fatigued out, and his throat bothering him like, choking him. He had an old pair of shoes on, and I had a feed of oats in my wagon, and I made him take his shoes off and put his feet on the bag of oats to cool them. We drove along about 100 yards until we came to a house on the right-hand side of the road. I asked a man standing at the gate to fetch the boy some milk, and he fetched out a pitcher of milk and three or four pieces of cake. He drank two tumblers of the milk, and it kind of revived his throat. He said his throat was very dry. He did not want to take any cake, but I made him and he took two pieces of cake.

I think I asked him then if he knew that the priest's housekeeper was murdered. I think that's the word I used, but I'm not positive about it. He says, "No," and kind of falls the same way again onto my shoulder. He was alongside of me. When we got to Bonny River, I stopped and got him his supper.

On the way to St. George after supper, he told McAdam and me a story about going fishing. Said he went out on a Thursday to get some fish for Father McAuley's breakfast or dinner, and only caught four fish. Said she was shouting at him for not getting any more fish than that, and he said the fish wasn't jumping. This was on the way from Bonny River to St. George. I can't remember whether he said any more to me, but when we got into St. George, he was in pretty bad shape.

He and I got out of the wagon in the yard and walked into the hotel. He was in such bad shape, that I took him into my room and asked Mrs. McGee, the man's wife that runs the hotel, if she would get me some water for him to have a bath. I searched him and found four coloured-cotton hand-kerchiefs, red and white, four white ones — soiled — and a silver watch. There was a black shoelace used as a cord on this watch, that I took off to put in his boot. Then four pieces of lead pencil and a little bag containing a pair of brass sleeve buttons, three shirt studs, and a piece of small brass chain. The watch was going. On the inside case, there were letters that he said he scratched on himself. "From Dad to Tom" and "Aug. 9, '05."

Mrs. McGee brought a big tub into my room and filled it with hot water. Collins had a bath. I got a pint of hot milk with ginger in it, and made him drink that. After he drank the hot ginger, I thought the best place for him was in bed. Before he got into bed, I warned him who I was and what business I was on; told him I was arresting him on a telegram charging him on suspicion of murder of this woman, Mary Ann McAuley.

I said, "Tom, I am going to ask you questions in regard to this murder I have arrested you for; you need not answer me unless you wish, but anything you say to me, I will take down in writing and may use in evidence against you at the trial."

He didn't answer me. He was in such bad shape, that I decided not to ask him any questions then. If a doctor had been there, I would have called him when we got to St. George; I thought he was in too weak condition to talk to that night. Our instructions are to get a doctor if a prisoner seems to require medical attention. But I thought the boy needed rest more than for me to bother him that night. I made him get right into bed and covered him with clothes. I stayed there with him and about an hour afterwards, I went to bed myself; put a handcuff — one on his wrist and one on my own — and we lay there until morning.

Chapter Eight

Saturday, August 25, 1906
Sunday, August 26, 1906

1.

It was past 7:00 a.m. and the proprietors and most residents of the Carleton House in St. George were already astir when Tom Collins woke up. Snoring on the bed beside him, forced to sleep on his back because his wrist was linked to Tom's by a handcuff, was Killen. Collins was feeling somewhat refreshed, but he was hungry and his muscles ached. His raw bare feet scraped painfully against the rough material of the blanket the police officer had thrown over him. He sat up on the bed and the movement disturbed Killen, who sputtered and opened his eyes. When he had his bearings, the detective unfastened the cuffs and went to the washstand, to splash water on his face from a basin. As he dried with a towel, he looked out the window into the new morning. Word probably had gotten out by now, and there could be considerable interest in his prisoner from the local citizens. Killen wasn't feeling too chipper. He had had no sleep while on watch at the train station all night Thursday, and had got blessed little last night cuffed to the prisoner. With any luck they would be back in Saint John with the prisoner today, and he would be back in his own bed tonight.

Chief Clark, who had gone back to Musquash on Friday chasing, as it turned out, a false clue, had received news of the capture and came down to St. George on the early train to take personal charge of the prisoner. He met Killen and Collins at the hotel, and they struck out right away for the city in the chief's rig, rather than take the train. They arrived at Dean's Hotel in Musquash and, feeling rather comfortable after one of Mrs. Dean's fine suppers, Chief Clark decided to spend the night there and drive in to Saint John Sunday. For Killen it was another restless night handcuffed to his prisoner. As he said later, he didn't get an overdose of sleep on the mission.

Killen's solicitous treatment of Collins after the capture was not uncharacteristic of the officer. He was born in the Lower Cove district of Saint John in 1853, to parents who were natives of the Parish of Carlingford, County Louth, Ireland, and who had left their homeland in 1847. Educated by the Christian Brothers, young Pat Killen began his working career as a longshoreman, and was actively involved with the Ship Labourers' Association. In 1881, he married Mary Theresa Lenihan, whose father had come from Youghal, County Cork. Mary had been born in Saint John's eastend and, prior to her marriage, had never set foot in Lower Cove, where she spent the remainder of her life. She would give birth to nine children, six of whom survived to adulthood.

In 1891, there came an opening on the Saint John Police Force when a cousin of Killen's left, and Killen, then thirty-eight years old, got the job. He was promoted to sergeant, then detective, before retiring in 1915, nine years after the Collins arrest. He died in 1928. The *New Freeman*, the local Catholic weekly newspaper, said of him:

> Throughout the city the news (of his death) was heard with sincere sorrow for he was a man with a big heart, and enjoyed a popularity which many years of service with the local detective force had engendered in the minds of the citizens. In his younger days, as a patrolman and later as a detective, he was strict in the discharge of his duty, yet his kindness of heart, his sympathy with the unfortunate, his genial disposition, enabled him often to temper the ends of justice with that broad sympathy for which this most kindly of men was widely noted.
>
> Detective Killen ably discharged the many difficult duties of a member of the local detective service. He had a knack of getting at the root of things, and

the solving of more than one knotty problem of the day lies to his credit. Few men know the city of Saint John or its citizens better and few men have been held in general higher esteem. He joined the local force in 1891 when W. Walker Clark was chief of police and in days when the lot of a patrolman was not an easy one. Faithful attendance to duty brought with it deserved promotion and he rose to be sergeant and later a member of the detective force. His period of service, without a flaw or a blemish, terminated in 1915 when he resigned.

Volumes could be written of the work of the late Mr. Killen while identified with the local force. Constant in his attendance to duty, unremitting in the faithful discharge of his office, he yet remained the kindly man with a cheery word for all, a man whose heart indeed was a very big one.

Killen's daughter remembers that a sofa in their Broad Street home was often occupied by one or other of her father's "charges."

2.

Killen: Saturday morning at the Carleton House at St. George, before the chief got there, Collins and me got up and dressed and had our breakfast. Starting into the dining room, I said, "I cautioned you last night and I am going to ask some questions of you." We went into the hotel office, and there was nobody there but the two of us. I took his statement and we were interrupted only once, when three clergymen came into the room. I wrote down what he had to say. I asked him his name, and he gave me his name as Thomas Francis Collins, aged twenty-one. Born at Liverpool, England. Then he gave me his story and I made notes as best I could.

"Last Monday," he said, "I got out of bed at Father McAuley's at 6:00 a.m. and lit the fire and attended to the horse. Mary Ann came down about seven and got my breakfast. After breakfast, she told me to get the horse out to go to town. When I got the horse ready, she told me it was too hot to drive out this morning, so I put the horse back again. She came to the stable and said something to me about cleaning the horse down, so I told her she was only making a fool of me like that. Mary Ann said she was not so much making a fool of me as I was of her, by going fishing all day and only catching four fish. I told her that Father McAuley didn't say so much to me about only catching four fish, so then she said I might as well stay at home and do my work.

"I went into the house to do some work. While I was there she came again to me and said, how was it that I could with two others catch about eight dozen fish on Sunday. I said, 'They were not jumping on the Thursday when I was there, and the Gross family could say the same.' Then I said, 'I'm not going to stand this, if you are going to keep on talking.' I told her I was going to put my coat on. I got my coat and left the house at about eight and walked to Elgin.

"I stayed in Elgin about one hour. While I was there I met Father McAuley, and he asked me what I was doing there. I told him I left. He asked me what for, and I told him that Mary Ann was shouting at me for going fishing on Thursday. So Father McAuley said, 'I didn't say anything to you.' I said, 'No, but she did.' He asked me if I would go back. I told him no. He asked me again and I told him I didn't know. Then he took me up to a house to stay, but I only stayed about five minutes there. Between five and six o'clock that evening, I started for Petitcodiac. I got there at 8:00 a.m. Tuesday. I got a ticket for Saint John. Paid $1.40 for the ticket.

"I got to Saint John about two o'clock. I started for Musquash, but turned back. Met a young man on Wednesday. He asked me if I was looking for work. I said yes. He said to jump on his wagon, and he drove me to the house. I stayed there all night and left about nine in the morning. The reason I left, I did not like that kind of work. I did not know about her being dead until you told me. I then kept going along the road until I was stopped. The reason I was going to St. Stephen was because I had a map."

Then the clergymen came in and Collins stopped talking. That was the whole conversation I had with him then. Him and I stayed around there in the hotel until the chief come in the train, and the three of us started in the wagon about one o'clock and drove up to Lepreaux. Stopped there, had a lunch there, fed our horse there, and then drove to Dean's. There we had supper and stayed all night, in the same position as down at St. George, him and I sleeping together with the handcuffs on both of us.

We got up Sunday, had breakfast and lunch, and then left with the team for Saint John. He seemed in much improved spirits riding with the chief and me in the wagon. He sang some and told us about himself, and some of what happened during the week he was in New Ireland at the McAuley residence. He seemed open with his statements, and never wavered from his story that Miss McAuley was alive and well when he left her there on Monday. He spoke willingly and without contradictions, but he didn't show any curiosity about her murder or how the body was found.

Collins told us he was born in Liverpool in 1885, and became of age on August 9 last. Comes of Irish parentage. Said his father, who was a well-to-do contractor, was dead, having been killed by falling downstairs. "How did that come about?" the chief asked him. He said he thought his father'd been taking too much beer. He had been in South Africa at the time, he said, serving in the war, and when he came back, he found his father was dead and his mother in ill health. He left with his mother the money he had received in wages while in the army, amounting to some thirty pounds, and then came to this country. He's heard nothing about her since, he said. Says he's unmarried and, in religion, a Roman Catholic.

He left his home when he was a lad and, along with a younger brother, saw active service in the Boer War. He reached Cape Town as an ordinary seaman, he said, soon after the commencement of hostilities. Corps were being organized and Collins, who was but a youth, was taken on as a bugler in a regiment of carabineers. "But I was as much developed then," he declared, "as I am now. After we went up country, I went on the strength of the regiment as a trooper." He claimed to have been present at the relief of

Ladysmith, and could give the names of staff officers and recite many incidents. If what he says is true, the force he was with must have covered much the same territory as that traversed by the 19th Brigade, which included the first Canadian contingent and some men from around here.

The only fight of any consequence that he was in, he said, was at Driefontein, sometimes called Poplar Grove. It was largely a cavalry action, and took place while on the march to Bloemfontein in March, 1900, after the Paardeberg surrender. President Kruger of the Boer republics, who was with the opposing force, was almost captured in that action. It was a day of hunger and thirst, of prodigious marching and precious little fighting, he said; but he passed through the engagement without mishap. He said the supply train had been left far behind by the march, and the night was spent without food, blanket or great-coat. Some of the men, near starving, gathered up some prickly pears and coaxed themselves to relish the fruit. Collins said he served through his entire enlistment period of fifteen months, and was honourably discharged. Said he re-enlisted, but shipped as a sailor.

For the last four or five years, he claimed, he's been a sailor and has sailed every sea. Previous to this visit, he said, he was often to Amherst, and also talked intelligently about New York, Philadelphia, Montreal, and other seaport cities. Three years ago he was in Saint John, he said, having come here on the *Numidian* of the Allan line. On this trip, he came from Liverpool three months ago on the steamer *Dominion* to Montreal. From Montreal, he tramped all the way down through Quebec and New Brunswick to Amherst. Said he was looking for work there and a man offered him employment on a scow going to St. Mary's Point in Albert County. When that job was done and he had been paid off, he tramped through the country until he was engaged by Father Mc-Auley at the New Ireland mission house.

Collins said he had three sisters. He even wrote to one of them to come out to Canada and he would take up a homestead, but she couldn't or wouldn't. His younger brother, he said, was a great athlete.

3.

Clark: During the drive up to Saint John, Killen and I didn't think it was necessary to handcuff the prisoner, and he talked most freely, telling the history of his stay in Albert County. He didn't hesitate to talk about his life at New Ireland, but of the crime he professed to know nothing. Killen had already taken his statement at St. George, and I cautioned him not to talk too much. Said he needn't answer any questions unless he wanted to, and that his answers could be used against him. But he didn't seem to mind talking.

He said he had quarrelled with Miss McAuley, but that he had left her in perfect health. "The whole trouble up there was with Mary Ann," he said. She was all the time nagging, and if he went fishing and did not catch as many fish as she thought, then she would say, "You are a liar." He said if he asked for a drink of water or would go for a drink, she had say, "Where are you going?" He would say, "For a drink." She would say, "There is no water in; go and get some." He said if he wasn't prompt in his work, she wouldn't give him his meals. He said the whole trouble with Mary Ann was that she was all the time nagging, nagging, nagging. Father McAuley, on the other hand, was always very kind to him, and Mary Ann never said a word when Father McAuley was there.

He said one day they had the gramophone started and it didn't work very well. He said Father McAuley put it outside the door, as I understood him, hoping they would hear it at the lake. But it was not working right, and he said he went in to fix it, and Mary Ann said, "Oh, Tommy is very smart. Tommy is very smart."

When he left there last Monday, he said, he had put the harness on the horse because Mary Ann wanted to go out. Then when he had done the work, she said, "It's too warm. I don't think I'll go out." He said she was cranky enough for anything, and he didn't know what to do. He went in and asked her again and she said, "It is too warm. I don't think I will go out at all." He said he couldn't stand any more of it and he just left. Said he didn't use the horse at all himself, just put it back in the barn and left it there with the harness on. He knew nothing about the murder, he said, until Detective Killen told him.

We allowed him to rattle on in the hope that by a slip of the tongue he might give his secret away, but the prisoner, as frankly as he seemed to speak, made no such break. He didn't ask any questions about Mary Ann, though, how she was found or anything else. He said only that she was well when he left.

During the trip up with Killen and me, he was mostly cheerful. He ate well and slept soundly, slept more soundly than Killen, I'd say. Collins is an all-round chap. He's seen a lot of the world and has, I believe, a pretty fair education. He seemed to take great interest in all kinds of athletics and especially in wrestling, in which his brother, he says, is a champion and has won many prizes. He's something of an athlete, too. He's a boxer and a runner. When he was on the run from Dean's on Thursday, he covered the distance from Musquash to Lepreaux, about twelve miles, in a little more than an hour — and he was footsore and pretty well done up when he started. A lineman saw him, and said he was moving along at a smart pace. He's got a good voice, too. Riding along in the wagon he sang and, though at times he appeared downhearted, he would soon brace up again. He entertained Killen and myself with some songs, comic and otherwise, but principally those of the sea. He may look like a boy, but he's a healthy speciman of manhood nevertheless.

When we got to Dean's Saturday evening, I went and got the brown square valise which Collins had left there when he ran away on Thursday. He admitted having left it there. It contained a pair of very wet drawers, a dry bath towel, a dry undershirt and a cotton shirt. There was a brush, two combs (a horn comb and a steel comb), a clothes brush, two neckties, six handkerchiefs (four men's and two lady's, one marked "Buffalo Exposition 1901" and the name "Mary Ann McAuley" worked in blue silk letters in the corner), one box of soap, a cake of toilet soap, matches tied with rubber bands, playing cards, a new razor in a case, one pencil, and one small case of court plaster.

Collins told me it was his property. I said, "Where'd you get these shirts? They're very large for you. They must be forty-two or forty-three." "Oh," he said, "I got them in Liverpool." The underclothing, of Scotch lamb's wool, were also too large for his frame, I'd have said. Of principal interest was this piece of wet underclothing. It was as wet as if it'd been wrung out in preparation to be hung up to dry. I asked him about it, and he said he got it wet in the rain. There were also some dark brown stains, suspiciously like blood.

4.

A large crowd of curious Saint John citizens gathered at the police station after supper hour on Saturday, eager to witness the arrival in chains of the fugitive. But word came late in the evening that he and his captors were spending the night at Musquash, and would not return to the city until the following day. The *Daily Telegraph*, in an editorial, complimented the police department, but reiterated its earlier criticism that word of the killing had been too slow coming out of Albert County.

AN ARREST

There will be general satisfaction over the arrest of Collins, the man named by the Albert County jurymen as in their opinion guilty of the McAuley murder. There would have been ground for grave and general public complaint had the suspected man succeeded in making his escape. Justice will now be done. If there is evidence sufficient to convict the law will be vindicated. The public mind will be relieved now that there is no longer any danger that the person sought may evade arrest. Collins will have a fair trial; probably a prompt and brief one. It is not necessary now to discuss the evidence upon which the crown may be expected to depend.

But the case suggests the necessity for a repetition of the statement that the authorities of Albert County erred in not giving the fullest possible publicity to a close description of the suspect as soon as possible after the discovery of the crime. Had this been done the missing man could scarcely have gone out of the county, and even if he had done so he would have been apprehended here.

Secrecy and hesitation in such matters belong to the old ways and the old days before publicity, properly employed, came to be recognized as the most effective of all known agencies for guarding the public against the escape of persons suspected of breaking the law. A fugitive murderer whose picture and description have been promptly and widely published is not very likely to escape the vigilance of the thousands of newspaper readers who are for the time being converted into detectives. In a country like New Brunswick where officers of the law are comparatively few in number the importance of fully and promptly utilizing the telephone, the telegraph and the newspapers in cases of this kind can scarcely be overestimated.

As early as nine o'clock Sunday morning, people were once again assembled on King Street east, awaiting the arrival as if it were a royal visit. The weather was perfect, a warm clear day, and by noon there was a straggling line of citizens along the edge of the old Loyalist burial ground. Some, after standing for as long as three hours, stretched luxuriously on the grass, seemingly casual and unconcerned, but with ears keenly alert. There were groups around the courthouse corner, about the morgue steps, and around the entrance to the station.

"Has he been heard from yet?" one could be heard inquiring occasionally of another.

"Yes, the team was passing through Fairville twenty-five minutes ago," came a response a little after noon.

"Time they were here then."

Sergeant Hastings, on house duty, looking out on the expectant crowd, was heard to remark in his droll manner, "The suspense is Killen."

At about three-thirty in the afternoon, there was a sudden movement from the square toward the station building. Men hurried up the station steps and, turning about, looked anxiously toward the corner of the jail building. Small boys raced down the street, chattering and pointing. The point of convergence was an open carriage approaching from Sydney Street. Sitting behind the single seat was Detective Killen and, in front, were Chief Clark and a rough boyish-looking stranger, with a brown straw hat in his lap. He was leaning comfortably back, and seemed to look upon the wildly informal reception with considerable complacence. Looking like a mere boy beside his burly captors, he appeared recovered from the pursuit and "in the pink of health." His demeanour, surprisingly — at least to the newspaper reporters who recorded the event — wasn't at all vicious, not in the least the popular conception of the cold-blooded killer. Pushed well back on his head was a blue cap. Around his neck was a soiled and wrinkled muffler. He wore mud-stained boots. He was clean shaven, with the exception of a growth of two or three days.

The crowd swept up the street like a chattering entourage, parted as the team stopped by the steps of the police station, then closed again around the carriage. When the motion stopped, so did the chatter and noise, as every eye fixed on the face of the fugitive. But Collins did not wilt. He displayed little concern for his position, and looked around him in a relaxed way — not in attempted bravado, but as if he were also a member of the mob and not its central figure. Turning to Chief Clark, he said: "Well, wouldn't this put you in mind of Barnum's caravan?"

He waited until the chief had alighted, then jumped briskly out and, escorted by the deputy chief, disappeared inside the station. A slight limp was noticeable and, as he went on into the guard room, the lameness became more pronounced. "Sit down there," said Deputy Chief Jenkins, pointing to the locker, and Collins did so. He seemed thankful to be seated, but his eyes flitted about the room.

"Collins is not a murder suspect according to popular fancy," one of the newspapermen wrote. "His features are regular. He showed no embarrassment. When asked a question he would smile slightly and answer promptly, but with a touch of deference. There was about him the look of the sailor. He is just the type that one would meet trudging around the streets during the winter port season. His hair is black and slightly wavy. His eyes are dark grey and prominent. His complexion is ruddy. He looked sunburnt, or as if he had been facing a powerful wind. He sat, with one leg crossed over the other, composed and attentive."

Collins was asked to stand, and measurements were made and noted by the officers: age — twenty-one; height — five feet, three-and-three-quarter inches; weight — 136 pounds; complexion — dark, red face; hair — black; eyes — grey; face — smooth; mouth — full; nose — straight, broad at the bridge; chin — short; face — short and narrow; teeth — front teeth good; arm extension — three feet, two inches; coat and vest — blue with grey stripes; trousers — grey with black stripes; cloth cap — size six; chest — thirty-four inches; collar — size fourteen and one half.

There was a tattoo mark, what looked like an attempt to make the letter "T," on one forearm, partially blurred. The prisoner said the mark had been made against the wishes of his father, who afterward tried to remove it. A number of scars were found on different parts of his body, including one of about an eighth of an inch between the third and fourth fingers of the left hand. "The prisoner is full chested. His ears are small. His forehead high. When smiling, his mouth hauls to the right side. He has three wrinkles running across his forehead. He usually wears his cap on the back of his head."

No third party was admitted to the deputy chief's private office while Collins was being interviewed, but twice during the time they were together there, the prisoner was escorted to the courtroom upstairs to sit for his portrait. As he limped awkwardly up the stairs, a reporter asked him questions. He gave a few pulls at the muffler tucked inside his coat collar. Queries bearing on the crime, he declined to answer.

"My 'ed feels a bit stiff," he said, speaking in a quick and somewhat throaty voice, "and my feet ache."

To judge from the few remarks credited him, observers noted, he seemed discerning and not without a streak of humour. After he had slept and bathed and breakfasted at St. George, he recounted his experience of the actual capture. "Oh, that revolver," he had said to Killen. "Why I think the men that 'ad hit were more scared of hit than me."

He was a model subject for the photographers.

"Just look there," requested the *Telegraph* photographer, indicating the window, and Collins, lifting his head slightly, gazed steadily as directed. He was photographed twice — once with the cap on and once with it off. As he stood up to descend the stairs, Chief Clark, remembering his comments about having once been a wrestler, asked with uplifted arms, "Is this the way they put up the arms in the old country?"

Collins for a moment looked amused. He seemed flattered that some reference had been made to his skill.

"Oh, I know both ways," he said.

He was taken to the city lockup and, on Sunday night, he ate ordinary jail fare. He consumed all that was brought to him, but complained there was no sugar in the tea. Later in the evening, he asked for papers and books, which were supplied, and which he hastened to read. He asked particularly for a Boston paper. But the strenuous activity of the past six days and nights finally claimed him, and by eleven o'clock he was sleeping on the cell bench, with the books and papers scattered at his feet.

5.

The legal disposal of Collins' case rested with New Brunswick Attorney General William Pugsley of Saint John. Pugsley was informed Sunday night at the Hotel Belle View of the capture. Asked what action the crown would take, he told reporters, "The first thing to do will be to have the prisoner identified. I have given instructions to have Rev. Father McAuley notified, and it is probable he will be in the city by Monday. I will consult with Chief of Police Clark, and the prisoner may be removed to Albert County. There will be no proceedings taken in this city or county."

Later, he instructed Albert County Sheriff Ernest Lynds to procure a warrant and to take all steps necessary for the removal of Collins from Saint John. "I do not know where the preliminary examination will be held, for Sheriff Lynds did not state what magistrate had issued the warrant. But the examination will, in all probability, be in either Hopewell or Albert. At the trial, I shall personally represent the crown."

Police Chief Clark made himself available to newspapermen as well, inviting a group of them into his office Sunday evening. He said he was well satisfied with the part the Saint John force had played in the capture. He warmly praised Detective Killen who, he said, had worked like a beaver. The chief added that the capture would have been easier had not Collins, chopping wood outside of Dean's hotel at Musquash, overheard Dean in conversation with Chief Clark on the telephone.

"You didn't find it necessary to handcuff him as you drove along?" a reporter asked.

"Do you think it would have been necessary with one of these on either side of him?" replied the chief, tapping a loaded revolver lying on the desk. He added, "The brown straw hat you saw in the prisoner's lap is one I wore when in the country. I wore a civilian coat, too."

Pointing out that the meals Collins had eaten since his capture seemed generous in quantity and quality, a reporter said, "We hear the prisoner is blessed with a reliable appetite."

"Eat!" exclaimed Chief Clark, "I wish you could have seen him!"

An exhausted Detective Killen was kept busy shaking hands Sunday afternoon and evening. Since Thursday his days and nights had been strenuous, the little sleep he had been able to get being snatched by the side of his prisoner, his wrist linked to that of the other. Collins spent his time in the lockup awaiting the arrival of Sheriff Lynds and Father McAuley, reading, eating, and occasionally whistling. In the local newspapers, he remained a hot topic. "He is and promises to remain for some time, a favourite subject for discussion. Budding criminal investigators have already and with almost uncanny ease, explained just what happened, and profess to know the suspect even better than he knows himself. 'You see it's like this …' — then the forefinger would commence to tap palm, and the suspect's inmost thoughts would be flung at a hungry public."

While Collins was the subject of curiosity, there was not a lot of local sympathy for his predicament. "Expressions of satisfaction are heard on all sides at the apprehension of the New Ireland murder suspect, and although occasionally one hears a word of sympathy for the youth who may by now be learning that the way of the transgressor is hard, there is a most general gratification that the prison bars are enclosing the man on whom suspicion so strongly rests as having committed one of the foulest deeds in the history of crime in this land."

Sentiments in Albert County may have been divided, however. Cigar salesman Curtis Boisvert, who had just travelled through New Ireland, caused a small sensation when he told a newspaper that most of the residents in that vicinity regarded Collins as an injured man who had not killed the housekeeper. He had talked with many people, he said, and only one household believed Collins guilty. "He had become well known while at Father McAuley's," Boisvert said, "and the majority of the neighbours express themselves as thinking rather well of him than otherwise. Many of the people do not hesitate in speaking of their suspicions of other parties than Collins. Not all the residents of the vicinity have been on good terms with the priest's household, and certain of these are regarded as by no means beyond suspicion."

Father McAuley, later in the week, took strong exception to Boisvert's version of events, particularly to his claim that some members of the community were not on good terms with his household. The priest said that everyone in New Ireland with whom he had talked believed that Collins had committed the murder. So far as enemies are concerned, he said, his household consisted of the late Miss McAuley and himself. "Miss McAuley was very generally esteemed among the neighbours, and I do not believe that she had enemies."

There was a great deal of talk concerning the robbery of the New Ireland rectory earlier in the summer, prior to Collins' arrival in the district. Father McAuley had been away from home, and the housekeeper, as was her custom during his absence, had gone to a neighbour's house to stay. A thief had broken in and stolen four bottles of wine. Charges were never laid, but it was now thought by some that the thief might have returned to steal again, after Collins had left the area, and killed Mary Ann in the commission of a second robbery attempt.

Albert County, meanwhile, was preparing for Collins' return to its jurisdiction. On Monday the charge against him was laid in Hopewell Cape before Stipendiary Magistrate D.W. Stuart, who would conduct the preliminary examination. He prepared a warrant for Sheriff Lynds to take to Saint John. There was local debate over where the court proceedings should be held, despite the fact that Hopewell Cape, the county's shiretown, had been given just two years earlier a spanking new courthouse. There was talk of holding the preliminary examination at Riverside, twelve miles away, perhaps because Magistrate Stuart resided there, but also because it would be a more convenient location for some of the witnesses. The people of Elgin were anxious, too, to have the examination held in their community, even though Collins would be incarcerated at the county jail at the Cape.

6.

On Wednesday morning Collins asked his jailers whether Father McAuley and Sheriff Lynds had arrived in Saint John yet. The two men were due that day on the express from Moncton, but there had been no sign of them at the police station. Collins remained outwardly undisturbed, as far as the authorities could tell. He seemed to relish his meals in jail — except the tea — and showed a fondness for tobacco, especially cigarettes. He continued to be an avid reader of whatever material his guards would bring.

Chief Clark and Detective Killen, having by now heard witnesses' stories that they had seen Collins in possession of what looked like a lady's gold watch, were pondering the whereabouts of the timepiece. If it had belonged to Mary Ann McAuley, it would be an important piece of evidence. That watch had not been found on Collins when he was taken into custody, and had not been in the valise found at Musquash. Perhaps it was in the second bag the fugitive had been seen carrying, but the whereabouts of that bag was also a mystery.

Killen located Daniel Lynch, who had been at John the Greek's Spruce Lake establishment when Collins showed up with Willie Dean, and took him to the police station to have a look at the prisoner. Lynch identified him as the man he had seen with a lady's gold watch at the roadhouse. Collins denied it, saying he had had only the silver watch that Killen found on him when he was captured.

"Well, Tom," said Killen, "this man will swear he saw a lady's gold watch in your hand."

"Well, I can swear, too, can't I?" said Collins.

The next day Killen drove down to Spruce Lake to interview Maggie Goguen, the Greek's waitress. While he was gone, Chief Clark decided to pay a visit to Collins in his cell. The chief had come to the conclusion that it was unlikely the gold watch would be found without Collins' help.

"You needn't tell me anything about it at all," he said to the prisoner, "but you have stolen a lot of property, and I would like to know something about the watch."

"I didn't have any watch," said Collins.

As the chief recounted the conversation later, he had then left Collins alone and walked back down the corridor. But when he returned later to the cell block, Collins said, "Well, I threw the watch away."

"Where did you throw it?" asked the chief.

"Oh," he said, "I lost it."

He told Clark it had happened after he had left the Douglas Spinney place at Lake Utopia Thursday evening. He had walked over the crest of a hill, where the old main road and the new shore road to St. George intersect, and spotted the still surface of the lake 300 yards away. He had decided he wanted a drink of water, and went down to the edge of the lake. He thought now, he said, that he had lost the watch somewhere between the tracks of the New Brunswick

Southern and the lake shore. Clark asked him to make a sketch of the place and he did, drawing rough lines on a sheet of paper, which Clark then labelled with place names.

When Killen returned from Spruce Lake later in the day, he went down to Collins' cell carrying some books for the prisoner.

"Good night, Tom," he said. "How are you?"

"Very well," said Collins, "but I told you a lie."

"What about?"

"About that watch," he said. "Didn't the chief tell you?"

"No, the chief didn't tell me."

Collins repeated the story he had told Clark, and a few days later Killen went to the area with Marshall McAdam from St. George. The two men searched through thick grass all afternoon, using Collins' rough map as a guide, but were empty-handed by dusk. Killen returned the next day with Douglas Spinney and two other men and searched the area up to 100 yards on either side of the road, but saw no trace of the gold watch. Killen said later, "I took off my shoes so I could go out in the water. It's very clear water with a gravelly beach, and I walked in the water nearly 300 or 400 yards looking on the bottom of the lake." The watch was never found.

Father McAuley and Sheriff Lynds arrived in Saint John Wednesday afternoon at five o'clock, but neither man went directly to the police station. The priest was the guest of his nephew, Joshua Ward of Dorchester Street, until Saturday, but the sheriff, who was staying at the Victoria Hotel, was expected to return to Hopewell Cape with the prisoner on Thursday's noon train, the only one which connected with Albert County. Father McAuley was expected to visit the police station the next morning, to identify the contents of the valise. A reporter called at the Ward residence Wednesday evening, but was told to leave because Father McAuley did not wish to discuss the details of the tragedy for publication. At 10:00 a.m. Thursday, Sheriff Lynds and Father McAuley arrived at the Saint John Central Police Station to meet Collins. Lynds went directly to Magistrate Ritchie's courtroom to have the warrant signed, and Ritchie told him to bring the prisoner before him. Reporters, hungry for any scraps of information, wanted to know what was said between the priest and the prisoner on their first meeting since the murder. Father McAuley, with a "kindly smile," told a reporter for the *Star* he had nothing to say on the case, that it was in the hands of the authorities.

"Well, could you say if the articles found in the possession of the prisoner are yours?" asked the reporter.

Father McAuley hesitated a moment, then said, "Well, I can say that he had very little when he came to me."

Collins was taken before Magistrate Ritchie, who abruptly told the prisoner he had not been treated fairly by the police. "This is the first I've seen of you," Ritchie said, "and, strictly speaking, you should have been in the jail, not where you were. That's all." Asked later by a reporter to explain his remark, Ritchie said, "According to the law, every man is innocent until proven guilty. Collins was placed in a cell in the police station Sunday afternoon with nothing but a hard board seat to sleep on, while he might have been lodged in jail and given a bed. It's a case like a person might hear of in Russia. The man Collins has the right to be treated like other prisoners and, if found guilty of murder, should then be placed in the cell that is arranged for convicts of this class."

Attorney General Pugsley, asked the next day about Ritchie's criticism, said he took full responsibility. Chief Clark had consulted him with regard to Collins' detention, he said, and, as he was not being held under a warrant, it was not necessary he should be taken before the magistrate. It was proper for the police to hold him until the arrival of the Albert County sheriff with the document. Pugsley said he had no doubt that Collins was made as comfortable as possible. After all, he had been given a bed and coverings.

Handcuffed, Collins was led from the police station at noon by Sheriff Lynds. Observers noted his flushed face, and speculated that the realization of his predicament may have begun to sink in. Father McAuley, asked by a reporter if he identified Collins, replied, "Yes, I could identify him with my eyes shut."

Father McAuley said goodbye to Collins just before he boarded the train. Regarding him "earnestly and without pity," he held the youth's steel-linked hands in his. "I suppose that I clasped his hand," the priest said later, "for at least a minute. I looked him squarely and steadily in the face and said that I hoped he would be good. He flushed slightly and I am sure that I saw tears gather." When he had met him earlier in the cell, Father McAuley said, Collins had shown no signs of embarrassment, fear or bravado. "We shook hands, and then he told me about his movements at the rectory. But I do not believe he is telling the truth." He had insisted, when questioned by the priest, that he left the axe on the woodpile at the rectory.

Sheriff Lynds and the prisoner left for Albert County on the *Atlantic Express* and, as they walked through the train-shed in Saint John, were followed by a curious crowd. While there were no disruptive incidents, Lynds and Collins were the centre of attention for the entire trip. At Salisbury, where they had to change trains for Hillsborough, onlookers in the station's waiting room pressed so close to Collins that he feared violence. Sheriff Lynds told him not to worry; he was prepared to prevent any assaults.

At Hillsborough station, not far from their destination at Hopewell Cape, a large crowd had assembled to see Collins. There were many comments thrown at him, but again no demonstration, as the two men left the train. Collins, still handcuffed, was placed in the mail wagon for the eight-mile drive to The Cape. He had little to say as they drove south along the wide river. As farm houses were passed, the little party was given close scrutiny by the residents. By 6:15 p.m. they had reached The Cape. The prisoner was taken immediately before Magistrate Stuart and the murder charge read. He did not plead and was remanded to the county jail, where he was the only inmate.

He appeared before the magistrate again on Monday, September 10. A large crowd had gathered to see the prisoner, who seemed agitated and uncomfortable. "He seemed to be haunted by an opinion that nearness to the scene of the tragedy would mean the existence of strong feeling against him as a suspect," a reporter wrote. His complexion was described as fair, his face as smooth, with the exception of his chin, which had a growth of whiskers, his eyes as full and "inclined to moisture apparently as if he were on the verge of a nervous breakdown." He kept his eyes downcast or gazing into a corner of the room during proceedings, and visibly trembled when the charge that he had murdered Mary Ann McAuley was read. His voice was low and indistinct when he answered that he would get counsel to defend him.

Leaving the courthouse, he was accosted by another photographer on the steps of the jailhouse. This time Collins was feeling less agreeable. "Have I got to have my picture taken again?" he asked the sheriff. "They have been doing nothing but taking pictures of me since they got me." The photographer got his portrait just the same. Sheriff Lynds told jailer Willard Porter to give the prisoner good and plentiful food, and Collins promised he would conduct himself well and give the jailer little trouble. In his cell, he began to write long letters to friends and relatives in Manchester, England, telling them of his predicament. He received replies — some would be publicized — as the legal apparatus of the British justice system worked its way through (and finally delivered its judgment on) the terrible event in New Ireland, which had disrupted the tranquility of the people of the county, and would continue to do so for the next fifteen months. But, so far as is known, the friends that Collins made while awaiting disposition of his case at Hopewell Cape would make far greater effort to keep him from paying the extreme penalty than any he might have had in the old country.

Chapter Nine

September-December, 1906

1.

Imagine the boy. He's just come out of the orchard on the slope behind the courthouse. He is slight, dressed in short wool pants, a cowlick of thick black hair flopping over his brow. He is carrying a stick on one shoulder like a rifle, and he seems to be involved in a conversation, though he is alone. He stops at the edge of the orchard, on a narrow path that comes out of a fringe of brush and canes, and watches the commotion in the field below. In the broad expanse between the courthouse and the squat stone building housing the jail is a turbulence of men, horses and wagons. The men yell and chatter at one another, and the brass and leather harnesses of the teams clink and rattle in the sunlight.

It is a warm fall day, the light golden yellow and green beneath the hazy sky, and the men sport white shirts without collars, or dark faded workshirts, and suspenders with silvery snaps. Some carry coats folded over the crook of an arm. They stand in clusters, gesticulating and guffawing loudly, and when they laugh — some of them — they lean back into it in a huge way, knees bent, thumbs hooked in straining suspenders, throwing their mirth at the sky from wide-open mouths. Others bend forward at the waist like a jackknife, peer into the ground, and slap a knee with calloused palm. When they are not laughing, they're solemn-browed, serious, looking straight down or all about, rather than into the face of the person they're speaking to, or squinting into the distance, into the sky. Occasionally they glance quickly over a shoulder, at the tree over there, or at the dog, leg kinked, nosing into the bush.

There are women, too, in long plain dresses, and they are standing on the lawns to the side, some with parasols and wide dark-coloured hats tilted on their hair, others with dusky straw boaters, a bright narrow ribbon tied over the crown and under the chin. The women chatter just as vigorously, though in more subdued tones. Their air is more steadily serious, and they stand straight-backed and motionless while they talk, hands clasped over their bellies. They seem to have brought a prerogative with them — solemn purpose perhaps. They nail the scene down like tent pegs. There is grave deadly work to be concluded here; a dead woman on the mountain; a young man's life on the scales here at the courthouse.

They're talking — some of these people — of Albert County's other killer, young Edward F. Cole, a Hopewell boy who, earlier in the year, had begun to serve a life sentence in Maine's Thomaston Prison for cutting the throat and bashing in the head of his buddy, John Frank Steeves, in a pasture at Falmouth, Maine. Ed Cole and John Steeves, who had grown up at Stoney Creek, Albert County, had crossed into Maine in April 1905 to escape the penalty for shooting a cow moose out of season in New Brunswick. John, for some reason, had begun acting as a liquor spotter for the sheriff of Falmouth just prior to his murder. After a time, his old friend Ed Cole was arrested and tried twice in Maine for the killing. On his way to prison after the second conviction, he had said to a reporter, "This is the last of Ed Cole." (Three years later, in 1909, Ed Cole, still maintaining his innocence, was visited in his cell by an acquaintance from the county. Ed was said to be quite happy, laughing and joking as though prison bars "could not suppress his characteristic good spirits.")

The boy on the slope, still watching intently, walks three steps out of the smoothly worn path and sits on the grassy incline, the stick between his knees. Turning his head, he invites his companion, who no one but himself can see, to sit beside him. "They've come to see this Collins," the boy says to his friend. "They're bringing him to the courthouse, there. Bringing him from the jail, across the field. He hurt a woman somewhere. Hit her with an axe. He's there, in that window." He aims the stick, butted against his shoulder like a rifle, at one of the tall windows in the back wall of the courthouse, sights along its length with narrowed eye, and slowly swings it across the field to his left over the gathered crowd, bringing it to rest on the barred aperture in the rear wall of the stone jail. In the dimness behind the bars, there's a white patch that could be the face of the killer.

Below the dust and buzz of the milling men and animals and carriages in the courtyard, the field slopes more sharply toward the distant river. Smaller county buildings, dating from the 1840s, perch on the bare field below the dominant pedimented portico of the courthouse. It's a grand building, the courthouse, as solid and angular as a silhouette. Just three years old, it was built for less than $5,000 (the county council alloted $4,000 for the construction — $1,200 of it from the Liverpool, London and Globe Insurance Company policy on the first courthouse — but gave the contract to H. Copp & Co, of Sackville for $4,495), after the fire in the summer of 1903 that wiped out most of the village; in all, twenty-one buildings, an old steamer tied at the public wharf, and a new steamer still in Warren Dixon's stocks waiting to be launched, went up in smoke.

The site of the courthouse, high on the hill overlooking the estuaries of the Petitcodiac and the Memramcook rivers, offers such an affecting vista to the poetic sensibility that it once helped resolve a civil action over payment of a debt for goods sold and delivered. The plaintiff, bored by the dusty rattling verbiage of the advocates, looked dreamily out of a courthouse window and, in a kind of rhapsody, watched the rush of the incoming tide, as it met the outflowing waters of the two rivers at their confluence with Shepody Bay, creating the playful sparkle of "The Merry Dancers" in the tumbling waters in front of the shiretown. Moved by the lovely vision of the rivers below the hill, and oblivious to his solemn surroundings, the plaintiff stretched out his hand toward the beautiful prospect beyond the window and broke into poetic recital. The sympathetic court, with a refined ear attuned to the suggestive allure of a fine strong metre, declared an adjournment, advocating to both sides that, if they wished to return after recess with relevant poetic renderings, their rhyming submissions could be appended with benefit to the official record of the proceedings.

When court reconvened, the enraptured plaintiff (known in the district as "The Prof") stood in his place before the bench, his commanding presence the centre of every gaze, and "in a voice redolent with the aroma of Lemon essence," delivered himself of an ode to the honourable court. "My hand is harsh, my heart is warm," he declaimed to the hushed room, adding in a wave of magnanimity: "None more regrets a deed of harm, and none forgives with nobler pride." Then, in rapture inspired by his own eloquence, he looked down in a pitying way on the lowly figure of the defendant, and declared "This is no place for a man like me; I can live without this sort of thing," and strode from the court, delivering himself into the lore of the county, under the influence of the magic of poetry.

Below the elevated site of the courthouse, large family homes are spread along the main road, some of them, too, built after the 1903 fire. A gravel road climbs the slope, winds round the back of the courthouse, and returns to the river road. More carriages and wagons are coming up it to add to the congestion. There are also people on foot, some having walked up from the public wharf far below after riding the ferry over from Dorchester Cape on the opposite bank of the broad blue-brown estuary. The layered red sandstone strata of the distant cape floats in grey haze beyond the swelling tidal waters, like another continent with its own mysteries.

The boy comes down the road with his companion to the courthouse porch, the floor of which is higher than his head. People are climbing the wide stone steps and disappearing inside the front doors, which stand open. The boy has been wanting to see inside the building, with its aura of circumscribed adult doings, but the broad windows with their fancy spandrels are so far from the ground that even a tall

man can't see into them. He and his companion have determined to edge inside with the crowd.

The building, seventy-two by forty feet, is constructed of
local wood as near to the style of the original as possible, with
four widely spaced fluted Ionic columns dominating the wide
porch. It is a building to study and to admire, with its
pilastered corners, its ornate fenestration, the square
louvred cupola, from the top of which rises a flag mast. Just
inside the door is an entranceway, with staircases on either
side leading to the public balconies. Directly ahead is the
doorway into the courtroom. The boy stands to the side, the
stick forgotten in his hand, as the men move past him into
the lower chamber. The women climb the staircases to the
upper balcony, confined there by virtue of their sex. The boy,
pushed to the side by the crowd, manages to peek around the
door casing.

The huge central courtroom is square, with an octagonal
metal ceiling supported by interlocked rafter beams, like the
upside-down hull of a ship. Douglas fir wainscotting anchors
the plastered walls, which give way to the pressed metal of
the ceiling. Slatted wooden blinds overlay the large windows.
The upper level of the public gallery rests on solid posts of
rock maple. On the lower level, the spectators' hardwood
benches, fastened to the sloping floor, open to the main
courtroom through wide wooden arches, decorated with
foliated scrolls at the upper corners. The public section of the
chamber is bounded by a hip-high wooden balustrade, with
a single gate running the width of the room.

The galleries face the judge's bench, which is perched
high on a raised platform. To the left, is the elevated
prisoner's dock enclosed by a gated railing; to the right, a
jury's platform with twelve wooden chairs; between them,
two expansive polished dark wood tables for the court officials and counsel. In the back wall, on either side of the
judge's bench, are doors leading to his chambers and those
of the jury, as well as rooms for the chief constable and his
deputies and, upstairs, storage areas for the exhibits of
evidence. Over the judge's head, in either corner, are small
railed balconies, each with a single wooden chair, on which

(if need be) could be seated county constables with firearms resting on their laps. Facing from opposite sides of the wide room are two large fireplaces of red brick.

Mystified and a little intimidated by the formal business of it all, the boy edges outside again, in time to see a small group of men, crossing the field from the jail, making their way to the rear entrance of the court. The man in the centre of the group is manacled; his eyes flit about the broad open field as he walks between the two constables, who move with solemn diginity as if preparing to take up the collection in a church service. The people still outside the courthouse look at him boldly, flinging his glance away as a dog unreflectively hurls the water from its fur. The prisoner appears to be acutely embarrassed facing these people in the open September air, but the route to the rear of the courthouse keeps a good distance between them.

2.

The preliminary hearing into the charge of murder against Tom Collins began Monday, September 10. The crowds, unprecedented in the county outside of political nominations, had the courtroom packed to the point of discomfort. The scene brought to the minds of some of the oldtimers Albert County's only other murder trial in memory — *The Queen vs Capt. Pye* — forty years earlier. Captain Pye, a native of Hopewell Cape, was tried for killing his mate at sea. Pye was convicted, but escaped the gallows by going "insane," and being sent to the provincial asylum where he died. One observer, who was more than casually interested in the current proceedings and who was seated in the lower level of the gallery, was Father Edward McAuley. He told a reporter that his home in New Ireland had since been broken up, and he had moved to Albert. He could not bear to live in the house where everything reminded him of Mary Ann and the horrible crime, he said, and it was thought likely that, before long, he would seek a change of parish. The priest had also attempted to discredit published reports that there was friction between himself and "certain residents of New Ireland or any other part of Albert County. I am now, and I have always been, on the best of terms with everybody in the county with whom I've come in contact."

Shortly after 11:00 a.m., Collins entered the courthouse for the first time. He was brought in through the back entrance behind the judge's pedestal, and he wore the same clothes he had been wearing when he was arrested. The baggy coat of blue serge was torn in places, while its collar was half turned out, almost obscuring the rough grey low-collared flannel shirt, hanging loosely at his throat. His grey trousers bagged about his seat and knees. The raucous chatter and laughter, which animated the courtroom, diminished into a hush as the prisoner was escorted to the witness table by Sheriff Lynds and Constable Coonan. He appeared to be at his ease, apparently unembarrassed, oblivious of the scrutiny from the galleries. He sat quietly, smiling occasionally at some jocular remark — "the synosure of all eyes," as one literate reporter observed.

His smile was described as frank, boyish and pleasing, and his facial appearance "decidedly in his favour." Numerous observers, seeing the young man for the first time that day, and despite the fact they had been following avidly the richly detailed, sometimes inaccurate newspaper accounts of his escapades, gave incredulous voice to an observation that was heard repeatedly whenever his case was discussed; that being that the young man simply did not measure up to the popular portrait of the hardened criminal. Moncton reporter Elmer Ferguson had this description: "Collins' face is distinctively not that of a murderer, unless it is a remarkable exception to the laws of physiognomy. His frank eyes look at one openly without flinching. While his complexion is ruddy, it is far from being dark. Ruddy cheeks are surmounted by close-cut black hair, and his smile is pleasing." (Ferguson would make a similar study of the physical appearance of hangman J.R. Radclive.)

Moncton lawyer Jim Sherren, who had come to The Cape to appear on behalf of Collins, also presented a physiognomical argument. "It is impossible for me to believe," he told Ferguson, "that Collins committed the terrible crime with which he is charged. In talking with him this morning, I was impressed with his general appearance, and his bearing and demeanour make it hard to believe that he is guilty of the crime charged against him. He has not the slightest indication in figure, physiognomy and otherwise, of a criminal, and his manner is far from that of the perpetrator of such a serious crime."

Sherren added that he would provide his client with a clean collar and tie tomorrow, hoping it would enhance his appearance. "Collins feels keenly the position in which he has been placed, charged as he is in a country where he has no friends, of such a horrible crime," said Sherren. "To me, as to others, he has maintained his innocence. I am convinced that he is not the murderer of Miss McAuley and that the matter will be resolved in another way."

Seated manacled at the table, Collins' hands trembled slightly as he brushed back the hair from his eyes. With the others jammed into the room, he was waiting for the proceedings to get under way. The word was that Premier Lemuel Tweedie himself, filling in for Attorney General William Pugsley, would come to The Cape to handle the crown's case against Collins. Justice of the Peace W.B. Dixon, in fact, had received a telegram from the premier asking for an adjournment of a few hours until he could get there.

3.

A Voice: Premier Tweedie come down for the Collins hearing, strange as it might seem. Wasn't there for the trials, but he did the hearing. He was a Liberal then — he had started off in politics as a Tory, but he came over to Blair's side (and into the cabinet, too) with some other Miramichi MLAs in the Northumberland County stumpage deal in the 1890s — and he had friends and enemies in Albert County. He was a big man, I remember, physically big, and friendly. People liked him, whether they liked him or not. He had been premier, I think, six years by the time the Collins thing got started, and he would be lieutenant governor before it was ended.

He was a lawyer up at Chatham, had a practice up there for many years. Went back to it after the politics. It's funny considering the Collins trials were at Hopewell, but R.B. Bennett, who came from Hopewell Cape and who become our Great Depression prime minister — and not too successful at it either — started his lawyering career with Tweedie. R.B. was a teacher first, after he left The Cape, and eventually got a job in Chatham, where he boarded with the Tweedie family. That would be well before the turn of the century. Mr. Tweedie got him interested in the law — must have seen potential in him — and R.B. started studying the law books with Tweedie in his spare time. By the time of the Collins thing, Bennett had gone out to Alberta and was making his fortune there, but he and Tweedie's family kept in touch over the years.

Now here's a story that Tweedie's son, Arthur, told old R.B. many years later, that shows what kind of a man Tweedie was. He was sharp for sure, but you had to laugh at him.

When he was about ten years old, as Arthur tells it, they had eight dogs, among them a large St. Bernard which they used to keep chained up, as he was a hen coop robber. One morning he got loose, and struck out downtown with about twenty-five feet of chain trailing behind him. His first stop was Jimmy Vanstone's butcher shop. Now Jimmy was cutting off some nice steaks for F.E. Neale, the lumber broker. Apparently the dog liked the look of them, because he grabbed the whole four pounds off the block and ran out the door. Jimmy was furious. He ran up Water Street toward Mickey Hickey's shoe store, but that dog outdistanced him. Jimmy's wrath at its height so overcame him, that he rushed on up to Tweedies's law office over Stothart's store, cleaver in hand and blood all over his apron.

Old Millet Salter was sitting at the desk in the outside office looking like Noah (with his long beard?), when Jimmy rushed in swinging the cleaver. Old Man Salter was frightened to death. Jimmy demanded to see Tweedie, who was in his inner office. In he rushes, with his cleaver and bloody apron.

"Well, good morning, Jim," says Tweedie, looking up calmly from his work.

"Good morning nothing," says Jimmy, fuming.

"Why what's your trouble?" says Tweedie. "Sit down and tell me what's the matter."

Jimmy, kind of forgetting himself, sits down. Then he jumps up real quick, and says, "Look, Mr. Tweedie, if a man's dog comes in to my store and takes four pounds of beef steak off my block, is the owner of the dog responsible?"

"Why, yes, of course," says Tweedie.

"Well," says Jimmy, "it was your dog."

"Well, well," says Tweedie. "How much was the steak worth?"

Jimmy's smiling now. "One dollar and sixty-eight cents," says he.

"A dollar sixty eight?" says Tweedie.

"Yes. A dollar sixty eight."

Tweedie purses his lips, sits back in his chair. "Mr. Salter," he calls to the outer office, "give Mr. Vanstone a dollar and sixty-eight cents."

He pauses, then adds, "And charge him five dollars for legal advice."

4.

By four o'clock Monday afternoon, Premier Tweedie had arrived at The Cape from Dorchester, making the trip across the river on Cole's Ferry (captained by another, though equally ill-fated, Ed Cole, who would go overboard into the river and drown on a summer day two years later). The hearing was reconvened and the premier, acting on behalf of Attorney General Pugsley, was accompanied by Clerk of the Peace M.B. Dixon. While the courtroom was comfortably cool, beads of perspiration stood on Collins' face, as the parade of witnesses began. At times a flush mounted his face, but these were the only evidence he gave of more than a passing interest in the proceedings. Even when the charge was read, and the words "did murder the said Mary Ann McAuley" spoken, Collins' eyes didn't drop. He sat and watched unmoved while Magistrate Stuart read the information, almost as if he were a spectator rather than the principal. Through the afternoon he sat, the only sign of nervousness being the incessant swinging of his feet. Sometimes he would call the attention of his lawyer, Jim Sherren, to points in the evidence on which he wanted particular stress laid, but for the greater part of the time, with hands folded in front of him, or resting on the arms of his chair, he listened to the stories of the witnesses.

Reporter Ferguson, taking note of the distribution of men and women present in the galleries for the hearing, wrote: "Among the male residents, and in fact among all the men who are in attendance at the trial, and they come from many and remote parts of the county, for it is seldom that Albert has a sensation, there is practically one opinion, the large majority of men being convinced that Collins is guilty of the charge. Among the ladies, and the fair sex are taking a deep interest in the trial, there being a large percentage present at the afternoon proceedings, the prisoner's open face and frank rather pleasing smile has made a highly favourable impression, and the lad has many champions among the ladies."

At the close of the second day, Premier Tweedie asked for an adjournment of sixteen days, saying he wished to call a number of witnesses from distant points in Carleton and St. John counties. The delay was granted. Some of the reporters were allowed into the jail to observe the prisoner at home in his small cell, and to talk to jailer Willard Porter, who lived with his family on the second floor of the stone-block building. In his small cell, Tom was reading everything he could get his hands on, and seemed especially anxious to get copies of the newspapers in which his case was being reported. He asked the newspapermen covering the hearing to send him copies of their respective journals. He also spent a good deal of time drawing, an art at which he was said to possess a certain amount of uncultivated skill. One day, as the reporters were cleaning up their copy paper at the close of a session, Tom asked one of them for some blank paper, which he evidently intended to use for copying pictures from the books and magazines he had been reading.

The hearing resumed for two days in late September and eighteen more witnesses were heard from. At the close of the second day, Premier Tweedie asked for a second adjournment, saying he needed time to locate William Dean Jr., son of the proprietor of the Musquash hotel where Collins had left one of the valises. On the last weekend of September, Detective Killen, continuing his investigation in the Elgin area of the county, found along the railway track near the village the other valise that Collins had been seen carrying from New Ireland.

Jim Sherren, meanwhile, who had written to Collins' relatives living in England, received replies. Sherren told the Moncton newspaper these letters were important to the case, because they indicated that Collins was of "respectable parentage in England. The letters go to show that the prisoner's story of his life and birth place were correct, and that he had led a very respectable life in the homeland." One letter, from a Liverpool Sunday school superintendent whose school Collins had attended, indicated the boy had been well thought of there. It said: "I need hardly say that I am extremely sorry to hear such sad news. For the short time that I had known Collins (about six or eight months), I had always found him a very steady, straightforward fellow, anxious to get on and do well for himself, and I cannot understand how he has gotten mixed up in such a serious matter. He became connected with our church through the football club, and came to our Sunday school several times, remaining connected with our church through the Football and Men's Recreation Club."

Sherren said he had also received a communication from a brother-in-law of the young man, saying that Collins' mother was still living in England, and the family felt terribly the position in which her son had been placed; to his relatives the whole matter seemed incredible. Sherren said he expected to receive further letters from other relatives within the next few days. And finally, he said Collins had told him that he had received a letter "from a young lady at home in which she expresses her sympathy for him, and asks him to come home and marry her if he gets clear."

When the hearing resumed in October, the crown announced no further evidence would be presented. In a wire to Crown Counsel Miles Dixon, Premier Tweedie wrote: "On consultation with the attorney general, and his opinion being that a very strong case has been made out for the commitment of Collins on the charge of murder, it will not be necessary to take further evidence in the preliminary examination; therefore, ask magistrate to close the matter and commit for trial."

Sherren immediately filed formal application for the dismissal of charges against his client. He said various features of the circumstances facing Collins needed commenting on, including "that the accused was a stranger in this country without a single friend and without any financial means, and when arrested he was not in a position to do anything towards procuring counsel or in any way securing anyone to look after his interests. The province made no provision in such cases and, before word could be received from England, the preliminary examination was practically over." Sherren said those who knew Collins on the other side of the ocean stated that he was a boy of almost exemplary character, and they could not in any way comprehend how he could be mixed up in, or could be tried for, such a serious offence. Sherren argued that the crown, in asking for numerous adjournments and then not putting on witnesses, had hardly been fair to the prisoner under the circumstances.

"If the crown had wanted the adjournment for the purpose of putting witnesses on when it came to conduct the case this day," he said, "the witnesses should have been on hand." Sherren claimed, too, that his case had been prejudiced by newspaper reports. He said, without specifying the incidents, that the crown should have supressed certain reports until the matter had been brought into court.

Clerk of the Peace Dixon, in his response, insisted the crown had intended to produce witnesses but, after discussing the matter with Premier Tweedie, who was unable to continue attending the hearing, and Attorney General Pugsley decided there was ample evidence already. "The question is not one to be determined as to Collins' guilt or innocence, that being a matter for a jury." He added there was no provision in law to provide counsel for Collins at the expense of the province, and the attorney general had no discretion to do so.

Magistrate Stuart accepted the crown's arguments. He added that he did not think the crown should be blamed for not supplying counsel for Collins, when they had no power to do so at this stage of the proceedings. He did think, however, that such things ought to be done if possible. "It is not my place to judge as to the guilt or innocence of the prisoner. That is a matter to be decided by a jury of twelve men to be selected from the body of this county, and these men I am sure will only be guided by the evidence adduced in the court. There seems to me, however, evidence to send the accused up for trial and, believing that, I will commit him for trial." Called upon by the magistrate, Collins rose and said he had nothing to say. "The accused," said the magistrate, "now stands committed." Trial was set to begin in the new year.

The murder weapon, meanwhile, still had not been found. In early November, Detective Killen went to the rectory in New Ireland with Sheriff Lynds to conduct a search. He spent two afternoons searching the premises, and came up with a double-bitted axe that had been tossed into an oat bin in the priest's barn. He believed he had the murder weapon, and took it back to Saint John with him. Nine days later it was announced that an analyst had been unable to find bloodstains, either on the axe or on a shirt which had belonged to Collins. Early in December, Jim Sherren decided to visit New Ireland personally "to gain a better idea of the locality and surroundings in which the crime was committed."

Four days before Christmas, Attorney General Pugsley was reported to have fears about being able to call an unbiased jury to hear the trial. He issued instructions to have fifty additional jurymen summoned for the trial, scheduled to open at the Hopewell Cape courthouse on Tuesday, January 15. This, with the ordinary panel and the members of the grand jury, would mean there would be ninety-five jurymen in attendance on opening day. Pugsley would conduct the case for the crown, and it was expected that thirty witnesses would give evidence. "The summoning of the large number of extra jurymen would appear to anticipate difficulty in securing the twelve men from the usual panel," the Moncton newspaper reported, "but there is quite an opinion here that there should not be much trouble in getting chosen the required number of unbiased men."

By now Tom Collins had been resident in Albert County jail for more than four months and, if newspaper stories were to be believed, he was rather enjoying his incarceration. After all, it was better than tramping about the winter countryside, penniless and hungry, trying to find work. His lawyer was saying that he personally was convinced there would be an acquittal in January. Over Christmas, some of the sympathetic women of the community baked holiday treats for him and sent them to his cell.

"Collins is taking things quietly in the jail," the newspapers told their readers, "and is said to be gaining in flesh and enjoying the best of health. He reads a good deal and tries his hand some at mechanical work, being just now engaged in the manufacture of a miniature ship to be presented to Constable Coonan."

Two days after Christmas, 129 days after the death of Mary Ann McAuley and 124 days after the capture of Tom Collins, the missing axe, generally thought to be the murder weapon, was found, quite by accident, by Sarah Williamson's step-daughter, Mabel, behind a piece of furniture in Father McAuley's own bedroom.

Chapter Ten

The First Trial, January 1907

1.

The January trial lasted nine days. Much of the evidence was tedious, repetitive. The prosecution had no witnesses to the crime, no physical evidence tying the accused to the crime, no dramatic confessions, no solid motive. Even the statement given the police by the accused following his capture was not admissable. Still, Collins was the only real suspect they had. And what the prosecution had against him was an elaborate congeries of circumstances, such individually innocuous particulars as a couple of valises, a pack of cards, a collar button, thirteen stereoscopic pictures, a bag with four pencils, a vanished gold watch, the outward manifestation of a guilty conscience, a degree of mendacity, an erratic flight, and an opportunity. The task of placing the circumstances before the jury and of maintaining the integrity of the charge that it supported, required many hours of testimony from the almost fifty witnesses the investigators had gathered from across the southern edge of the province.

Tuesday, January 15. With steel cuffs linking wrists, Collins was brought into the crowded courtroom through a door at the front, to the left of the judge's bench, perched like a pulpit on its dais. He walked briskly, almost jauntily, looking alertly at the spectators seated in the galleries. He was dressed in the same blue serge suit that he had worn three months ago during the preliminary examination, with a white collar, dark tie, and a silk handkerchief tucked inside the collar. He had gained weight since October, and there was a touch of prison pallor in his skin.

Led by Constable Herman Coonan, he walked to the small railed prisoner's dock, elevated slightly on a platform in front of the judge's bench. He sat on the wooden chair in the dock and leaned forward, elbows on his knees, linked hands slack-wristed between them. In the warmth of the courtroom, the pallor soon left his face and was replaced by a bright flush. There were brick fireplaces on either side of the large room, and these had been fired up early in the day. Turning on his chair and looking about the hall behind the prisoner's dock, he smiled occasionally at familiar faces.

Seated at two long tables in front of the bench were four men: Harrison A. McKeown of Saint John and J.C. Sherren of Moncton for the defence, and New Brunswick Solicitor General Wendall P. Jones of Woodstock and C.N. Skinner of Saint John for the prosecution. Amongst the spectators was a group of curious barristers from the area anxious to watch McKeown and Jones at work. McKeown's reasons for undertaking Collins' defence have been lost in time, though it is known that he was working for virtually nothing. William Burns, the editor of the *Albert Journal*, reported in October that Jim Sherren had been communicating with Collins' relatives in the old country, and was retained by them to defend the young man. It was thought some of Collins' "friends" from England would be present when the trial got under way, but no one made the trip. Several local women, however, who would continue over the next several months to take a keen interest in Collins' fate, occupied seats in the segregated overhead galleries. The ground floor benches, sloping back from the railing which separated the business end of the courtroom from the public, were accessible only to the men; the ladies had to labour up the stairs to the balcony.

Mr. Justice George F. Gregory of the New Brunswick Supreme Court, who had come down from Fredericton for the trial and was not feeling well that morning (had, in fact, delayed the start of proceedings for an hour), ordered the handcuffs removed as soon as the room had been called to order. Collins seemed to display keen interest as the proceedings began and, in a steady voice, replied, "Not guilty" to the charge read against him. Judge Gregory, peering at the panel of grand jurors, declared that if any of them had contributed to the fund raised at Hillsborough for Collins' defence, "you will please retire as you cannot be allowed to sit upon the jury." One man departed, leaving twenty-one to consider whether the charge against Collins ought to be proceeded with.

Solicitor General Jones rose to his feet and turned to the grand jurors, addressing them at some length. "We cannot," he intoned, "be influenced by anything except the evidence offered, and not by anything we hear or read. The evidence will be principally of a circumstantial nature, as is often the case in criminal matters. The crown will produce between thirty and forty witnesses, who can testify to some facts which the crown believes will have a bearing on the guilt or innocence of the accused. The crown puts it forward that Mary Ann McAuley was murdered on Monday morning, August 20, and that the prisoner is guilty of that murder. I believe that sufficient evidence will be offered to show that the prisoner is guilty. We cannot produce any evidence in regard to the striking of the blow, but Doctor Murray has stated that the wounds could not be self-inflicted."

Judge Gregory, addressing the indictment, told the jury there was no evidence of "improper assault" upon the body of the murdered woman, and it was quite difficult to ascribe any motive for the crime. "You will have no difficulty in finding that the poor woman was murdered, her life taken by violence, that she was felled with an axe and was dragged out to the woodshed and left. Then you will have to face the question, who committed the crime? You have the circumstances, you have the prisoner's going away, and nothing but misrepresentation from that time on. Circumstances related in the evidence will have to be taken into consideration in coming to a conclusion as to whether there is sufficient facts upon which to find a true bill."

It took the twenty-one-member grand jury just over three hours to find a true bill against Collins. He would stand trial for murder. The selection of a jury, which began immediately, took considerable time, with numerous objections from the defence and the prosecution, but twelve men were eventually selected. Judge Gregory then adjourned the court until Wednesday morning, when Father Edward McAuley would be the first witness.

2.

Harrison Andrew McKeown, the Saint John lawyer with the dignified bearing, the piercing eyes, the heavy moustache and deeply cleft chin, who had come to The Cape to defend Collins, had a checkered career as a politician. His public life began in 1890 at age twenty-seven, so young that he was tagged with the label "the boy candidate." (The name stuck with him, and would be recalled in his obituary forty years later.) He was attracted to politics at a time when rock-solid partisanship was still in the future, and Andrew Blair was just beginning to put together the coalition that was to become the New Brunswick Liberal party.

Born in 1863 at St. Stephen of English-Canadian ancestry, McKeown was a son of United Church minister Rev. Hezekiah and Elizabeth (Harrison) McKeown. He was educated at Mount Allison University, Sackville, where he befriended English professor W.M. Tweedie, cousin of Lemuel Tweedie of Chatham, who would become premier of the province and McKeown's political boss. McKeown settled in Saint John, where he began to practise his profession. One of the city's more eligible bachelors, he fell in love in 1901 with a young lady named Edith A. Perkins. They were married in Boston in November and returned to Saint John at the end of the month.

Two days before Christmas, Edith's illness was announced in a local newspaper's regular column, "The Smallpox Situation." She was one of ninety-seven victims in the city in the closing weeks of that year. J. McGinty's boarding house on the corner of King St. East and Carmarth Street, where the couple had rooms, was quarantined. Edith was removed to the isolation hospital the next night. On December 26, her condition was reported as not serious. On December 29, she was said to be resting easier. On December 30, her condition was said to be causing considerable anxiety and was described as very low. She died the next day. She was twenty-four years old, a bride of less than two months.

McKeown was devastated. A month later, he wrote to his friend, Professor Tweedie in Sackville: "My dear Morley, I have just read yours of some days ago. Frank brings me up the letters from the office and I recognized your well-known handwriting. I can do no more just now than simply thank you for your kind letter of sympathy. I am absolutely beaten down to the ground by this blow. I have absolutely no idea of what I will do in the immediate future. I have not been at my office since and only go out in the air for about half an hour when weather is fine. Yours in great sorrow, Harry."

McKeown recovered from the loss, however, and resumed his political career, which had begun in 1890 when he won the St. John County seat in New Brunswick's house of assembly for the Blair administration. Two years later, he contested a city seat, but lost. He was successful in 1899, however, and the following year was named minister without portfolio in the Liberal administration of H.R. Emmerson. In 1903, fifteen months after the death of his wife, McKeown was appointed solicitor general by the new premier, Lemuel Tweedie, and held the post until January, 1904, when he resigned to contest a federal seat in Saint John. He lost twice — at a byelection in February and again in the general election in November. He returned to his law practice.

McKeown was a commanding presence, with the gifts of a public speaker whose voice carried to all parts of an assembly hall. He had a fighting style of speech, vigorous diction, and a ready wit. The story is told of a meeting at which he was speaking in support of a controversial policy of Sir Wilfred Laurier. A heckler interrupted with a series of questions on an entirely different matter. Without hesitating, McKeown replied in detail. The questioner sat down and the audience applauded vigorously. When the meeting ended, however, McKeown quietly called a reporter aside and suggested he not publish the answers. "I made them up as I went along," he said.

He was known as a clever man, a clear thinker, a splendid, even brilliant jurist, fluent, vigorous and learned, and a

man who made friends easily. In January, 1907, he made the
decision to defend the vagrant immigrant, Collins, against
the charge of murdering Mary Ann McAuley, even though
Collins had no money to pay for his defence and it would
mean McKeown would have to spend some time at Hopewell
Cape. It was a high-profile case and the evidence against his
client, though it was all circumstantial, seemed strong.
McKeown's former political boss, Premier Tweedie, had acted
for the crown at the preliminary hearing in September. Now
McKeown would be appearing for Collins against Wendall
Jones, his own successor as the province's solicitor general.

Before the Collins story was played out to its end, Mc-
Keown would be remarried, re-elected to the house of assembly, and appointed attorney general by another Liberal
premier, C.W. Robinson. (Tweedie had resigned earlier in the
year to become lieutenant governor, and was succeeded by
William Pugsley, who himself resigned shortly after to accept
a federal cabinet post; Pugsley was in turn succeeded by
Robinson.) In April, three months after Collins' first trial,
McKeown married Agnes Grace Burpee of Saint John.
Professor Tweedie was his best man. Following the reception
at Ravencliffe, the bride's home, the couple went to Halifax
to board *S.S. Empress of Ireland* for an extended European
tour.

The honeymoon apparently forced a delay in Premier
Robinson's effort to complete his cabinet. In any event, he
denied reports that the attorney general's portfolio "had been
hawked about the country from lawyer to lawyer. I can only
say that I was influenced by the fact that Mr. McKeown's
experience and standing at the bar, his well known ability
as a skilful debater both in and out of the house, coupled with
his residence in the city of Saint John, where he will be easily
accessible to all those having business with the chief crown
officer of the province, made him pre-eminently fitted for the
occasion."

McKeown would continue his public life until the year
before he dropped dead, at the Westfield ferry landing near
his summer home on the St. John River in 1932, aged sixty-
eight. He would serve on the Supreme Court of New

Brunswick, for eight years as Chief Justice of the King's Bench Division, and end his career as chairman of the board of the Railway Commission of Canada.

3.

The courtroom at Hopewell Cape was packed on Wednesday, the second day of the trial, for the testimony of Father McAuley. The bereaved priest, known only by name in some areas of the county, especially the more prosperous Protestant river communities peopled by families descended from sea captains, shipbuilders and lumber merchants, was in the witness box for the entire day. Some surprising material came out in his testimony, notably the accidental discovery of the murder weapon in his own bedroom weeks after the police investigation had been concluded. He also told of the burglary of his home a few weeks before the murder.

Collins, seated in the railed enclosure facing Judge Gregory and guarded on each side by a constable, was not indifferent to the proceedings, but his attention wandered at times when the testimony seemed only marginally relevant. Stretched back in his chair, his head tilted and resting against a corner of the dock, he gave each speaker intermittently close scrutiny — by turn, as the morning wore on, Prosecutor C.N. Skinner, a thin hawk-faced man with a heavy moustache and chin whisker; McKeown; Judge Gregory; and Father McAuley.

Father McAuley's presence drew the largest attendance since the trial opened. In the overhead galleries surrounding the courtroom were scores of women, some of whom had driven a considerable distance, while downstairs the seats were again filled. Giving his clear and concise testimony, the priest displayed little impatience at the long series of questions. Skinner, a well-known legal and political figure of Loyalist descent, began the examination by asking the priest the extent of his parish. Father McAuley said he had five missions, and described their locations. His residence, he said, was in New Ireland near his church.

"Speaking of last year, had you a housekeeper?"

"I had a housekeeper last year until August."

"What was her name?"

"Mary Ann McAuley — a second cousin of my own."

"Was she a single or married woman?"

"A single woman."

"About what was her age?"

"Fifty-two years."

"She was a relative of yours?"

"Second cousin."

"State with reference to her health and her physical state."

"Oh, her health was generally good — always able to do her duty, with very few exceptions."

"What is ordinarily called a well preserved woman?"

"Yes."

"And were her habits active?"

"Very active — very smart."

Father McAuley told how he met and hired Tom Collins, and of subsequent events at the rectory the week before the murder.

Father McAuley: I first met Collins at the McAnulty house at Albert village on the eleventh of August, Saturday it was. Mr. McAnulty partially introduced him by asking me if I wanted to hire a man. I said I did, but I would rather wait until later on. The three of us were standing near together. I was on the station platform, and so was Mc-Anulty, and Tom was below us. I hadn't seen him before this time, but understood he had come in on a scow from across the bay. Then McAnulty asked Tom if he would go with me for ten dollars a month. I looked sharply at McAnulty, but I gave no consent to ten dollars a month. I said nothing at all then, but afterwards I told Mac, I said: "I didn't say anything about ten dollars." Said I: "I wouldn't give him any more than seven dollars a month." Then McAnulty said, "I don't think that man will suit you."

But I talked to Tom anyway after dinner and decided to take him in with me. I asked him something with regard to his cutting wood and taking charge of a horse — I thought if he didn't know much about it I could teach him if he were willing to learn and work. I asked him where he was from, and I understood him to say that he was born in Sligo, which is in Ireland, but afterwards he told me his father was born in Sligo. He said he'd come in to St. Mary's Point at Harvey, crossing the bay from Nova Scotia on a scow out of Amherst.

We arranged on seven dollars a month and he was satisfied. I made arrangements for him to come in to New Ireland with me on Monday. I'd intended to go home on Sunday, but I had a call which took me to Hillsborough, and consequently I didn't return until Monday afternoon about a-quarter-past three. Went straight to McAnulty's again and fed the horse. We left there — Tom and I — at five o'clock to go home to New Ireland, about ten miles from Albert village.

He showed me right away that he knew little of horses. Just outside the village on the way to New Ireland, there's a large steep hill that the road climbs. It was the warmest part of a warm day in a very warm week. Last August was as hot a month as I remember in the thirty-odd years that I've served in New Ireland. As we went up the hill Tom walked, and as we came to the watering place about halfway up the slope, I asked him to take off the check rein to give the horse a drink. He didn't understand what the check line was. I told him it was that which was made fast to the hook, so by that he saw, and after the horse had drank he put it on again in its place and walked up the hill ahead of me. It seemed clear that he knew nothing about the harness of a horse, but then he hadn't told me that he did.

We reached the rectory about twenty minutes after seven that evening. It's a long hard ride from Albert to the parish house, much of it uphill, and steep pitched at that. Mary Ann was there, of course. She came out of the house as we pulled into the yard and, after I'd got out of the wagon, and she helped him untackle the horse, put the rig in the carriage barn and the horse in the stable. I told her who he was, why he was there, and asked her to show him how to feed and water the horse — she's very capable with the horse.

After we'd eaten, I sent him with my axe down to William Williamson's, which is about a mile east of Chapel Hill, to get the edge sharpened. Mr. Williamson is a good woodsman and had a stone for grinding an axe. My axe had a double-bit, and one edge was badly chewed up with a large gap in it. The other edge was in fairly good shape and it was that edge that Mr. Williamson worked on. He would have sharpened the other, too, but he told Tom that it was very dull and he didn't have the time that night.

Tom started work on Tuesday morning. I looked out and saw him at the woodpile with the axe, trying to split a block of wood that had been sawn off with a crosscut saw. I saw he didn't understand it very well, and I went out myself and showed him how to do it. I think I split the block, or started it pretty well for him. He had been commencing at a knotty stick, and I said, "Don't try these knotty pieces, because you won't get along very well with them." They were sawed hardwood, birch and maple, and he was to split them for the stove. I said: "There is no use of commencing with that, because that is too heavy for you."

I guess he worked away at it as best he could all day. I didn't watch him, being busy at the church — the church is right by the house about five or six rod away — and busy in my office in the rectory, getting ready for my visit to Albert Mines and Fredericton Road missions on the weekend. I was planning to leave Friday afternoon with the mail wagon, so I wouldn't be needing Collins to drive the horse for me. I don't think he could harness the horse anyway, but he had no occasion to try at all that week, as the horse wasn't used.

On Wednesday, he went at the wood as usual, and carried water from the spring behind the house when asked by the housekeeper. I remember him going out to the barn, where I saw him at work cleaning the wagon and the harness. I said to him, "That is all very well, but I would rather you would keep at the wood, because we want some wood split up for the fire." That is all I said to him at the barn. I don't remember anything more from that day.

On Thursday morning, I gave him permission to go out to the lake between nine and ten o'clock to get a few trout. The lake is part of the property of the church; it's a good distance from the rectory in the hills behind it. There's a road runs straight out there from the house, and there's an overnight camp with a stove and bunks. Mr. Gross and his family

— Albert Gross, he's a postal clerk from Saint John — were out there, staying most of the week.

Tom went out Thursday morning on foot and he stayed all day, didn't come back 'til supper time, about five o'clock or thereabouts, and then with only three or four fish. He come back in with Mr. Gross, who had a span of horses with him. Wanted to leave them with me so he wouldn't have to take more hay out to the lake for them. Said he'd be leaving Saturday morning and could he leave them in my barn 'til then. I said I could keep one horse for him, I hadn't the room for two, and I would send Collins up to a neighbour's, Mr. Duffy's, with the other horse to keep 'til Saturday morning.

I wasn't very well pleased with the hired man staying so long at the lake and coming back with so few fish, and I told him so. But I told him in a pleasant way — I didn't show any temper or anger whatever. I said, "You've been a long time away today." Mr. Gross said he'd had Tom cutting down some alders from the shore of the lake so they could have a view from the clubhouse to the water. Said I: "That is alright then that he didn't catch many fish." And Mr. Gross said, "There were some children with him in the boat, and they were making a noise, scaring away the fish." Then Tom took the horse over to Duffy's place and nothing more was said on that score.

The next day — Friday — Michael Teahan, a neighbour who has his farm a few miles to the west near Teahan's Corner, came down with his son, Everett, to show Tom how to get through the wood. They sawed wood there all the forenoon, the three of them. Michael Teahan had brought his bucksaw down, and they just sawed while I was there. I don't recall that he brought an axe, but my axe, the one that Mr. Williamson had sharpened, was there. I think they worked 'til they had their tea, between five and six probably. Of course, I wasn't there by then.

The mail had arrived, somewhere I should judge about a-quarter-past three or nearly four that afternoon, and I got ready to go out in the mail wagon to Albert. I was going to Fredericton Road for Sunday mission. I went to McAnulty's in Albert to remain the night, and then caught the train for

Salisbury at six o'clock Saturday morning. When I got to Salisbury I drove immediately out to the Fredericton Road, eight miles.

Before I left home I told the housekeeper to see that the furnace wood was got down into the cellar and piled up there while I was away; to tell the boy to do it. There were shingles and kindling wood and cord wood. I also told Mary Ann they could go fishing at the lake on Saturday. That would be Michael Teahan's family and the housekeeper, and I think she spoke of Mrs. Williamson, that she would like to go, and I said it was alright. I told her to take the boy with them. I also gave instructions with regard to going to Albert on Monday morning to get some groceries for the house. I gave her two dollars, one dollar in paper money and two fifty-cent silver pieces.

Skinner asked Father McAuley what he knew about his housekeeper's gold watch.

"Oh, I saw the watch two or three times. I paid no very particular attention, any more than it was in very bad shape. She had it in Boston, she told me, and the jeweller there didn't do any kind of a job, and she sent for it and got it returned."

"Do you remember any marks on it?"

"Well, I believe she had ... "

McKeown objected to the witness entering into evidence what he merely believed.

"Just tell us," said Skinner, "as your memory serves you what you can remember."

"Her initials I can't distinctly remember."

"You don't really remember any of the marks or numbers, I presume?"

"No."

"Do you know if it had any on it? Sometimes if you hold a watch you will see it has some marks or initials on it, but can't tell what they are."

"Well, I wouldn't like to say that I could say what initials were on it."

"But were there any marks on the outside of it?" Skinner persisted. "If you have any memory of any marks, not that you remember what they were, you can state it."

Father McAuley said he had no recollection.

"You can speak to the best of your recollection," Judge Gregory interjected, "but if you haven't any recollection, do not pretend to give any."

Father McAuley said he could not recall whether there were marks on the watch case, or whether there were none at all.

Skinner entered the two pieces of luggage — the second had been found by Detective Killen in bushes by the railway tracks near Elgin — into evidence. Item by item, he pulled out the contents for Father McAuley's identification. Inside the telescope valise were a towel, two undershirts, an outside shirt, a clothes brush, soap and a soap dish, a hairbrush, a comb, a razor, a pack of cards, a collar button, and a number of handkerchiefs, including one of silk, with Mary Ann's name sewn on, that he had bought at the PanAmerican exhibition in Buffalo in 1901.

Inside the gladstone bag, which he identified as one he had bought in Portland, Maine, in 1893 or 1894, were a stereoscope with broken glasses, thirteen stereoscopic pictures, a soap holder, a pencil holder, a comb with a holder, four coloured handkerchiefs, and a bag with four pencils. All the items had been in the rectory when he had last seen them. Also found in the bags, but not belonging to the priest, were a shaving brush, a cardboard box with shaving soap, a number of soiled handkerchiefs, a watch key, two neckties, and a pair of drawers.

He identified by the stitching a pair of reins that had been found along the rail line near Elgin. "They were re-sewed last year by a saddler at Elgin," he said. "I remember I was out in a rain storm and they came apart. They're the ordinary lines that I use with the old harness. I always took them off the bit and hung them up with the rest of the harness." He had another set of reins that he used with the new harness, he said. He identified the bloodstained overalls found in the woodshed, and said they had been hanging in a corner on a nail. "I never used them in this county. I bought them down in Charlotte, and I used them once only in Charlotte fishing."

Two axes, wrapped in cotton, were brought into the courtroom. The double-bitted axe with a gap in one edge was identified and entered in evidence as axe "No. 1." The second axe, the one found in the feed bin in the barn and thought to belong to Tommy Mellen, was marked "No. 2" and entered. Father McAuley told the court how axe "No. 1" had been found only last December standing behind a commode in his bedroom.

McKeown, in his cross-examination, attempted to shed some light on the nature and disposition of the accused.

"I felt kind of favourably with regard to him," said Father McAuley at one point.

"You saw nothing to indicate any bad behaviour?"

"Nothing. I felt charitably towards him from the first."

"Was he profane?"

"I never heard anything."

"You thought he smoked?"

"I saw a small pipe with him. He showed it to me. He got it as a present from some friends in the old country."

McKeown spent a good deal of time with the priest, going over a sketch of the church property and the interior of the rectory. He asked for more precise details about the discovery of the body on Tuesday, and about the layout of the wood-shed. Father McAuley told of sending Jimmy Doyle to the neighbours to look for Mary Ann, after she could not be found at the rectory that night. He said he had been confused and could not understand why she was missing. He said he walked up and down the verandah while he waited for Doyle to return. "I didn't seem to want to rest at all."

"Were you nervous?"

"Yes."

"Were you getting a little angry, too?" Judge Gregory asked.

"Well," said the priest, "I couldn't say I was very well pleased. At the same time I couldn't say I was very angry. I was more nervous than angry. I was alarmed. There is no doubt about it. I was so confused I did not know what I was doing. I was disappointed at not finding her there." He said the disorder of the rectory had made him very apprehensive, but he had never thought that he would find her dead.

Father McAuley admitted that some items that seemed to be missing from the rectory, such as postage stamps, rings and a small valise belonging to Mary Ann, were not found either in the two bags or in Collins' possession when he had been arrested. McKeown asked whether the mission house had been broken into in July, a few weeks before Collins arrived in New Ireland.

"I was absent when this happened," said the priest. "I would only know from the housekeeper. I had got some groceries from Saint John, some canned things and some corned beef, and amongst the rest I had a half dozen bottles of Irish whiskey. And when the parcel arrived in the house — this is all from the housekeeper — she opened it, and took out the meat and put some more pickle on it, and put those canned things away in their places, and put the liquor down in the cellar. When I got home that evening the first word she said to me, she said, 'There has been a burglary committed here.' And she told me there was only one bottle of whiskey left there, and I saw that, and that is all I did see. The other bottle she took to a distant part of the mission and made it a present to an old lady who was not very well. There were also two bottles of wine in the cellar which were tampered with, and the other four bottles were missing."

"Were any attempts made to find out who did this?" asked McKeown.

"I never accused anybody myself, because I don't know."

"There was suspicion attached to a person down there, was there not?"

"By the talk of the people."

"But there were not steps of any kind taken?"

"No steps. I didn't bother any more about it."

"Now then," said McKeown, "the occasion when this robbery was committed was an instance when you were away?"

"Yes."

"And when she was away?"

"Yes."

"It is a fact that you were away when this other tragedy was committed?"

"Yes."

McKeown pointed out that the weekend before the murder, Mary Ann had made arrangements to go to Albert on Monday for groceries. If she had gone as planned, he asked, "whoever came there that day (Monday) would be liable to find the place unoccupied?"

"Yes," said the priest, "locked up, but unoccupied."

Father McAuley said he kept wine at the rectory at all times for church purposes.

"In parts of the country you live in down there," said McKeown, "there is a pretty well defined taste for alcohol?"

"Oh, I suppose amongst some there is."

"Have you ever heard of illicit stills being in operation down there?"

"Yes."

McKeown asked whether the priest knew of the circumstances surrounding the robbery and beating of a pedlar in New Ireland district during the summer.

"I heard something about it," he said. "The fellow had called at my house that day, though he wasn't inside."

Skinner objected to Father McAuley being asked to testify on matters about which he had no personal knowledge.

"I know nothing," said the priest, "but what people talked."

McKeown continued: "It was this last summer?"

"Yes."

"Was it prior to or after the tragedy?"

"It was prior to it."

Father McAuley said both he and Mary Ann kept some money at the rectory; he himself had $140 in a box in his closet.

"Do you know," asked McKeown, "whether it was a matter of knowledge among the people there?"

Skinner objected to the question, and it was not answered.

McKeown asked the priest to go over details of the discovery of the axe in his bedroom. It had been found December

27, just a week before the opening of the trial. Father Mc-
Auley said it had been found behind the commode by Mabel
Williamson, who was acting as his housekeeper. He had
ordered that it be put back behind the washstand, and then
notified the Saint John police. He said the axe had been
standing upright behind the commode, but the top of the
handle had been obscured by a splasher, a piece of material
which protected the wall from spatters. He said he had not
been present when Detective Killen had unsuccessfully searched the room during his investigation earlier.

Court was adjourned at 5:30 p.m.. Father McAuley had
been on the stand since morning.

4.

On Thursday, Doctor G.A.B. Addy of Saint John, a bacteriologist and pathologist who said he had been educated at
McGill College, and Albert County coroner Doctor Suther
Murray were the chief witnesses. Doctor Addy said that as a
bacteriologist, he was often called upon to analyze blood and
other stains. He said he had found definite bloodstains on
the sharp edge of axe No. 1, the one found in Father
McAuley's bedroom, but no blood was detected in stains on
Collins' clothing, nor was there blood on the second axe found
in the oatbin in Father McAuley's barn. He said he could not
state positively the age of the stains.

"Can you state approximately?"

"Not after a certain length of time, say forty-eight hours."

Solicitor General Jones drew his attention to another
stain on the axe, white in colour.

"I think it was put on after the bloodstains," the witness
said, "because the blood is partially obscured by the white
stain." A piece of wood from the smashed closet door panel
in the priest's room was produced. He said the white stain
on the axe was similar in colour to the paint on the door, but
he would not like to account for it, as that would require a
chemical test, which was out of his line.

In cross-examination, Doctor Addy said he had found only
one bloodstain on the axe.

"How can this stain be produced?" asked McKeown, referring to the axe.

"It can be produced by sinking the axe in any flesh with blood in it."

"For instance, if you sink it into a piece of beef, will it produce the same stain?"

"It would. We tell human blood from other blood by the size of the corpuscles, measuring them with an instrument for that purpose. When the blood dries up, these corpuscles shrink in size, and it is only when the bloodstains are fresh that we can tell them apart."

"Then you couldn't tell whether the blood on the axe is the blood of an ox or a man?"

"No, I could not."

Prosecutor Skinner asked the doctor to clarify his remarks about the sequence of the wounds.

"From the stains on the axe," he replied, "I would think that the cut on the brain was done first. Judging from those stains, I would not think that the throat had been cut first."

Asked about decomposition, he said that heat and air conditions had much to do with it. Many circumstances have a bearing, and it could be hastened by extreme temperature. "That is," Skinner added, "if the extreme temperature is proven."

Doctor Addy said it would take about six hours for a dead body to cool and, after cooling, a state of rigidity sets in. At the end of twenty-four hours this was well defined, and at the end of forty-eight hours decomposition generally starts. The temperature has a great deal to do with conditions, as a warm temperature would tend to hasten decomposition. A stout person would decompose sooner than a thin or emaciated person.

Doctor Murray was called to the stand. He recounted his examination of the body, and described the wounds.

"Would the axe marked 'No. 1' make such a wound?" Skinner asked.

"The marks on the axe would indicate that the wound was as deep as the blood mark upon the blade. Such a wound would cause death."

"Would death be instantaneous or would the person linger?"

"I think it would mean death within a few minutes."

Doctor Murray said when the throat was cut, the arteries on one side were severed deeper than on the other. "I think the throat was cut before the body was placed in the pit."

He said when he first saw the body Wednesday morning, August 22, death had taken place about forty-eight hours before; decomposition had already started.

Cross-examined by McKeown, he said rigidity had not passed away when he first saw the body, it being noticeable in the limbs. The wound in the head would cause death in from eight to sixteen minutes, and if the throat had been cut within that time the deceased would probably still have been alive.

5.

The expert testimony completed for the time being, the prosecution began to weave, piece-by-piece, the circumstantial web in which it hoped to snare Collins, calling to the stand one after another over the next four days, the people Collins had encountered as he made his way from New Ireland to Lake Utopia. The defence, meanwhile, persisted in its attempt to draw an unflattering portrait of the New Ireland area and its people. Some of Father McAuley's neighbours confirmed stories they had heard about the burglary at the rectory, and about a pedlar who had been beaten and robbed of his wares.

"Don't you know," McKeown said to Michael Teahan, "of a certain pedlar having gone a certain distance through New Ireland this summer laden with fairly valuable goods and having disappeared, and never heard of again?"

"I have heard only hearsay."

Skinner objected to having hearsay reported, but Judge Gregory allowed the questioning to continue. If there were blunders made by his court, he said, he would rather they be in favour of the prisoner.

Teahan said he had heard of the pedlar incident some time last summer. "I think it was in July."

"Did you hear of the name of any certain people in New Ireland connected with the disappearance? I don't want to know who they are and am not going to ask."

Skinner objected again, saying it was an attack on the whole of the people there. Judge Gregory suggested the question be rephrased.

"Can you," McKeown asked, "give us the names of any people in New Ireland said to be connected with that disappearance?"

"Yes, by common hearsay," Teahan replied.

McKeown next asked Sarah Williamson to admit that Tom Collins had visited her house on different occasions the week before the murder only to get liquor. "Didn't you know what he came to your house for?"

"No, I didn't ask him."

"Don't you know that he came to your house to get some liquor?"

"He did not," said Sarah. "I didn't have any liquor."

When McKeown said nothing further, Skinner rose and asked Sarah, "He didn't ask you for any liquor?"

"He did not."

"He got none from you nor any member of your family?"

"No, we do not keep liquor at our house."

On Friday afternoon, the court was jammed once again, this time to hear the evidence of Sarah's stepdaughter, Mabel, who had taken over housekeeping duties at the rectory following the murder, and who had found the missing axe believed to be the weapon. The upper and lower galleries were crowded, with all seats occupied, while many other spectators stood in the aisles. A reporter noted that Collins by now seemed to be enjoying the proceeding.

Dark-haired and pretty, Mabel was the sixteen-year-old daughter of William Williamson and his first wife. She had returned to New Ireland early in December to run Father McAuley's household. It was an unusually mild Christmas season and, on December 27, Mabel had opened a window to air the priest's bedroom. A stiff breeze blew in, and she noticed that the linen splasher hanging above the commode was rumpled. She ran her palm over the fabric to straighten it, and a hard object behind the cloth bumped against the wall. Gripping it, she knew immediately it was an axe. She pulled it out, held it up, and looked at it for a long time. Then she put it back.

When Father McAuley returned from the church, Mabel had asked, "Did you keep an axe in your room?"

"No," he said.

"Well, I found one," she said.

She had led him down the hall to the bedroom and pulled the axe from behind the washstand. Father McAuley looked it over. "It's my axe alright," he said, and put it back. Later that afternoon, he had sent word to Detective Killen in Saint John that the long-sought axe had been found.

Judge Gregory, listening intently to Mabel's testimony, expressed surprise that the axe had not been found earlier.

"How long had you been at Father McAuley's before you made the discovery?" he asked.

"A little over three weeks."

"Are you there now?" he asked.

"No, sir, I'm here," said Mabel, prompting a burst of laughter from the galleries.

"It seems strange to me," the judge persisted, "that you were there four weeks, attending to Father McAuley's room, dusting and cleaning this commode, and did not happen in some way to strike the axe. Does it not appear strange to you that you did not find it before then?"

"Yes, sir, it does, but I didn't."

"Is it your belief that although you were there three weeks and did not see the axe, that it was there all the time?" Judge Gregory asked.

"Yes, sir, I think it was all the time."

McKeown was also curious why the axe had not turned up sooner. "Don't you think Detective Killen would have found the axe if he had made a thorough search of the room?"

"I should think he would," Mabel replied. She said that though she had been cleaning the room, she had not moved the furniture.

"But if you had been looking for anything in the room," said McKeown, "you would have found it, don't you think?"

"Yes, I think I would. I would move everything in the room."

"One last question, Miss Williamson. If there had been any wet blood on the axe when it was placed there, it would have left a trace, would it not?"

"Yes," said Mabel, "but there is no blood on the splasher, for I examined it thoroughly."

The trial continued into the weekend and it began to look as if it would take most of the following week. The circumstantial case against Collins continued to build, but it was not clear what line of defence would be laid out. McKeown's associate, Jim Sherren, told a reporter that a number of witnesses would give evidence on Collins' behalf. Albert jeweller Peter LeBlanc described the watch he had repaired for Mary Ann in April. It was a six-sided American Waltham seven-jewelled model in a gold hunting case. The initial "M" was engraved in Roman on the outside cover, and on the inside was the initial "M" again, along with the full name "McAuley" in French script.

The stains on the blade of the McAuley axe were widely discussed, and it was passed around the jury box. McKeown, who had brought a strong lens for close inspection of the blade, handed the instrument to the jurors. "That paint looks as if it had been put on with a brush," one of the jurymen remarked. Judge Gregory said it didn't look like paint at all, rather as if the blade had been dabbed into a ball of putty. He added that until it was proven what the stain on the blade was, the jury was free to form its own opinions.

Father McAuley's commode, meanwhile, was beginning to figure so strongly in the case that McKeown suggested it be brought to the courthouse. The solicitor general said arrangements had already been made with Detective Killen to bring it down from New Ireland, along with the broken closet doors. At this point, Father McAuley's ninety-pound Newfoundland dog, nails clicking loudly on the hardwood floor, came ambling into the courtroom, passing in front of the judge's bench. As if it were a signal, Judge Gregory chose the moment to adjourn proceedings until Monday. On Sunday the judge relaxed as a guest at the Riverside home of former New Brunswick lieutenant-governor, Senator A. R. McLelan.

6.

It wasn't until Tuesday morning, a full week after the opening of the trial, that Saint John police detective Patrick Killen, was called to the stand. There was a great deal of interest in what he would have to say about the murder weapon and how he might have missed it in his searches. The two closet doors with the broken panels from the rectory were produced, along with the commode and illustrations depicting the location of the axe. Killen described the pursuit and capture of the accused. The night of the capture, he said, he had warned the prisoner that he need not say anything, and that everything he did say would be used in evidence against him. Collins made a statement the next morning, he said, but the warning had not been repeated. When McKeown objected to the statement being read in court, Skinner said he would not press the point. He conceded it was doubtful the statement would be admissable, since Collins had not been warned immediately before making it.

Killen: I came up to the house to look for the axe on the seventh of November, I think it was, Sheriff Lynds and I. We got to the house about three o'clock in the evening, I think. The sheriff had a key that opened the east door of the outside kitchen or woodshed, and after we got in there he told me there was a key in one of the rafters that would open the kitchen door. I found it and opened the kitchen door and went in, and all the other doors were open to us after we got there. We went in there, went through the house, looked all through it, and particularly the priest's bedroom. I searched the bedroom and didn't find anything in there. I looked in the closet. I looked behind what they call the bureau, more of a chest of drawers than a bureau. I looked under the bed and lifted the mattress up off the bed. I have no knowledge whatever of ever looking or seeing that commode. We went out of there and went into the basement, and we searched the basement.

It was snowing pretty hard up there, and the sheriff was going home again after we got through, so I asked him to drive me to the house I was going to stop at, and he drove me to Mr. John Duffy's, and I stayed there all night. The next morning I got Mr. Duffy, an old man, to come to the house with me, and I searched the pit where the body was found, and the shed. There was a big pile of shingles there and an old pickaxe, and I took the pickaxe and hauled over the pile of shingles, and I looked underneath the floor that was in the shed, and I didn't get any trace of an axe there.

I went to go to the barn then, and I found the barn was locked, and I had no key. It was one of those hasps that goes on with four screws. I went into the priest's office, and in a drawer I found a screwdriver, and I came out and unscrewed the hasp off the door and went in, Mr. Duffy and I. I searched the lower floor of the barn, the stalls, looked down the closets — there was two closets in the barn. I went into the hayloft and searched around there. Took a hay fork that was there and upset the hay, and got no trace of it. I had my own electric lamp with me, and coming down the stairs there was the grain boxes there, one quite large and the other not so large. The big one had a cover on and was locked, and the small one had no cover on it. It was very dark.

I was coming down at the foot of the stairs, and I put my lamp down in the oat box or grain box, and standing right up in the corner of the box, in the lefthand corner as you face the box, I found an axe standing right up and down straight in the corner. I took it up and looked at it, and it answered the description of the axe I was after. I didn't know of any other axe being there. I made up my mind I had the axe. So I took it out and showed it to Mr. Duffy; and Mr. Duffy wanted to see the room where the doors was broken, and I took him into the room and he looked at the doors, and we went out and locked the house and started for home.

Killen, believing he had the murder weapon, took the axe back to Saint John where it was tested for bloodstains. He didn't return to New Ireland until late December, when Father McAuley notified him that Mabel Williamson had found the second axe behind the bedroom commode.

"I went down into the cellar again that day," Killen told the court. "I had heard that the throat was cut, and I thought that there might be a knife or razor. There is a hot-air furnace in the cellar, and I hit the tin pipes, thinking if there was anything in them it would jump and rattle. But I found nothing. I went around the wood pit again that day, me and another man. There was a lot of cordwood in it then. We searched the place and then piled the cordwood up."

In his cross-examination, McKeown wanted to know why Killen had no recollection of the commode being in the priest's bedroom when he had first searched the premises.

"I don't know. All the other things are as plain to me as you are. But I have no recollection of seeing the commode."

"And you made what you considered to be a thorough search of the room?"

"I have to say that I came out of the room believing that the axe wasn't in the room."

"You are an experienced and skilful searcher, aren't you?"

"Well, I don't know. You might say I had more luck than skill."

"You do a great deal of searching?"

"Yes, I do all the searching, or help to do it, nearly, that is done in our town." Killen said he had been in the police service since 1891, and had a great deal of experience searching for missing goods.

"I would give a great deal," he told McKeown, "to have the credit of finding the axe, and I would be willing to work the rest of the year without any pay to have the credit. I was sure when I left the room that I had made a thorough search for the axe."

A new technical witness, Prof. W.W. Andrews of Mount Allison University in Sackville, was called to analyze the stains found on the axe. A graduate of Toronto University, Andrews had been professor of chemistry and physics at Mount Allison for seventeen years. He provided long, elaborate, detailed testimony, aimed at tying the blood-stained McAuley axe to the cuts in the closet doors. But, though he was able to say the paint on the axe and the door were similar, he could not say with certainty that the cuts in the door panel had been made by the McAuley axe.

"Is it paint on the axe?" Judge Gregory asked.

"There is no question about that."

"In what respects does it correspond with, or differ from, the paint on the door?"

"It seems with this limited means of testing to be the same kind of paint."

McKeown attempted to draw a line under the professor's unwillingness to state explicitly that the paint on the axe had come from the closet door.

"So far as the identity of what you saw on the axe and what you saw on the door is concerned," he said, "except that both contain lead, that is all you can say about it?"

"Yes; both have iron and both have lead and similar tint of colour."

"You could make no tests to unquestionably affirm or disaffirm the identity of the paint on each?"

"You mean by that, paint of the same mixing?"

"Yes."

"To make an absolute test would be impossible, because two samples might be the same. We would have to go the whole round of everything that was commonly used in paints, but we have not material enough on the axe to do work of that sort."

"And you did not?"

"No."

"And therefore you can't say they are the same?"

"Oh no. They are strongly similar."

Pointing to the large cut in the hall closet door, McKeown asked, "Supposing that cut had been made with an axe that had been smeared with blood and had not been wiped off, and was made within fifteen minutes, and was the first stroke made by the axe, would you not in a stroke like that expect to find some indications of blood on the door?"

"I certainly should," Professor Andrews replied, but he added he had not been asked to test the door for the presence of blood.

Andrews was on the stand about an hour. Collins displayed no more than usual interest in the proceedings. He watched closely at times, seemed indifferent at others, his demeanour not unlike that of a spectator who had little at stake in the outcome.

7.

Father McAuley was recalled. He said that of the six razors in his possession, two had been taken from the rectory. One was found in the stolen valise, the other was still missing. When Skinner pointed out that Collins had taken a razor to William Williamson to be sharpened and that Williamson had loaned him one of his own, the priest said he had no knowledge of Collins' razors.

"Up to the time when the axe was discovered behind the commode," said Skinner, "did you ever see it or have any knowledge of it — brought in contact with it in any way, directly or indirectly?"

"No way whatever," the priest replied, "and, I think, I'm pretty sure the last time I remember seeing that axe was the time when I went out to show the prisoner how to split a stick of wood."

"And you feel sure you never saw it until the housekeeper discovered it behind the commode?"

"Quite certain, quite certain."

"Did you have any knowledge at all, one way or the other, of anybody, so to speak, having or seeing or doing anything to that axe, painting it or anything at all, from first to last?"

"No knowledge whatever."

McKeown's associate, Jim Sherren, asked Father McAuley whether he had been using his bedroom and the commode since moving back to the rectory in November. He replied that he had.

"Would you," said Sherren, "give me the name of the person who was suspected of burglarizing your house?"

"Suspected?" said Father McAuley.

"You told us there was a burglary committed at your house and suspicion pointing to someone. Will you give us the name of the person suspected?"

"Well, I don't say it myself."

"You knew of it?"

"I knew of it being said."

"Did you know the name of the person mentioned?"

"Oh, I know the party very well."

"A neighbour of yours?"

"Neighbour."

"Live in that district?"

"Lives in that district."

"There was a party, a neighbour of yours also connected with a pedlar being robbed — there was a mention of that thing?"

"Oh ... " Father McAuley hesitated.

"Well, it was mentioned?" Sherren persisted. "Reported around?"

"Yes, reported around."

"That was also a neighbour? Handy to you?"

"Yes, it was."

"Those neighbours of yours would know if you were out of New Ireland? They would know whether you were holding church there on Sunday or in your other missions?"

"Yes, they would know that alright, but wouldn't know when I would be away or back."

"When you didn't have church in New Ireland they would know you were in some other part of your mission?"

"In some other part of my mission."

"Your districts lying so far apart you would never get home before Monday next, or very seldom?"

"Well, the long days in summer I would get home Sunday evening if not stopped somewhere else."

Sherren asked whether, on the the weekend the murder occurred, people in New Ireland knew that he would not return to his home until the following Wednesday.

"I don't know it was known to all the people," he replied. "It was known to the housekeeper."

"You didn't give the name of this neighbour who it was suspected burglarized your house," said Sherren. "An entrance was forced, was it not?"

"Entrance was forced by a back window looking out into the shed."

"Who was suspected of that?"

"I didn't suspect him," Father McAuley replied.

"Who was the party," Sherren persisted, "the housekeeper and the neighbours there fixed on as the person who was guilty?"

Skinner intervened, though he did not offer a formal objection to the line of questioning. "It does seem," he said, "where a party that someone would start a rumour against, where the witness has no knowledge of the matter at all, to have a man's name brought into court, might do a man a great deal of injury and might be very unjust. If they press Father McAuley for a name, he will have to give it, unless I object. But I will not go that far if they choose to stain any person's character."

Sherren did not relent. "Well, Father McAuley, will you give us the name of the party?"

"In the first place," replied the priest reluctantly, "I said here now that I never accused the party whom other people talk about."

"I understand that."

"If you want the name, the name is John Duffy."

"How far from your place does John Duffy live?"

"About a mile or so, maybe a little less. He's the postmaster."

"Is it not at John Duffy's place this pedlar was supposed to have been robbed?"

"That is another Duffy, Patrick Duffy, right opposite."

"They are brothers, are they?"

"No, they are cousins."

"Tell us as near as you can what the circumstances connected with the pedlar business were?"

Skinner intervened once more. "If he knows any circumstance I am not going to object. But he must not tell circumstances of which he hasn't any knowledge."

"He is not asking what he knows," said Judge Gregory, "but what he knows to have been said — reports."

"As far as I am concerned personally," said the priest, "I know nothing as regards that. If you want hearsay, there may be different versions."

Sherren began another question, but was cut off by Skinner's objection.

"There can't be any objection taken to the form of the question," said Judge Gregory, "he is being cross-examined. If you wish to shut it out altogether, that doesn't go to form."

"When the question he proposes to ask," Skinner argued, "is something like drawing up the indictment of a man who is not here to to defend himself, I think it is using the court for purposes that are not legitimate. But I am not going to object."

"Ask your question in any form you like," said the judge.

"Did you ever hear this version?" asked Sherren. "That a pedlar came to this Duffy's, who was a neighbour of yours, not very far away; that he stayed there overnight; that he had his travelling kit with him and left the house in the morning, and going to the next house he found quite a large number of articles had been taken; that he returned to the Duffy's wanting the articles to be restored; that he was beaten almost to endanger his life; is that, or not, a version circulated in that district?"

"Well, I didn't hear it altogether that way," said Father McAuley. "I heard something about a watch being taken from him, and that a woman had struck him with a stone on the head."

"Did you hear anything else?"

"Duffy asked the man to pay for his horse that night, and himself and his breakfast, and I did hear the person partially objected and ... "

"A quarrel arose?"

"Well, I can't say what kind of quarrel, but the pedlar ..."

"The pedlar got hurt?"

"Well, that was said. Some said he didn't get hurt at all."

"And it is also reported, is it not, that the pedlar lost some of his goods?"

"Reported."

"You heard that goods were lost that time?"

"I heard nothing more than about the watch, that some party had taken a gold watch, or losing the watch."

"And he was badly beaten?"

"I didn't hear that exactly, but somebody struck him with a stone."

"Did you ever make any investigation as to who had burglarized your house?"

"None."

"And rumour in your district connected those two Duffy families who are almost neighbours of yours with those two things?"

"Yes."

"Did your housekeeper ever express a dislike for living in that district?"

"Well, not to me."

"Have you heard that she had?"

"Well, no. Other people have said it is a very lonely place."

"It is lonely. Is that all?"

"That is all I recollect. She seemed to be quite satisfied there, so far as I ever knew. She always considered it a healthy place and got good health there."

"Evidently," Sherren mused, "it wasn't a very healthy place."

"It is healthy alright in the way I mean," countered Father McAuley, "a good place for consumptives."

Sherren was finished, but Skinner had a further question about the pedlar affair. "You were going to tell something a little while ago concerning this pedlar business and Duffy, and counsel stopped you telling it."

"After the affair," said the priest, "I heard the pedlar had gone away, and he went to the mail driver's house, Thomas Campbell; either got his wagon or his horse to drive. I heard he went to John Connors and Connors wouldn't give him any law, and he proceeded to Elgin and got no law there, and then went to Moncton. Said he would go to see his brother in business there. The pedlar remained in Moncton, and his brother came back for his horse and goods that he'd left at Thomas Campbell's. He'd left them there on the ground, seemed to act very strangely. Thomas Campbell took charge

of his goods and put them away. And as far as I could hear
he came back, this brother from Moncton, about two or three
days afterwards, and got the goods and got the horse and
wagon and returned."

"That is the whole story as you heard it?"

"That is about it."

"I mean the rumours?"

"The rumours; different versions of it."

"There may have been some little difficulty among them
— you don't know?"

"Don't know," said Father McAuley, "but as far as any
theft was done, I don't believe it at all."

"But they started with the idea of doing away with the
pedlar?" asked Skinner.

"Well, doing away means different things. Disappearing
is, I think, the word that was used."

"There is no pretense the pedlar was killed?"

"Oh no, he disappeared himself."

Father McAuley said the Duffy family was very decent,
the whole of them; some of his best people, honest and
upright in every way. Kate Duffy, his former housekeeper,
was a cousin of John and a sister of Patrick, the two men
mentioned in the rumours.

Sherren was on his feet again, asking how John Duffy's
name could have been connected with the burglary if he was
such an honest man of good reputation. Skinner objected to
the question. "I think it is improper to go to work and try a
man who is not here." But Judge Gregory was also curious.
"How do you account for it?" he asked the priest.

"Well, I don't know how to account for it exactly, for my
part," said Father McAuley. "I said about stuff being taken;
don't know who took it."

"The rest is what gossipers chose to say about it?"

"Chose to say about it, and there it is."

He denied that Mary Ann had ever told a neighbour that
she was glad she had not been home on the day of the
robbery, as she didn't know what might have happened to
her. "I never heard that, and I don't believe she ever expressed herself so to one of the neighbours."

(A month later, Stipendiary Magistrate Charles Morris of Harvey came to the defence of the Duffy name in a letter published on the front page of the *Albert Journal*. Morris wrote that it was because of his advice that the incident involving the pedlar had stood in a mysterious light in the county, thus allowing Collins' attorneys to bring it up "as a side issue in the defence of an atrocious murderer." As a result, "I feel it is my duty to Mr. Duffy to place the matter in its true light before the public."

One day last summer, he wrote, a "foreign pedlar" spent the night at Patrick Duffy's house. The next morning the man attempted to sell some of his goods to Duffy's brother, Edward, who "through mischief, made fun of his goods and called them nothing but trash." The angered pedlar became so abusive that Patrick asked him to pay for the keep of himself and his horse — an uncustomary breach of New Ireland hospitality — then to get off his property. This further enraged the pedlar, who not only refused to pay, but accused Patrick of stealing his goods.

Was the unfortunate trader then thrashed? Morris put it this way in his letter: "If the pedlar was insulted, consider the fact of an honest upright man being charged in his own house with theft, and if he took the law on the spur of the moment in his own hands, would it be considered a grave crime?" However it may have been, the pedlar hightailed it to a local magistrate and demanded law, charging Patrick Duffy with theft and assault. The magistrate declined, saying the charge was preposterous. But when Duffy heard what the pedlar was up to, he drove immediately to Morris and asked for a warrant to have the man arrested for publicly slandering him.

Morris' advice had been for Duffy, who was in "an excited state of mind," to waste neither time nor money over what a foreign pedlar was saying about him. "He was too well known for it to have any effect, and every person who knew him would brand it a lie and an absurdity." It was good advice at the time, said Morris, and, unfortunately as it now turned out, Duffy had heeded it and had let the matter drop.

As for the slur that New Ireland was a land of illicit stills
and moonshiners, Morris added in his letter, neither Patrick
Duffy, an honest and industrious man of about forty years,
nor his eighty-year-old father, an upright man who had lived
all his life in New Ireland and who sired a large and respectable family, had ever tasted "illicit whiskey or any other kind
of liquor.")

8.

With Father McAuley's second appearance, the prosecution
case was complete. But, in a surprising move, McKeown
announced the defence would call no witnesses, and suggested to the bench that he should have the right to address
the jury last. Judge Gregory disagreed. McKeown asked for
an adjournment so he could consult with his associate. He
returned after the recess to deliver, for two hours and thirty
minutes, his address to the jury. The reporters thought it "a
splendid plea on behalf of the prisoner, forceful and impressive." Collins sat through it flushed, anxious, apparently
concerned now. He leaned back in his chair, resting his head
for a time on the rear rail of the dock, then leaned forward,
chin in hand, the indifference he had been displaying
through the week noticeably absent.

"At times," one of the reporters wrote, "Collins smiled at
acquaintances in the room, but the smile was without the
genuineness shown earlier in the week, while his eager
watchfulness of the court proceedings occupied his entire
attention. For the greater part of the time, his right hand
covered the lower part of his face, but his keen grey eyes,
brightened by the nervous strain now becoming apparent,
followed every movement and gesture of the speakers."

The courtroom was packed to the point of discomfort,
every seat occupied, every inch of standing room bearing a
human body. Rising to begin, McKeown had in his hand a
piece of paper which, he said, was a letter from the superintendent of Christ Church Sunday school in Liverpool,
England, relating to the accused. He said he would not read
the letter unless counsel for the crown consented. Skinner
balked. McKeown, feigning surprise, remarked that when he

conducted cases for the crown, he never objected to anything going to the jury which would tell in favour of the accused. Skinner relented, saying it could be read, along with another from the manager of a Liverpool club, as long as the letters of inquiry from the defence counsel were entered as well. Both letters spoke favourably of Collins' character.

McKeown based his argument on six essential points: that Collins, admittedly a thief, had no motive to kill Mary Ann McAuley, and in fact had had an amiable relationship with the woman; that the circumstantial evidence in this case, not least because motive had not been proven, was insufficient to convict; that the forensic evidence did not prove that the woman could not still have been alive when Collins left New Ireland early Monday morning; that the crown had not been able to rule out the possibility that someone else (especially in light of earlier burglaries at the rectory) could not have committed the murder; that, if Collins had killed Mary Ann that morning and then hidden the axe before leaving the rectory and meeting Harbell and the others, he could not have failed to get bloodstains on the cloth behind the commode; and that, in any event, when he did leave he did not behave in the manner of a man who had just committed murder.

"It is essential that motive be established," McKeown argued, "and the evidence must show not only that the circumstances were consistent with the accused having committed the crime, but that no other person might have committed the crime. I do not think any among you believe that the prisoner committed the crime to cover up a theft. It is a terrible thing to commit a murder, and it would require a long servitude in crime to qualify one of us for that offence. The great law authorities have put motive in the very forefront of the considerations which govern circumstantial evidence. However strongly circumstances may weigh against the prisoner, there must be some motive. Have we any motive here? The crown has spared no efforts in its laudable desire to inflict punishment for this offence, but in the mass of evidence presented has there been anything of motive? The parties who saw Miss McAuley and the prisoner at the lake fishing, who saw them at their home, and Father McAuley himself, testify that their relationships were amiable and friendly.

"If this boy were a murderer at heart, it will occur to you that there were many better opportunities. Murder is a crime which lends itself to darkness. There are degrees in crime, and no man guilty of the crime of murder, fleeing for his life, would seek the highway and carry a few soiled clothes and generally act as the prisoner did. A man who puts his hand upon that sacred citadel of another's life, does he go up and down, as this boy did, before the house of his victim, when, for all he knew, neighbours might at any time drop in and discover the corpse of his victim? Murders do not walk the highways back and forth, but as Cain of old, flee as from the avenging angel and from their fellowmen. Would any sane man, who had committed murder, travel from house to house and into public houses, in one of which he sings, dances and plays the piano?"

McKeown said it was an "awful and sinister fact that the axe was not found until three months after the tragedy. I don't believe that any man, just after he had committed murder, would want to hide his axe when there lay the body of his victim. What to him is the axe, when the mangled body lies a few yards away? Where are we arriving at in this most mysterious case? Piece these things together. Remember there were no bloodstains on the boy's clothing. Remember that he acted like a thief, but not like a murderer. Remember the stains on the axe. When all these circumstances are considered, I do not know how you can find him guilty."

It was ten minutes before five o'clock in the afternoon when McKeown finished his plea to the jury, but there was no thought of bringing the court to adjournment. Skinner stood immediately and began to address the panel on behalf of the crown. He would orate for three hours, not including a break for supper. "The peroration," it was written later, "was one of the most eloquent ever delivered in a New Brunswick court."

Skinner told the jury that McKeown had greatly exaggerated certain points about circumstantial evidence, and had laid too much stress on the need to establish a motive. "The prisoner told the priest the housekeeper had been nagging at him, and this in itself might provide a motive. While it has not been proven that the prisoner knew Miss McAuley was going to have him discharged, still this might also be a motive. The hand that would lift the axe and plunge it into that poor woman's brain could do anything. There was nothing too bad, nothing too outrageous for that hand to do. There is no hard and fast rule with regard to circumstantial evidence; every case stands upon its own merits, and there are many cases in which, if you could not convict on circumstantial evidence, you could not convict at all. If the doctrine of circumstantial evidence was that laid down by Mr. McKeown, the country would be rampant with murder and nobody convicted. There was never a crime committed, but that someone else might have done it. But does it follow that because someone else might have done it, the one found guilty is not guilty?"

Skinner argued that the murder could have been done much earlier than daybreak, so the blood had time to dry on the axe blade. "The facts go to show that he spent the night there and gathered the things he took with him after she was dead, for how would it be possible for the prisoner to commit the breaking in of the doors if Miss McAuley were still alive? The stealing and breaking must necessarily have been done after the murder." He sneered at the claim that somebody came and killed her after Collins had left. "The defence got up the pedlar story — which might rightfully have been objected to, although I allowed it to go — and forced it on the jury to show that someone in the neighbourhood might have come in and killed Mary Ann. But is not that an absurd claim? There is not a particle of proof to show that different persons committed the different crimes in the McAuley home. There is no evidence of anyone being there after the prisoner left, except the deaf man who found the horse wandering the next day."

Skinner went on to say that "we know nothing about the habits and characteristics of this young man. Mr. McKeown contends that Collins had only tried to get away because he stole. I believe Collins stole those things and then ran away because the housekeeper had been already ushered into the great beyond. We must deal with the facts as we have them. Collins was very near the border when arrested, which leads us to believe that he was trying to get out of the country, but was having difficulty on account of lack of money. The defence has argued that his behaviour shows him to be a thief, not a murderer. I think it goes to show the murder was the primary thing, and the theft secondary. Surely the conflicting stories were told to cover a more atrocious deed than a robbery. Do you think it possible that any living man could go through the string of lies he did only to cover up a little stealing?" He decried McKeown's insinuation that there was something sinister in the axe being found where it was. "The detective admits he was not entirely careful in making the search, and that he did not look behind the commode. There is no evidence to warrant the conclusion that the commode was purposely overlooked, as all the searchers had been very sincere in their desire to find the axe. The axe was discovered there and that is the whole story about it."

9.

For more than ninety minutes the next morning, Judge Gregory presented his charge to the jury, speaking strongly against the innocence of Tom Collins. He seemed convinced that Collins had smashed the closet doors of the rectory, had committed the thefts, and had killed Mary Ann in order to get away. During the recitation from the bench, which an incredulous McKeown interrupted twice to question points made by the judge, Collins sat in the dock with his head tipped back, watching Gregory's every movement and gesture. His face was pale and his lips tightly compressed. Not for a moment did he turn his eyes away from the bench.

The room once more was packed. Every inch of standing room was taken, and many spectators from outside the village had brought their lunches with them so they could retain their seats through the adjournment. When the jury retired shortly after noon, the court officials had to clear one of the upper galleries for them, crowding other parts of the building even more. The attendance of women was especially large, and a number of clergymen had also taken an interest, among them Rev. Mr. McNintch of Surrey, Rev. Mr. Warden of Hopewell, Rev. I.N. Parker and Rev. Z.L. Fash, both of Hillsborough.

Leaning forward from his high perch behind the bench, Judge Gregory's voice rolled out into the still room.

Gregory: The time has come when we must discharge our duties in regard to this most serious and solemn case. I am entirely free from any desire to reach either a conviction or an acquittal, and I hope you, the jury, hold the same attitude. You are bound by your oaths — you as jurymen, I as judge — to do this. Being chosen to ascertain the facts, being chosen to hear the evidence, and from it exercise your very best judgment in determining and pronouncing what are the facts, you will see how necessary it is that you should clear your minds of all motives, of all bias, of all disposition to give effect to anything else than that which has been told to you in evidence, under the solemnity of the oath by the witness. You should do your duty with solemnity, with responsibility, and, without fear and upon the evidence adduced, say whether or not the prisoner is guilty of the murder of Mary Ann McAuley.

I want to consider the nature of circumstantial evidence. In some cases, it is possible to have witnesses who can give direct evidence of having seen the crime, but these cases are very few, in comparison with the cases that are proven by circumstantial evidence. The value of testimony is estimated differently. Cases proved by circumstantial evidence leave more duty for the jury. You must draw natural inferences, and must not avoid drawing them simply because you wish not to. This case that we have before us is one that is to be passed upon on circumstantial evidence, but in my opinion, circumstantial evidence of such a character that violent presumptions arise from the facts that are proved, and about which there can be no doubt. They are not presumptions for which you have to look abroad and grope, as it were, in darkness to draw your inferences, but I think the facts that are proved will give you no great difficulty in applying your reason to them, and drawing from them the natural and necessary presumptions that properly appertain.

The prisoner's counsel has sought to show the prisoner did not strike the fatal blow, but that somebody else did. However, he did not tell you how you could conjecture that anyone else had committed the crime, and circumstances fail to tell who else could do it. He argues that another man may have called at the McAuley home on the day the murder was committed. Where is there any room for the slightest conjecture that anyone else was there, when everything that was missing from the house was found on the prisoner?

When the prisoner conceived the idea of stealing, we cannot tell; nor can we tell when he conceived the idea of murder, if he is guilty of that awful crime. It is immaterial which crime he committed first, although it is my opinion that he first committed the murder, if he did that deed, with the intention of robbery. Considerable stress has been laid by the counsel for the defence on the subject of motive, but I believe there was abundant proof of motive. The criminal needs no stronger motive than that of escaping. If Collins committed the crime of stealing when Miss McAuley was still alive, what stronger motive could he have for committing the murder?

The closet doors have been produced. One use the axe has been put to, I think, has been made pretty clear. It seems to me so. It is as you may think, namely, to beat down or batter in the panels of those two doors. We then have the admission and the proved fact that this man pillaged the place and carried off his booty. Not very much, not as much as he was looking for, not as much as he would have found if he had taken time and gone further, because there was some left behind that would have been perhaps the most valuable to him of all; but we have him beating down the closet doors searching for booty, and booty he carried off, and he is confessedly a thief, and in the commission of that deed he must have had the axe in his own hand. He is the man; must be the man, I would judge. It is for you to say if you can see any other inference from it. You then have him with the weapon causing death in his hands and working and using it, and that, apparently, after the bloodstain got upon the axe by the dealing of the foul blow to the deceased.

It is to the evidence you are to look for your doubts if you are to find any. Do not dishonour your intellects by imagining any doubts, unless you can point to some part of the evidence on which they may rest. However, you cannot doubt that that axe found behind the commode was the one that did the murdering, because the marks show it. You cannot doubt it is the one that broke in the doors, and you cannot doubt but what the prisoner broke in the doors. The prisoner used the axe, because he comes confessedly acknowledging himself as a thief, and of the things taken out of those rooms where this breaking of doors was done.

As far as the location of the axe when it was finally found is concerned, I can see no reason why any doubt can be found from that circumstance. It matters little who placed the axe behind the commode. The detective was made shamefaced about it that he had not found it long before; the house was locked up during the interval, and there is nothing in the world that you can put your finger on to throw any light upon the subject. Do not be mystified by nothing. Do not waste your time in thinking and trying to ferret out, as we wasted our time in ferreting out that incident, which I do not know what it furnished to the learned counsel and while it occupied our time in finding it out, we have accomplished nothing more than that something mysterious has happened in getting that axe there, or else that Detective Killen was careless, and everyone else who looked for the axe made a very superficial search.

I have shown you the connection between the use of the axe in the murder and in the theft. I have shown you, and the evidence shows you, that the use of the axe in the theft, was clearly by the admission of the prisoner in his hands. It's my duty only to point out the facts as I see them. No one else has been shown to have been at the McAuley home but the prisoner. Do your duty according to your conscience, exercise your intellect conscientiously so that each of you will be able to say that you have done your duty.

At 2:10 p.m., Thursday, January 24, Judge Gregory took his seat once more on the bench. There was an instant hush. The subdued murmurs which had been rustling through the courtroom, as spectators discussed the possibilities of the case and speculated on the outcome, were silenced as if a switch had been thrown. Sheriff Lynds entered through a door beside the dais. He told Judge Gregory the jury had reached a verdict. Collins was sent for. He entered the court with the constables, his bearing erect, his face flushed, his manner tentative. The *Transcript* observed:

With ruddy cheeks and bright eyes, Collins looked like a school boy prepared by motherly hand to face the sharp frost of a winter's morning. Around his throat was wrapped a long, light grey woollen scarf, his head was covered with a dark cloth cap, and he wore a black overcoat reaching to his knees. His wrists were linked together with steel cuffs and, as he reached the dock, he held out his hands to the attending constable and the manacles were removed. His cap was lifted off, and the scarf removed from around his neck. He was assisted out of his overcoat and took his seat in the chair. He gave to the constable a letter, which was transferred to his counsel.

The sharp touch of frost had brought a warm glow of colour to the cheeks of the prisoner, but in the warmth of the courtroom, his cheeks became pale as during the morning session. He glanced nervously at the judge and, as he took his seat, his eyes wandered for a brief instant to the corner gallery almost above his head. In the meantime, with serious air and downcast eyes, the jury had entered the courtroom. Coming in by the door to the right of the judge's bench, the twelve men who had as with one mind agreed upon the fate of the prisoner, filed across the room and took their place in the jury box which occupies a corner of the floor. Here in the railed enclosure they sat while Collins, with one last quick glance around, dropped into his seat, threw his head back and waited. The quick return of the jury came as a surprise to many. Up to the last days it had been the universal opinion that the jury would disagree, necessitating a new trial. Why this belief was given tolerance, it is impossible to say, but nevertheless it was the general opinion among those who have been closely following the trial.

Clerk of the court M.B. Dixon rose, his voice startling the quiet courtroom.

"Gentlemen of the jury, have you found a verdict, and if so, who will answer for you?"

Harvey Stevens, a farmer from the Hillsborough area, stood in the front row and replied, "We have."

"How is your finding?"

"Guilty."

Collins flinched. His face changed slightly, the flush returning to replace the pallor, but it was the only outward sign of emotion. McKeown was on his feet immediately.

"Your Honour," he declared, "I ask for a crown reserve of this case on the ground that, in your charge to the jury, you committed technical errors. The specific part of the charge to which I object is that in which Your Honour instructed the jury as follows: 'The prisoner's counsel is not bound to show that his client did not do the murder, but he is compelled to show that someone else did it.'"

"I did not so direct the jury," protested Judge Gregory.

"Nobody will admit quicker than Your Honour," McKeown replied, "that if that expression did fall from your lips, it would be incorrect."

"It would."

"Further, in Your Honour's charge, from place to place throughout, Your Honour treated it as a fact fully proven that the prisoner had broken the doors in the house with the axe, and directed the jury from that standpoint."

"I will not assent to your request at this time," said Judge Gregory, "but I will hear you later."

Solicitor General Jones, rising impatiently, asked that the sentence be passed. "Thomas F. Collins, stand up," called the judge. Collins stepped to the front of the dock; one hand reached for the rail as if for support, and stopped; then both hands went behind his back and clasped, and Collins stood calmly awaiting sentence. Judge Gregory's voice broke into the silence which had frozen the room like a stoppage of time.

"You have been tried by a jury of the county, with sufficient hearing of evidence, and a watchful and able defence, and still you have been found guilty of the murder of Mary Ann McAuley, on the twentieth of August last. You have conducted yourself throughout the trial with composure and coolness, which might lead one to think that you, for yourself, either felt innocent and confident of a verdict in your favour, or that you were indifferent and prepared for the worst conclusion, and had steeled yourself to meet it with composure.

"I cannot help saying that I am entirely in accord with the finding of the jury. Your counsel has said all that could possibly be said, not in your favour, for scarcely anything could be said in your favour, but against the conclusiveness of the proof against you. He has watched every word of the testimony with a keenness and an astuteness of which you cannot have a full appreciation, probably, for want of your legal knowledge. He has, by every artifice known to the profession, sought to create or discover a doubt as to your being guilty of this fearful crime. He failed to find, in my opinion and in the opinion of the jury, anything in the course of the case that could raise a presumption or even a hope of a favourable verdict. He failed to find the least evidence that could give rise to doubt about your being the guilty one.

"You have just heard your counsel ask for reservation of the case. That means that he thinks he may argue, and successfully have it held, that in some part of my charge to the jury I committed an error. I would advise you not to hope so much for that as to make your preparation to meet your God. If you do not by virtue of the sentence I am about to give, you will assuredly have at some time to face our God and to answer to Him.

"The sentence of the court is that you be taken hence to the place from which you came, and there kept in close confinement until Thursday, the 25th day of April, and that on that day, you will be hanged by the neck until you are dead. And may God have mercy on your soul."

The words seemed, momentarily at least, devoid of sense, like the syllables of a nonsense rhyme. The congregation sat in frozen time, briefly, silently, dazedly one. Then, as quickly, they began to breathe again.

The *Transcript*:

It was at once a pathetic and solemn scene. The deathly silence of the courtroom was broken by the sound from the gallery of a woman's sob. Tears were flowing from many eyes, while in the surrounding galleries women sobbed audibly. Many men, too, were visibly affected, sitting with heads bowed. Collins was perhaps the most unmoved person present, nor did the slightest outward sign betray the awful import of the sentence. After standing for a few seconds, he stepped back and resumed his seat. He whispered across to his counsel and spoke a few words to Mr. McKeown. Judge Gregory, whose voice had scarcely regained its composure, turned to the jury and thanked them for the able manner in which they had done their duty.

Collins was outwardly composed as he held out his arms to be assisted into his overcoat. He put on his cap, wriggled into the tight-fitting coat, wrapped the long woollen scarf about his neck, and then stretched out his hands for the handcuffs. The gate of the dock opened. He walked steadily out, making one or two remarks to the constables by his side, and with erect bearing passed out the entrance on his way back to the jail. On the path over he smiled, looking backwards over his shoulder, and made one or two laughing remarks to the constables who, one on each side, led him back to the place of confinement.

Silently and with bowed heads, the crowd made its way out of the courtroom and filed away.

Chapter Eleven

The Second and Third Trials, February-October, 1907

1.

Ten days after Tom Collins was sentenced to hang, Father Edward McAuley died of heart failure at New Ireland rectory. It was Sunday, February 3; he was sixty-two. The priest had complained of chest pains since giving his demanding testimony at the trial, but he did not rest from his work and was planning to have service at St. Agatha's the day he died. He was stricken early in the morning and his housekeeper, Mabel Williamson, frightened by the severity of the attack, sent a messenger for Doctor Suther Murray in Albert. The doctor, an old friend of the priest, arrived at 10:00 a.m., but it was too late.

It was generally believed that the strain of the past few months, following the murder of Mary Ann, had much to do with undermining the priest's health, which was not robust at any time. Father John Savage of Moncton, a long-time friend who went to New Ireland to take care of funeral services, said he had no doubt but that the strain occasioned by the tragedy and subsequent events had much to do with Father McAuley's sudden death. "I regarded his return to New Ireland after the tragedy as nothing short of heroic. He had to face conditions there that would daunt many a man. It was difficult for him to secure anyone to stay in the house after all that had taken place there. He had only an old man and a young girl to do the work around the home for him, and yet he laboured on faithfully."

Father Savage said his lifelong friend was a good and faithful and highly esteemed priest. "His whole pastorate had been one full of discouragements. He had laboured to lift up his young people, to show them the ways of a better life, but he never saw the results of his work. As soon as the young people attained manhood and womanhood, they moved away from the New Ireland community, and Father McAuley was never able to see the good effects of his teaching."

Father McAuley was laid to rest beside the grave of his murdered cousin. If Tom Collins, waiting in jail at Hopewell Cape for word on his attorney's latest legal maneouvres, had any thoughts on the demise of his former benefactor, no one has recorded them. The last rites of Father McAuley, Father Savage told a reporter, wrote the last chapter in a tragedy which had shocked and moved an entire province.

But it was far from the last chapter. On February 14, Defence Counsel McKeown appeared at the Supreme Court building in Fredericton to argue his motion to have the conviction of Collins quashed. Six judges sat on the bench, including Judge Gregory, whose direction to the jury contained the contentious points under review. At McKeown's request, Judge Gregory had reserved the case for the Supreme Court to consider three points: "Did I err in not adequately directing and impressing the jury that the whole burden of proving the prisoner's guilt was upon the crown? Was there error in my assuming it proven that the prisoner had the axe in his hand in the committing of the theft, and generally directing the jury from that standpoint? Was there error in directing the jury that the desire of the prisoner to make practicable his theft and escape would be sufficient motive; and if they were satisfied the prisoner was the one who did the killing, there was no need for searching for or proving a motive?"

As it turned out, the decision rendered by the Supreme Court hinged only on the second point. McKeown argued that Judge Gregory's strong charge to the jury, which included the statement that the axe used on the doors was the murder weapon, had been virtually a direction that the prisoner was guilty of the murder. Inasmuch as it was the sole province of the jury to determine, either by direct testimony or by inference drawn from proven facts, whether the prisoner was guilty, it was a misdirection, McKeown argued.

Arguing for the crown, Skinner said that inasmuch as no defence had been laid down for Collins, the judge's charge was simply a fair comment on uncontradicted testimony. The entire defence rested not upon facts tending to dispose of the guilt of the accused, he said, but on McKeown's attempt to raise a fictitious doubt in the minds of the jury. "The prisoner had no defence; his defence was Mr. McKeown's address, and the address, I concede, was a remarkable one in point of ability."

"And," remarked Judge D.L. Hanington from the bench, "I have no doubt a remarkably ingenious one. That was what he was there for."

"Indeed," said Skinner. "Mr. McKeown drew a vivid picture to the jury of their deathbeds, and held up to them that when they came to die, this verdict would stare them in the face and disturb them."

"But," Hanington pointed out to Skinner, "you had the reply."

As the arguments progressed, it became clear from many of the remarks made from the bench, that Collins' chances for a new trial were good. At one point, Judge Gregory was moved to ask his colleagues, "Why don't you just say that *I* found the verdict, and not the jury?" When the Supreme Court decision came down a week later, it was unanimous: Collins must be given a new trial. Chief Justice William Tuck pointed out that Judge Gregory was confined to his home from injuries sustained a short time ago, but that he agreed with the majority opinion and believed the case should go down for a new trial.

The opinion was unequivocal. From the published judgment:

> Throughout his charge, Judge Gregory seems to assume that the prisoner is guilty, and his strong reasoning throughout is to that effect...
>
> He tells the jury that they can not doubt that this (the murder weapon) was the axe that broke in the

doors, that the prisoner broke in the doors, and that the prisoner used the axe. It is wrong, because, first, what the judge asserts was not proved, and, secondly, if there was evidence from which a jury might infer guilt, the facts were not left to them...

There is no evidence by any witness that Collins had the axe in his own hand, nor that he broke down the closet doors...

It is clearly an error that a trial judge should tell a jury not only the inference they must draw, but that there is no doubt as to any important fact or inference from that fact...

He went too far in presuming himself that certain matters were in fact proved, which were material to the case, and should have been left to the jury to determine whether or not they had been proven...

There is no question but that we should order a new trial so that all the facts, without any expression of opinion from the judge, should be left to the jury to find if true or not."

Collins, meanwhile, took quite calmly news of the decision that he had escaped his April date with the hangman. His jailer reported that he handed Collins a paper, and the prisoner read it with no emotion, showing neither approval nor disapproval. Since his incarceration, in fact, Collins had found no fault with his opponents, but he (or someone else) did publicly thank his supporters. A "card of thanks" appeared in the *Albert Journal* early in February, which read, "Thomas F. Collins now incarcerated in jail at Hopewell Cape desires his deepest gratitude conveyed to all who so kindly contributed toward securing additional counsel for him." He was grateful, too, to those who sent him fruit and reading matter. He passed his time reading or drawing or playing the harmonica, on which he could fashion simple tunes. On Feb. 14 he drew a valentine for the jailer's daughter.

2.

Late in February, a poem entitled *The Collins Trial*, penned by "A.E.T.," appeared on the front page of the *Albert Journal*. In fifty blank verse lines arrayed in a rather well-wrought metre, the opposing attorneys stand and argue for the life of the prisoner. The poet sets the scene: "Six days had the shire been crowded with clamoring masses of mortals." Then on the evening of the sixth day, with "darkness unfolding her pinion," McKeown rises to his feet and "intently surveying his hearers ... in tones of deep pathos, appealing, thus spake to the wavering jurors." After reminding them that "two sides has a story, / Although the one side may be crimson, the unseen may be colored still darker," McKeown's general intention seems to be to scare the hell out of them. He's given, among others, these lines: "Behold you the boy in the dock there, with youth on his features imprinted, / Before him the path of a lifetime, Shall you bar it forever against him? / Shall you lay that fair form by yon prison to be marred by oblivion's ravage? / And you haunted by stern apparitions for hastening a soul on its journey?"

But "mercy ne'er usurps justice," and the crown attorney is on his feet, beseeching the jury to acknowledge the "guilt vile and tragic." Says he: "You are not to regard your decision as affecting the prisoner's welfare. / But affecting the welfare of many, hence I warn you not mercy but justice ... Mete forth to the man only justice, untainted by dread or emotion. / The safety of homes depends on you, so therefore consider in candor."

The poem closes with a vivid scene of pervasive silence in a cold courtroom, as a stern judge advises Collins to prepare himself to be punished for his "vile, atrocious" crime. "'Discard every fancy of freedom, commend each fond hope to oblivion, / One door to you now is thrown open, one door which admits to the gallows. / I plead with you, charge you, implore you, prepare now to meet your Creator, / May the God of all wisdom attend you and your undying soul give a welcome.' / Thus the sentence of death was presented in the morning of life — Friend, how solemn."

There was a more prosaic discussion of the case in the pages of the *Journal*. A front-page letter late in March, above the name "New Ireland," in colourful language takes to task the Supreme Court for its decision to grant a new trial, scorning the assertion that the crown had presented only circumstantial evidence. There are many places on the continent, says the writer, where Collins' trial would have been made "quite short and his neck made quite a bit longer in short time."

The letter, evidence of the depth of emotions stirred by the case, continues: "Think of a poor lone woman in the prime of life a mile distant from human aid dropped down in the peace of her own home and at the very door of a Christian church, yes dropped down by blows from an axe in the hands of her assailant as though she was a wild beast in search of prey. The butcher in the slaughter house would show more leniency to the ox he was going to slaughter for the market than was shown to this poor lone woman in the peace of her home, yet the slayer of this woman is awarded a new trial."

The writer berates McKeown for, in an effort to save his client, having broadcast "his trashy pedlar story," thereby injuring the reputation of the whole community, and demands a retraction of his "insinuations" or an apology, "otherwise he will get a chance to have it threshed out in some law court in Albert Co." The letter blames Collins for the death of the priest, who, with his housekeeper, would still be living "happy and well in their comfortable home, had not the arch fiend sent his agent, a demon incarnate in the person of Collins," to destroy it.

The diatribe, containing "some of the most barefaced assertions which I ever saw in print," proved too much to ignore for another correspondent, who signed himself "Justice." His response chides "New Ireland" for posing as a superior "of the learned judges who heard the appeal," and derides the claim that there was any other — "not one jot or tittle" — than circumstantial evidence presented. It commends McKeown for the "fearless" discharge of his duty, and points out that the mystery surrounding the axe — "Where was it when the room was searched?" — is sufficient to cast doubt on the conviction. Collins, he argues, deserves "every ounce of fair play that British law will give him." It is written "in letters of gold that a man is innocent until he is proven guilty, and if a judge happens to be overzealous and charges a jury a little too strongly, that same British justice intervenes and takes away any bad effect which might possibly have resulted in consequence."

Charles Morris, the Harvey magistrate married to Father McAuley's niece, wrote to the *Journal* to counter the assertion of "Justice" that the axe could not have been missed if it had been, for the entire time before its discovery, in the priest's bedroom. He points out that the rectory was vacant for much of that period and that, owing to a badly positioned heat register, the room was too cold to be used as sleeping quarters in the winter. In fact, he argued, it was by merest chance — the hoisting of a window and a strong gust of wind — that the axe was found at all.

Morris closes: "Mr. Editor in conclusion, in my humble opinion in this case of murder it is not British Justice to allow men to discuss the innocence or guilt of Collins in the columns of the *Albert Journal* over a *Nom de plume*. The men who aspire to discuss the ruling of the Supreme judges or the innocence or guilt of Collins, should be possessed of manly spirit enough to write over their own names, and if they refuse, the waste basket is the proper place for their letters."

In the next issue, appeared this statement from the *Journal's* editor: "As far as the *Albert Journal* is concerned, the controversy about the New Ireland tragedy must cease. A number of letters have been received this week for publication, but they have been consigned to the waste basket. There is nothing to be gained by a controversy. The matter is of too horrific a nature to be weekly presented to the reading public. Collins will have another trial in June, and it will be for the jury to say whether he is guilty or not."

The public debate in the Hillsborough weekly paper ended, but Collins continued to receive intermittent attention in the provincial press. In March there was a report that the prisoner had received a letter from a sister, who said she was glad he would get a new trial. Her fiancé also wrote to say that Collins' mother had been injured in a fall. Collins, the report observed, "was apparently a good deal affected by the news."

Premier Pugsley, meanwhile, was asked in the provincial legislative assembly about the cost of holding a second trial. "The government," he replied, "recognizes the fact that the case is a hard one. It is to be regretted that, owing to a misdirection on the part of the judge, it will be necessary to have a second trial, which will largely increase the cost. With regard to relieving the county, the matter is one of considerable difficulty for, under the law, the county must pay. The government, however, will be prepared to pay for the expenses of the arrest and for the expert testimony of Doctor Addy and Doctor Andrews. Further than this I am not able at present to say." (Two years later, in April, 1909, the provincial government agreed to pay from its treasury $2,500 to defray in part the expense incurred by the Collins trials — about half the total cost.)

3.

The second trial began on Tuesday, June 25. This time William H. Tuck, chief justice of the Supreme Court of New Brunswick, was on the bench. Solicitor General W.P. Jones appeared again for the crown, while Collins was represented once more by James Sherren and H.A. McKeown, the latter recently returned from his honeymoon vacation in Europe. Judge Tuck was an elderly, clean-shaven man, except for a wispy growth of side-whiskers, which extended to his shoulders like long tendrils of pale moss. He impressed the gallery with his physical and mental vigour, his intelligence, and the business-like way in which he ran the court. He complimented the people of Albert on their new courthouse, which he called a credit to the county. Judge Tuck dispensed quickly with the case of a small thirteen-year-old fatherless boy from Caledonia, Freeman Collins, nabbed Sunday at midnight by Constable Hyslop inside Thomas Peck's store in Albert. The weeping boy pleaded guilty to the charge of entering with the intent to steal — a charge which, if he were a man, would have given him seven years in the penitentiary.

Eliciting the boy's promise that he would lead a better life, the judge said he would deal with him as leniently as possible, but would have to give him some punishment. The sentence was two months in jail.

Attendance at the opening morning session was small, though it picked up considerably by afternoon. It was a raw windy day for late June, a cold drizzle adding to the rather unpleasant conditions. But waning interest in the case may have been as much a contributing factor in the relatively small attendance as the weather. Selection of the jury was a more laborious ordeal than at the first trial. Seventy-one men were called. A great many, subjected to vigorous examination by a vigilant defence, were rejected. "It was surprising," noted an observer, "the number of men who stated they would be governed by the old evidence." Judge Tuck, however, claimed the matter of having previously formed an opinion was of no special importance, the question being whether the mind of the man was such that he could give an honest verdict on the evidence presented at this trial. Five men were selected from the first panel of twenty-one and only four from the second panel of twenty. By mid-afternoon the twelve had been selected, all but one identified as farmers. They came from the four corners of the county. It was expected this trial would take as long as the first; it would last for seven days.

When the grand jury had been dismissed, Collins was brought to the courtroom by Constable Rose and Constable Coonan. He had changed little in appearance since February, still pale but rather more fleshy. He was neatly attired, sporting a white collar and red tie, but, taking his seat in the dock, he seemed to observers not in the best of spirits. He was nervous, fidgety, serious, but occasionally glanced around the galleries, nodding in acknowledgement of a greeting from an acquaintance. He listened attentively as Solicitor General Jones gave his opening address, his head thrown back and resting on his hand against the railing. But, according to one newsman's account, he seemed to take particular interest in Jones' account of the finding of the axe, showing considerable agitation, moving about in his chair uneasily, his face flushed perceptibly.

The lineup of witnesses was virtually identical to that of the first trial. Court officials were called to read the transcript of Father McAuley's evidence from January. A great deal of attention was paid once again to the stains on the axe, but with no greater degree of resolution than that achieved at the first trial. A new witness, twelve-year-old Browning Day, said he had been a member of a fishing party at the New Ireland lake which had been joined by Collins. He said Collins had told him that he expected Mary Ann would be cross at him for wasting his time and catching only one fish. The boy added that Collins did not "act very nice when he caught his trout, striking it against the boat and swearing at it."

As the trial wore on and the weather improved, more spectators began to gather. The axe and the commode figured largely in the defence's cross-examination of witnesses, as McKeown and Sherren attempted once more to convince the jury that the axe could not have been behind the commode when Detective Killen searched the rectory and, hence, could not have been put there by Collins. Two new witnesses, Clara Barrett and Laurie Bulmer, told of passing by the rectory Sunday, August 19, at about ten o'clock at night and of seeing a light both in Mary Ann's bedroom and in Father McAuley's office. They were especially struck by the light in the priest's office, because they knew that he was not at home. The prosecution also called two new witnesses from Fredericton Road, apparently to establish that the priest had indeed been in that area, some forty miles away from New Ireland, on the weekend of the murder.

The fifth day of the trial drew to a close. It was Saturday, June 29, and Judge Tuck agreed to a longer adjournment so that court officials, witnesses and the jurymen could celebrate the July 1 holiday weekend. After supper, the courtroom adversaries joined the judge on an excursion to "The Rocks," a geological marvel on the mud-flats where the Petitcodiac and Memramcook Rivers empty into Shepody Bay south of the village. Solicitor General Jones, McKeown,

Sherren, Police Chief Clark, Detective Killen and Judge Tuck were driven the few miles to the site, through the warm, buzzing June evening along the ridge overlooking the Petit-codiac. The Micmacs believed that the powerful Fundy tides had been created by a monstrous whale, friend of Glooscap the Giant, and that the Rocks were members of their own people, once enslaved by the whales of Fundy and turned to stone when they attempted to escape.

Chief Justice Tuck told hovering newsmen that, while there was reason for believing court proceedings could legally be continued on July 1, the public holiday, he had great respect for Canada's natal day and would not think of sitting. On Sunday he attended church service with Chief Clark and the jurymen, while McKeown took the opportunity to continue his sightseeing, visiting the famed underground lake near Albert Mines with Detective Killen. On Monday afternoon, the jury members were taken for a ride into the country, but an unexpected shower dampened their pleasure somewhat.

The pleasant hiatus of the weekend proved to be a quiet prelude for a surprising move by McKeown on Tuesday, when the trial resumed. As the crown closed its case, Jim Sherren rose to make a dramatic statement to the crowded courtroom. He repeated the claim made in January that Collins was friendless and alone in a strange country, and that he had no money to hire detectives to search out witnesses to give him support. He said what small funds had been furnished the defence came from charity alone. He laid great emphasis on the fact that no blood was found on Collins' clothing, and said that someone else must have gone to the rectory and killed the woman after Collins left. Sherren reminded the jury that Detective Killen had been so certain the axe was not in the rectory following his search that he had remarked to Sheriff Lynds, "The axe is not in there."

Then came his startling announcement. The jury, and the eager throng that filled the court, would see Collins himself stand at the bar and declare with his own voice that Mary Ann McAuley had been alive and well when he left the rectory on that warm Monday morning in August. "We will put the prisoner on the stand," Sherren declared, "and you gentlemen of the jury and this honourable court will hear his statement, and he will fully explain to you, satisfactorily, I trust, many of the points which may appear true." It was an unexpected manoeuvre. McKeown and Sherren apparently had re-evaluated the strategy they had employed in the first trial, and had found it wanting. In January, McKeown evidently had thought that his oratorical powers, had he been allowed to address the court last, would carry more weight with the jury than Collins' credibility as a witness in his own behalf. This time, since the defence again would not have the last word, they decided an appearance by Collins, if it went well, could help his case.

Another departure at the second trial was the admission into evidence of the handwritten transcript of Collins' statement to Detective Killen the morning after his capture. Killen had admitted at the first trial that he had failed to warn Collins that his statement could be used against him, and the prosecution had not attempted to have the statement entered. This time the transcript was admitted, and the defence did not object.

4.

Standing easily at the witness-stand with one hand resting on the rail beside him, Tom Collins spoke in a clear voice, relating his experiences in a manner which, to an attentive Judge Tuck, showed considerable intelligence and education. "Part of his story seemed fairly plausible," one of the newspapermen wrote the next day, "but in many points was decidedly weak. He showed deep embarrassment under Mr. Jones's cross-examination." Though he was on the stand for more than an hour, Collins' evidence was largely anti-climactic for anyone following the case closely. He repeated details he had given Detective Killen about his family and his youth in England, saying he had followed the sea since he was thirteen. He was one of six children, his father having died in 1901 and a sister just a few weeks before the trial. In his twenty-first year he had come to Canada — May, 1906 —

arriving at Montreal on the fourth of June with fifteen shillings in his pocket. He had stayed there a few weeks, then came east.

He had seven dollars, he said, when he was hired by Father McAuley, and still had it when he left. He had told the priest that he knew nothing about farming or horses, in fact, had never harnessed a horse. The night that he arrived, he said, Miss McAuley had unharnessed the horse and shown him his duties. On Tuesday, the priest showed him how to split wood, but he didn't understand the work, and made poor progress. He told of the fishing trip on Thursday, when he had caught only one fish. Mary Ann told him he would have done better if he had stayed home from the lake, but there was no quarrel. He said he opened a tin of cream and put some in a glass of water, but Mary Ann didn't mention the matter to him. He said he had not heard of her wanting him dismissed. She used him well and he bore her no ill will whatever.

On Sunday afternoon he paid Duffy's wife the fifty cents left by Albert Gross for the care of the horse. After supper he went to Williamson's, taking a small can of water to drink, as the water at the rectory was warm. He got back from Williamson's about seven o'clock and did not leave the house that night. He and Mary Ann sat for some time on the verandah talking of his travels, and he went to his room at nine o'clock. He heard Mary Ann moving about in the kitchen for awhile, then things got quiet. He got up and went to Father McAuley's room, where he took some stereopticon views, putting them into a valise that had been left under the bed in his own room.

He rose at six o'clock Monday morning, took some more things from Father McAuley's room, but did not break the doors or use the axe on them. After making the fires, he did the chores at the barn, and was piling up shingles in the woodshed when he saw Mary Ann in the kitchen. She was dressed in a kimono, moving about the room tending to her duties. She came out and told him to go in and get his breakfast. He did, and Mary Ann went to the barn. After breakfast, she told him to clean the horse and showed him how to harness the animal. When it was ready, he held the shafts of the buggy while she backed the horse between them and did the hitching. She spoke to him again about not catching more fish, and he told her if she did not stop talking about it, he would leave. Mary Ann was not dressed for the planned trip to Albert. She spoke of it being very hot, and said she might not go until evening. She picked up a pail and left the building, heading for the spring behind the church. That was the last he saw of her. As soon as she was out of sight, Collins said he put on his coat, retrieved the valises, and struck out on foot, crossing the road and going through the cemetery on the north side of the road opposite the rectory. He went through the bushes for about fifty yards, then returned to the road. From that point on, he said, his travels and statements had been faithfully and truthfully reported by the various witnesses. He heard nothing of Mary Ann's death until told of it by Detective Killen.

When he was at Dean's Hotel at Musquash, he heard the telephone bell ring. Although he could not hear what was said, he thought Father McAuley might be looking for him because of the valises and other things, so he left in a hurry. He had Mary Ann's watch when he left the rectory. She had given it to him some time before, saying they were going to Albert and she would drop him at the watchmaker's, where she wanted him to get it repaired. He had the watch at John Martin's place at Spruce Lake, but lost it later. He supposed it had fallen from his pocket, while he was drinking from a stream. He did not wash his clothes after leaving Father McAuley's, and any dampness in them was from perspiration.

"Now," said McKeown in a stern voice, "I want to ask you, did you strike Mary Ann McAuley with an axe?"

Collins replied, with firm voice and unwavering gaze, "No, sir."

"Did you," asked McKeown, "commit this foul murder?"

"No, sir."

"Did you break open the doors of Father McAuley's closet?"

"No, sir."

McKeown was finished with his examination.

Solicitor General Jones stood beside the long polished table in front of the bench to begin his cross-examination. He had razors on his mind. Father McAuley had testified at the earlier trial that several were missing from the rectory. What happened to them? Collins said he had taken only one of the priest's razors, leaving the others behind. The suggestion that he had thrown one away was not true. Collins said he knew that Mary Ann was physically stronger than he and could have overpowered him, and if he had met her as he was making off with the valises, he would have given them up. In fact, he said, the reason he had turned back to the rectory after setting out on foot Monday morning was that he intended to give her the valises and to ask her to let him go.

He did not smash the doors in Father McAuley's closet and was not looking for money, he said. He repeated the story of Mary Ann giving him her watch. He had not intended to take it with him, but forgot he had it until he reached Forest Glen. Then he thought of returning it to her if he had a chance. He said his story to Aylesford Mitton about Miss McAuley giving him two dollars was merely an excuse. He admitted making up the story he told at Ruth Leaman's — that the priest's horse had been stolen — in order to deceive them and get away with the valises. When he left the property Monday morning, he said, the horse was in the yard. He never saw it again. He denied positively that he was looking for the horse in order to get away with it. He asked Tilman Bannister if he had seen the horse along the road, he said, because he had noticed Bannister looking with suspicion at the valises he was carrying.

"You have made up a great many lies, haven't you, Collins?" the solicitor general said.

"Yes."

He said he told Miss McAuley on Monday morning, after she had referred again to the fishing trip, that he would take his coat and leave. He was not cross, but intended to go while she was at Albert. The reason he gave for leaving was that he did not like the work, and he had made up his mind to go on Sunday, when they came back from the lake. In connection with the light being on in the priest's office, he said Mary Ann told him it was because Father McAuley might return unexpectedly. He had intended to leave the articles at Mrs. Williamson's, but she was not at home when he passed by. He went out the Kent Road, because he knew it led to Elgin and he wished to give the valises to Father McAuley. But he changed his mind because he became afraid that the priest would have him arrested. He said he was told by Detective Killen how and where the body of Miss McAuley had been found, and he afterwards saw it in the papers. He had found the two valises because Miss McAuley had told him to put them under the bed in his room earlier in the week.

"When did you stop being an honest man?" Judge Tuck asked.

"When I stole from Father McAuley," said Collins. "Before that I did nothing that wasn't straightforward and honest."

"Why didn't you go on the witness stand at the last trial?"

"Because I was advised by my counsel not to."

McKeown's address to the jury, described as a splendid effort, set forth in ringing tones and eloquent language, was virtually a repeat of the ideas he had presented to the jury at the first trial. This time, however, he referred to Collins' own testimony, and asked what more an innocent man could do, than to subject himself as Collins had to the cross-examination of the learned counsel for the crown and to any questions that the bench or the jury might ask. He said Collins' story on the witness stand was practically the same as that given to Detective Killen after the capture, and to McKeown himself when Collins was under the shadow of the gallows. And it was the same story he would tell, whether he went out of there a free man or under sentence of death.

In his argument, described as full, clear and logical, Solicitor General Jones said it was the most natural thing in the world for the prisoner to deny his crime. He said the jury could not for a moment believe that Miss McAuley ever gave the prisoner her watch; it was too unreasonable. "In fact, you can't imagine any reasonable or rational story that would fit in with the innocence of the prisoner. The circumstances are too strong against him." Why would Miss McAuley put the valises in his room, when there were plenty of other places? Where was she when Collins was passing back and forth in front of the house? Would he do such a thing if she were alive and well? Was not the whole thing a tissue of lies and most absurd?

5.

Chief Justice Tuck had the last word, and a cranky one it was. If anything, it was even stronger against the prisoner than that of Judge Gregory in January. While he did not place the bloody axe in Collins' hands as had his predecessor on the circuit court bench, Judge Tuck completely discredited Collins' claim that he was given the gold watch by Mary Ann.

"I was curious to know," he said, "how he [McKeown] was going to account for having Mary Ann McAuley's gold watch upon him. I could not conceive of his explanation. Can any ordinary mind believe it, gentlemen, that she would give him her valuable watch on Sunday night to keep all night and take to the jeweler's the next day when she was going to accompany him? And the way he says he lost the gold watch; is it reasonable that he stopped to drink at a spring and that the watch dropped from his pocket?"

Immediately the chief justice finished his charge, an aghast McKeown was on his feet.

"Your honour," he said, "might I ask you if you could not charge regarding the watch more favourably to the prisoner?"

"In which way?" asked the judge.

"I have no hesitation in saying to your honour, that your charge has been much stronger against the prisoner than was the charge at the other trial," said McKeown.

"I may have spoken with a louder voice."

"I did not touch upon the watch," McKeown continued, "but the learned solicitor general addressed the jury regarding it, and now you, your honour, have strengthened his argument. I did not touch upon the watch."

"You ought to have done so," His Honour snapped.

Solicitor General Jones intervened.

"I object," he said, "to Mr. McKeown addressing the jury further."

"Yes, yes," replied Judge Tuck.

"You ought not to do this," said McKeown.

"I, as chief justice, have the right to preside here and have the last word with the jury," he declared. Then turning to the panel seated on two rows of chairs to the left of the bench, he said, "Gentlemen of the jury, the responsibility is now with you. Take the evidence as it has been given and do your duty faithfully and fearlessly."

After three hours of deliberation, the jury was completely divided. They reported their disagreement to Judge Tuck, and he told them to try again.

"Can we find a degree of guilt?" one of them asked.

"There are only two findings," replied the judge, "guilty or not guilty."

But the next morning, the result was the same: five in favour of conviction, seven against. It was generally believed that the seven jurors who had voted for acquittal were strongly opposed to finding a conviction for a capital offence, the penalty for which was execution. The solicitor general told the press there would undoubtedly be a third trial in September. Since the first had resulted in a conviction, overturned on appeal, and the second in a disagreement, he believed it was the duty of the crown to secure a decision in the matter, if possible.

McKeown said the finding of the jury was partially satisfactory though, of course, he had hoped for complete acquittal. He attributed the difference in the results of the two trials largely to the care shown in the selection of the jury. Each juryman had been subjected to an examination as to whether or not he had formed an opinion concerning the case, and as to whether such opinion would prejudice him in considering the evidence. More than forty of the panel of seventy, he said, admitted, when questioned under oath, that the opinion they then held would probably be influential. The twelve selected, while most admitted having formed an opinion, said they would not allow the opinion to influence them after hearing the evidence.

McKeown said that, unquestionably, the clear and un-hesitating answers to all questions put to Collins produced a marked effect on the jury, and he attributed the result to a considerable degree to the prisoner's own testimony. While there remains a large body of opinion in the county adverse to Collins, he added, those who had been in close contact with him during his imprisonment nearly all believed he was not guilty. "Of course, I am thoroughly convinced of his innocence of the crime charged." He said he did not speak to Collins after the trial, except to say goodbye and that he would see him again in September.

(In an unusual development, in the midst of the third trial, the seven jurors from the second who had voted for acquittal issued a statement to the newspapers disclaiming the conventional wisdom about their decision. "Sir," they wrote, "will you kindly allow us space in your paper to contradict a statement which has been circulated through the press. It was reported that the reason that some of the jurymen voted for acquittal in the last trial of Thomas F. Collins, was because they did not believe in capital punishment. This statement is false and misleading, as our conclusions were based solely upon the evidence which we did not think strong enough for a conviction.")

So it was back to the cell for Tom Collins once again. He dropped out of the news for the rest of the summer, except for a small snippy item in the *Albert Journal* in late August which noted, "The prisoner looks well and gives orders concerning his food and drink much the same as though he were in a hotel. Often the notices for a change of menu are in writing. The visits of the prisoner's woman friend from Hillsboro still continue."

6.

The trials of Tom Collins, as they ranged through the seasons, went from January frost to the warm and myriad shades of June green; now they would be surrounded by the pleasant primal colours of autumn. Judge D.L. Hanington of

Dorchester was the third member of the province's Supreme Court to be sent to Hopewell Cape to preside over the crown's proceedings against the accused killer. Judge Hanington, fully-bearded with closely cropped hair and deep-set dark eyes, was disposed to get things over quickly. He decreed that court would start earlier in the mornings, and that some evening sessions would be held to expedite matters.

This time, 121 citizens were summoned to appear for jury duty, the largest panel assembled in the history of the county. Selection of the jury, as McKeown had pointed out following the second trial, was an even more crucial element in the resolution of the case. Both sides questioned the men closely. Solicitor General Jones, bearing in mind the popular belief that jurors at the second trial declined to convict Collins because of the death sentence that would follow, was especially interested in their views on capital punishment. Eighty-eight men eventually were set aside by either the prosecution or the defence before the panel was complete, seven because they declared themselves opposed to capital punishment.

Though the newspapers reported that interest in the trial continued to be intense all across the province, actual attendance was considerably lower than before, in part because it was harvest time. "The Collins trials," a Moncton newspaper claimed, "are unique in the criminal history of New Brunswick, if not in Canada. It is the first time, it is believed, that a prisoner sentenced to death in the province was granted a new trial on the grounds of misdirection by the court — thanks to a legal technicality picked out by the clever defence counsel — and it is also the first time, not only in the history of the courts of New Brunswick, but in the history of the courts of Canada, that a prisoner has been tried three times on the same charge of murder."

Meanwhile, another fund to pay for the defence had been established, this time in the Moncton area, though neither the names nor the motives of the interests behind the effort not survived. Chief Justice Tuck had pointed out at the last trial that Collins was extremely fortunate to have a man of the calibre of H.A. McKeown working for him for a pittance;

his services, said the judge, usually went for fifty dollars a day.

As court opened, Collins was back in the dock, looking much the same as in the summer, though the pallor of his face was more pronounced. He was neatly attired in dark blue serge with a light four-in-hand tie. He wore no vest this time. He was calm and composed as usual, and soon assumed his familiar pose of leaning back in the chair, the back of his head resting against the palms of his hands, fingers threaded, eyes intently watching the judge. "A stranger happening into the courtroom this afternoon," a reporter mused, "would never think that a murder trial was in progress. The small attendance was noticeable, there being besides the officers scarcely a score of spectators in the whole house." It was a busy time of year for the rural people, and some of the witnesses were called with a view to their own convenience as much as possible, as they were anxious to get home to continue work on their farms.

The presentation of evidence was very much a reprise of proceedings at the first two trials. But this time, in cross-examination, Jim Sherren asked Doctor Murray, the coroner who had examined Mary Ann's body, whether he had held an inquest following the death of Father McAuley in February.

"No," said Doctor Murray.

"What did you ascribe as the cause of death?"

"If it is material to this matter," Judge Hanington interjected.

"I will merely say," the doctor replied, "if it is not material, I do not think it is worthwhile my answering the question. I have no objection to answering it. There is a professional etiquette between the patient and the doctor, and that is why I do not answer."

"Then I withdraw the question," said Sherren.

McKeown recalled Doctor Murray later in the trial so that he could question him more closely on the bloodstains in the woodshed, and any light they might shed on the timing of the killing. It was a ghoulishly fascinating, ultimately pointless exercise, but it demonstrated once more how difficult it was for the attorneys on either side to get precise physical evidence.

"How long would it take — estimate a person's throat were cut like that," McKeown began, "how long would it take by gravitation for the body to empty itself of blood?"

"I couldn't say positively," Doctor Murray replied. "It wouldn't take long. I had occasion to use a knife just a short time ago in a case where the patient had died, all used up with rheumatism and very much disfigured, so they couldn't get the patient into the casket. They sent for me to straighten out the patient. Well, there was an oozing of blood when I made the incisions, but I couldn't positively state how long it would ooze out. It would be more or less from the nature of the patient than otherwise."

"What I want to know is, the throat being cut in the way it was, in regard to those conditions, how long do you think it would take for the blood to drain itself from the body by gravitation?"

"Of course, all the blood wouldn't come out."

"All that would really come?"

"I don't know that I have any particular data to go by to state exactly the time it would take, and I don't know that I have any authorities."

"You couldn't give any idea?"

"I couldn't give any authorities."

"I gather from the way you answered other questions the flow would be slow?"

"Yes."

"There would be no spurting out?"

"No, it would be slow, but as to the time, I couldn't state."

"There was a pool of blood on the floor by the mat and by the overalls?"

"Well, of course blood makes a good show."

"Judging by the impression, I gathered there was quite a large amount?"

"Quite a flow."

"Could you give us any idea how long the body would have had to lie there to make the pool of blood you saw?"

"I couldn't state."

"Do you think it would in half an hour?"

"I think it would."

"You think it would take half an hour for that amount of blood to ooze from the body?"

"Well I should think the flow of blood would be stopped inside of half an hour."

"He is asking you," said Judge Hanington, "how long it would take for that quantity of blood to flow from the cut."

"I couldn't answer that exactly."

"Was there as much blood on the floor as there was down on the shingles?" asked McKeown.

"I think there was more."

"Was there quite a little bit of it on the shingles?"

"Well, you see it trickled down through the shingles and I couldn't tell how much was there, but it appeared there was more on the floor than on the shingles."

"Relatively?"

"Yes."

"Twice as much would you say?"

"Well, as I stated before, you see they stated it had run through the cracks on the floor, which I didn't examine underneath, but some of the other witnesses stated something had run through, but my opinion would be there was quite a bit more on the floor than on the shingles."

"Would your opinion be the blood had ceased to flow from the body when the body was put on the shingles?"

"I don't think entirely."

Judge Hanington intervened again. "Would all the blood flow out of the body after death? Wouldn't it depend on how the body was lying?"

"Somewhat."

"And if the body was hauled along the floor might that not start it again?" asked the judge.

"Yes."

"And if the person or animal," the judge continued, "was struck very dead, would there be as much flow of blood as if not struck so dead?"

"No."

"And," said Judge Hanington, "you say this blow would strike them dead?"

"Well, substantially so."

"All of the blood then," Mckeown resumed, "that would ooze in the position that the woman was lying in on the floor might have gone out, and the change in her position might have brought some out afterwards?"

"The change in position would bring some more."

"You can't give us any idea as to what amount of time it would take for the amount of blood you saw indicated there to leave the body?"

"I couldn't give you."

"It would be a slow flow?"

"A slow flow."

"It would ooze slowly?"

"Slowly."

"How much blood is there in the body, in a woman of her time of life and preservation and size?"

"Well there would be about a gallon; perhaps not quite that much, in her condition."

"How much would you say it would take to make those stains you saw there on the top of the floor?"

"I think from a pint to a quart would make it."

"Then whatever had gone down underneath on the timbers, as there will be some testimony to show, would be in addition to that?"

"Yes, there might be a pint would make what stains were there alright."

"Would it make any difference as to the amount of blood that would flow, according to the way she lay on the floor? Say if she lay on her face, would more flow than if on her back?"

"I don't think there would be much difference in that after death."

"She would bleed as much one way as another lying down, would she?"

"Well, there wouldn't be very much difference."

"Then from what you saw you would conclude, wouldn't you, that all the blood had left the body that would leave it, before she was moved from the floor to the pit?"

"Oh, I don't know, I couldn't tell. As I said before I couldn't tell what quantity had trickled through the boards on the floor, and therefore I don't know whether all the blood had ceased flowing before she was moved or not, that would naturally flow after death. I couldn't tell."

"Thinking it over, how much would you think now it would take to make those stains?"

"I think I said a pint could make all the stains I saw."

"Could you say how long she would have to be there before a pint or quart would flow from her?"

"I couldn't say, because there were large arteries cut."

"Do you think half an hour?"

"I wouldn't think she would have to lie there that long."

"Perhaps not more than a quarter of an hour?"

"That would be about my judgment, maybe a little more than that."

And so it went.

While it was widely expected that Collins would be put on the stand to tell his story once again, those who had come hoping to hear him would be disappointed. His counsel decided not to call him nor any other defence witnesses. Though Jim Sherren would say later that Collins had not been well enough to testify, McKeown gave another reason to the court in his closing argument. "It makes little difference," he said, "whether the accused himself goes on the stand or not, for it might be responded that one guilty of a great crime would have no hesitation in denying it on the witness stand."

7.

Judge Hanington gave a very carefully worded charge to the jury. He did not put the bloody axe in Collins' hand as had Judge Gregory at the first trial. "The law is for me," he told the jury, "the facts are for you." He asked more general questions about the evidence that had been laid before them. The principle involved in circumstantial evidence, he said, is this: "You must be satisfied of the existence of the facts from which you draw your conclusions; you must be thoroughly satisfied, not that the fact was possible, but that it existed, and not absolutely satisfied, but satisfied beyond a reasonable doubt." He defined a reasonable doubt: "You must be satisfied of the fact so that if you had to act upon that fact in some most important and serious matter of your own personal concern and that of your family, you would take it for granted that the fact exists and you would act upon it."

"You are practical men," he added. "Let me say there is no tribunal under the face of Heaven that is so well qualified to decide as to facts as is an independent, impartial, intelligent, honest jury. You are living in the country and you are acquainted with the ways of living in the country, with the circumstances of the country, with what takes place in the work of the country, in the action of individuals, and you are identified with them more than any man can be who sits upon the bench."

An important question that must be considered carefully, he said, is this: When did Collins, who admitted carrying goods away with him from the rectory, pack the valises? Did he do it in the presence of the woman? If not, where was she? And what was his knowledge of her whereabouts? Why would someone chop at the closet doors in the rectory? Would they do so in the knowledge that the housekeeper was alive and in the house? Why wasn't the job of breaking into the closet finished? Was the person disturbed while chopping at the door? By what? Would a wagon passing by on the road outside disturb the person? How did the axe get behind the commode? The police say it wasn't there when the room was searched. Could the police have made a mistake?

"If the axe wasn't there, by whom was it put there? If you find it wasn't there, and wasn't put there until after he (Collins) was met on the road, then I say you could find him not guilty; but if it was put there that morning before the prisoner left there, and was accidently not discovered by the detectives, then, if you believe that, that is a very different state of facts. You are practical men, and you may know that you have looked for things yourselves and your wife or some member of your family may have found them in the very place you looked. I do not mention that to say that the axe was there, but it is for you to draw your conclusions as practical men as to whether the axe was there or not."

Hanington also did not charge as strongly on the watch as had Judge Tuck at the second trial. He did say, though, that Collins' explanation for having Mary Ann's gold watch "struck me as a strange thing, but it is for you to say." He spoke to a current rumour that county officials were beginning to complain about the cost of trying the accused murderer of Mary Ann McAuley. "I imagine," he said, "that is a rumour without any foundation. The expense to Albert County is not an ingredient in this at all. If this murder took place, and there seems to be no doubt that it did, then the blood of the victim cries to Heaven for vindication — I am not saying too much — and it is upon the county of Albert, not to seek a victim, not to convict a man who is not guilty, but to see to it that every reasonable expense is incurred and every trouble is had to see that blood is vindicated. I am satisfied that in this county of Albert, which I know pretty well, nowhere, in no heart or breast of the community, is there any such feeling, and the question of expense has nothing whatever to do with the results in this case."

Judge Hanington urged the jury to accept that the question of capital punishment had no place in their deliberations. "Capital punishment has been the law of this empire for over a thousand years. Capital punishment is not commanded by our empire and our law alone, but it is the command of Almighty God. *Whosoever sheddeth man's blood, by man shall his blood be shed.* In case a life be taken, in case that life, a part of the essence of the Almighty himself, that life that never dies, in case that life is sent back to its Maker before he calls for it, in case of wilful, deliberate murder, the blood of the murderer is the expiation, as far as this world goes, of that murder."

The jury retired at 10:50 a.m. At 2:35 p.m. it returned with a verdict of guilty. Collins was sentenced to be hanged on Friday, November 15.

8.

The *Transcript*'s headline the following day:

Thomas Collins' Wonderful Nerve Did Not Forsake Him.

The trial, which has lasted seven days, has been carried through in a manner which has been creditable to all concerned, and the result would appear to be only one that could reasonably be expected. Judge Hanington's charge to the jury was most favourably commented upon and was certainly a model of impartiality. The counsel for the defence considered it absolutely fair and satisfactory.

Intense silence fell on the throng of people that filled the building. All eyes were turned on the prisoner, who stepped lightly into the dock, laid down his cap and took his seat. He showed a consciousness of the presence of the supreme moment, but in the trying hour when the tick of the clock would tell his fate, his wonderful nerve did not forsake him. Pale but with marvellous composure and motionless and erect of figure, the youthful prisoner stood in the dock and watched Judge Hanington as the fateful words were uttered, never once giving the slightest trace of emotion during the terrible ordeal.

In a low tense voice, Judge Hanington asked Collins whether he had anything to say why sentence should not be passed.

"I have nothing to say."

"You were taken into the service of Father McAuley," Judge Hanington continued, "a warmhearted and kind clergyman, and there in the quiet hours of morning, while the priest who trusted you was absent from his house, you betrayed your trust and took an innocent life by striking down most ruthlessly a lone and harmless woman. I do not know how you could be betrayed into such sin. God alone knows. I implore you now to seek forgiveness of Almighty

God and prepare for that moment a few weeks hence, when you must stand before your Maker, when your spirit which God gave you will be ushered back to His presence.

"Personally I have not the slightest doubt of your guilt and I admonish you with all kindness and earnestness to seek repentance and that consolation that is not withheld from the vilest by the blessed God who said *Though your sins be as scarlet, they shall be as white as snow; though they be red like crimson, they shall be as wool.* Yes, though as red as the blood of that sacrificed woman whose life you took away. You have only a short time to live and I implore you to make good use of that time. It is now my solemn and imperative duty to pronounce upon you the sentence of the court, which is that you be taken hence to the place from whence you came and there kept in close confinement until Friday, the 15th day of November, when you will be taken to the place of execution and hanged by the neck until you are dead, and may God have mercy on your soul."

Chapter Twelve

"Not a proper person to be executed"

1.

Hopewell Cape 1907

Please Mrs. Milburn:

Could you kindly send me your daughters Florence, her address, hoping you are all well at home also Florence. I am getting along alright myself. Mr. Porter and Mrs. also Laura are doing nicely (also the chickens). So I think that I ought not to have written you this short note, without my first asking your permission hoping you will excuse me for taking this liberty.

I remain sincerely
Thomas F. Collins
Hopewell Cape A. Co. N.B

Sara Milburn lived with her husband, Asa, her son, fourteen-year-old Jim, and daughter, Florence, at Curryville, a small scatter of houses on Demoiselle Creek, a few miles over the hills due west of Hopewell Cape. The Milburns were friends of Willard Porter, the Albert County jailer, whose family lived at The Cape in an apartment directly over the cell block. Laura was their thirty-year-old daughter. Laura and Florence, who was twenty, were also friends, and it is likely that Florence met Tom Collins while she was visiting the Porters. It was said at the time that Tom had an eye for the girls. The note to Mrs. Milburn was written on rough blue-lined paper torn from a scribbler. Her response to it, if there was one, has been lost in time.

On another sheet of paper, Tom drew a picture of a woman wearing a long-belted blue winter coat with fur on the collar and hem. The face is tiny, and she appears to be carolling, her small mouth shaped in a singing "O." On one hand at her waist is a fur muff; the other holds a sheet of paper. On her head, a blue-brimmed hat with large showy feathers. Scrawled up one side of the sheet of paper in large-lettered handwriting is the signature "Thos. F. Collins." Again, at the bottom of the sheet is written "Tom Collins."

Tom's residence for more than a full year — the county jail — was (and still is) a two-storey structure built in 1845, the year the politicians were at work cutting Albert off from Westmorland County and proclaiming Hopewell Cape the seat of the new county government. The squat lower half of the building was constructed from cut stone with walls twenty-six inches thick. The jail sat solid on the hill like a boulder, hunched near the classical grace of the courthouse and the other scattered county buildings, overlooking the grey-brown waters of the Petitcodiac and the homes and public wharves of the shiretown. Strung along the front of the building was a split rail fence following the contours of the sloping field. The wooden second floor level of the jail provided living quarters for the jailer, whom the county paid eighty dollars a year for services rendered.

A visitor would climb the pyramid of seven wide stone steps, with the moulded iron railing set into them, to thump the heavy front door of the jail, fitted with snug precision into finely-cut stone jambs and lintel. Overhead, resting on four posts, was a steeply-pitched porch with a wooden skirt, into the front of which was cut a window. Inside the front door the visitor would face, across the room, a portcullis-like iron grillwork made of widely-spaced pronged pickets like upright spears, closing the cellblock off from the lobby and the stairway to the jailer's apartment.

The centre cell of the block, with its low vaulted ceiling of rough-textured stone, was called the dungeon. It served as the drunk tank and, when necessary, the solitary confinement cell. In the centre of the concrete floor was fixed a heavy ring bolt to which a recalcitrant inmate could be shackled.

The three-inch-thick iron-reinforced wooden door, with a six-inch-wide keyhole for the latch bolt lock and another hasp lock at the foot, had an eight-inch-square aperture at mid-level with a sliding panel for mealtimes and, perhaps, wood fuel in season. The single window, set into the two-foot-thick stone wall, had two sets of bars; the inside grate made of five round iron bars six inches apart passed through three flat iron crosspieces; the wider outside grate had five square bars set a foot apart. The comforts included a straw pallet thrown on the floor without a bed frame, and a small wood stove.

Tom Collins had spent some time in the dungeon, but for most of the year was detained in the smaller, but more homey cell beside it. This small room was used primarily to segregate prisoners awaiting trial on more serious criminal charges. It was furnished with wooden bunk beds. It had a plank floor, a plaster ceiling, and a cast-iron wood stove. Inmates of the jail were not treated harshly, most being residents of the county who in a rash liquor-fuelled, usually harmless episode found themselves momentarily outside the confines of the law. Prisoners were often released to help with the harvest during haying season, to work on dyking crews on the tidal marsh, to swing a pick and shovel on a road crew, to work bent-over in the gardens and potato fields of the local residents. The more harmless occupants of the jail were permitted to keep their jackknives, so they could while away their time whittling on small chunks of softwood or carving initials into any wood surface within their reach.

These were quiet days for Collins, who had little to do in his cell but to read, talk to his visitors, and await word on the commutation request. Since there were no legal grounds to support an appeal of the last conviction, the final hope of Collins and his supporters was that the federal government of Prime Minister Wilfrid Laurier would set the sentence aside. It was a pleasant time of year. Looking through the barred window at the rear of his cell, Tom could see children in an apple orchard on the hill behind the jail. The girls in long dresses, the boys in shorts, they moved intently beneath the branches among the dark and scaley trees, picking the red-green fruit from the ground. One of the larger boys reached up to a low-hanging branch and, gripping it in both fists and lifting his feet from the ground, shook more apples free, the young ones laughing and skittering away. Across the quiet afternoon, Tom could hear the faint pulses of the fruit striking the ground, the high careless eternally durable voices of the young ones making play of their work.

Collins was still buoyant in October when a newspaper reporter gained admission to his tiny cell to talk. "With the day appointed for his execution only four weeks away," the reporter wrote later, "Collins, in his cell in the county jail, preserves the same calm composure that has characterized him from the start."

When the *Sun* correspondent talked with him awhile, he appeared in excellent spirits, laughing and chatting pleasantly. He is enjoying the best of health, though is somewhat thinner in flesh, this being due, he claims, to the physical exercise he takes in his cell. The prisoner evidently hopes for the best, so far as the commutation matter is concerned, but is prepared for the worst, and if the death sentence is carried out there is little doubt he will go unflinchingly to the gallows. He says he is innocent and has nothing to fear. Looking the reporter square in the face, the prisoner said, 'I tell you now, as I have told from the beginning, I did not do it, and this story I will tell when I stand with the rope about my neck at the gallows.'

The prisoner speaks as though he might be sent to the penitentiary, but providing the death sentence is carried out, he assured the reporter that he would stand the ordeal firmly. The prisoner says he eats and sleeps well, and he still reads with avidity the magazines and papers sent him, and busies himself drawing pictures, at which he is quite adept.

He plays the mouth organ considerably and entertained the scribe with *Blue Bell* and *The Good Old Summertime*, the performance, which was a very creditable one, necessarily having a pathetic side, which interfered somewhat with the visitor's enjoy-

ment of the music. Collins speaks very gratefully of
his counsel, Sheriff Lynds, and others who have used
him well, and appears very appreciative of acts of
kindness towards him.

2.

The legal wheels continued to turn, inexorable as the country
seasons, but not as visible. On the last day of September,
Judge Hanington, in a scrawled script on Supreme Court
letterhead, wrote from his Dorchester home to the federal
department of justice, reporting on the trial, conviction and
sentence. Within eight days, Sheriff Lynds, warm-hearted,
amiable, anxious, was reluctantly looking for professional
help. He addressed a plea to the federal minister of justice.

"I shall be very much obliged if you will let me know at
your earliest convenience whether or not I can procure the
service of Radcliffe, the official executioner, to carry out the
sentence of the law upon Collins at the date named. If I
cannot procure the services of Radcliffe, is there any other
person whose services could be procured in his place and who
has the necessary experience? Your early reply will very
much oblige. Your obedient servant."

Two days later, from Ottawa, he had a less than encouraging response from E.L. Newcombe, deputy minister of
justice. "Referring to your letter of the 8th instant, the address of J.R. Radclive, the hangman, is 54 Fern Avenue,
Toronto, but this department has no communication with
him, nor can I give you any further information about an
executioner. The local authorities are charged with the administration of the criminal law in the provinces, and if you
require any instructions you should communicate with your
attorney general."

Within three weeks, a new attorney general for New
Brunswick would be named, and he would be H.A. McKeown.
Following the trials, McKeown had decided to resume his
political career and, earlier in the month, had won a by-elec-
tion for a seat in St. John county. (He once explained that he
was being "jocular," when quoted by a reporter as having
said, "I never intended being a politician, and my political

life is an accident which will not be followed any further.")
On October 28, Clifford Robinson, who in June had succeeded
William Pugsley as Liberal premier, asked McKeown to be
his attorney general. It is unlikely that McKeown's accep-
tance of the cabinet post had anything to do with his desire
to save Collins' life, but both he and Premier Robinson would
write letters of support to the federal authorities.

On October 11, the federal justice department asked
Judge Hanington for a transcript of the evidence presented
at the September trial. It was sent a week later. Sheriff
Lynds, meanwhile, lost no time taking his grievance to the
new attorney general. He would take no part, he declared, in
the hanging of Tom Collins. Two days after his appointment
to the New Brunswick cabinet, McKeown wrote to the deputy
minister in Ottawa:

"Fearing it might get into some other channel and be
overlooked, I am writing to say that I have addressed to the
Minister of Justice a communication concerning a little difficulty which has arisen in Albert County in consequence of
the High Sheriff of that place declining to execute the death
penalty on Thomas F. Collins, who has been convicted of
murder. You will see from the letter to the minister, which
goes forward by this mail, that I am inquiring as to whether
anybody could be got to relieve the sheriff of that duty. I
would be very much obliged if you would favour me with a
reply at your earliest possible convenience, and if there is
anybody available by the department, I would like to secure
him for the work, in case the petition for a commutation is
not granted." This time the reply came from the acting
deputy minister, but it was no more agreeable. "I am afraid
the department cannot be of much assistance," he wrote
McKeown.

McKeown's letter to the minister, A.B. Aylesworth, was
somewhat stronger. He wrote that Sheriff Lynds was
prepared to resign his office rather than execute the death
penalty himself. "I may add that a largely-signed petition for
commutation is on its way to your department, and as the
evidence was wholly circumstantial, I think the ends of jus-

tice would be met by commuting the present sentence to imprisonment for life."

Aylesworth's reply was firm, if rather disingenuous. He could in no way interfere with the carrying out of the sentence, and if the law takes its course "the duty of the sheriff in the matter is clear." He added that the matter of clemency rests with the Governor-General-in-Council and "I cannot anticipate, much less forestall, the decision." What he did not say was that his department could have a role to play in recommending clemency. While an order-in-council is made by the governor general, it is in effect a cabinet decision approved by the governor general. And in the case of applications of clemency, the cabinet would rely heavily, if not exclusively, on the recommendation of the minister of justice.

Collins' supporters in the county, however, weren't waiting for the politicians to resolve the matter. On October 1, a number of petitions asking that the death sentence be commuted to life imprisonment began to circulate throughout Albert and Westmorland counties. No one person was given credit for the crusade, but Jim Sherren had agreed to take the petitions to Ottawa. McKeown, asked by reporters about the petition effort, denied having anything to do with it. According to the newspapers, "Several ladies of Hillsborough were, it is understood, the first to suggest the step, and the suggestion was followed up by several prominent residents in the county." It was the only course open to them and, because the evidence was circumstantial, there was considerable optimism that the death sentence would be set aside. The *Albert Journal* reported, "There is little doubt in the community that Collins is guilty, but there has been and is now in some quarters a strong feeling of repugnance against the hanging taking place."

The text of the petition recounted the details of the crime and the three trials, then stated: "The evidence against the boy was wholly circumstantial. From the time of being accused he reiterated his innocence, and at the second trial he went on the stand and gave evidence in his own behalf, denying his guilt and accounting for his movements on the day in question. At the time of the third trial he was broken in health in consequence of the long strain involved in being put on trial for his life three times within nine months, and he was unable to take the stand in his own behalf. Your petitioners would therefore humbly pray that his Excellency would be pleased to exercise his power by reprieving the sentence of the young man from capital punishment to imprisonment for life, and as in duty bound will ever pray."

The petition was circulated throughout October, receiving more support in Westmorland County and the northern section of Albert, and when Sherren took it to Ottawa in early November, it bore 488 names (not the 800 to 1,000 names reported in the press), including those of some of the jurors who believed Collins was guilty.

3.

A woman living in Halifax, a former resident of Moncton, was moved by newspaper reports of the efforts to save Collins' life to write a confession to Jim Sherren. The letter, dated October 20, begins: "Having just read the steps you are taking to save the life of Collins, I am pleased to be able to tell you that I know that John Sullivan went to the gallows an innocent man." Sullivan was a man hanged at Dorchester several years earlier for the murder of Mrs. Dutcher of Meadow Brook. The letter writer claimed that she and her daughter knew all along that Sullivan was innocent. Not only did she see Sullivan as a passenger on a train with her at the very time that he was alleged to have been murdering the unfortunate Mrs. Dutcher, but she also saw the very next day the man who was the real killer. This man, she claimed, appeared at the door of her home in Moncton, drenched "from head to foot" in blood, asking for food. Notwithstanding his appearance, she fed him and he went on his way.

"I have heard poor Collins trial all through," she wrote, "and I firmly believe he is innocent also. I am writing you this letter that you may believe me Sullivan should never have been hanged. I do not wish my letter published, at least my name, but I trust if you read it to Collins it may comfort him to know that there is one who believes him innocent."

The *Transcript*, which published the letter, posed the obvious query at the end of its report: "The only question that might arise is that if the woman knew all these facts which she professes to, why did she not come forward at the time of the trial, and thus save Sullivan from the gallows?"

4.

As the pressure from Albert County continued to mount, the acting deputy minister of justice in Ottawa was studying the transcripts of the evidence. On Saturday, November 2, he sent a memorandum to the minister. "Upon reading the report of Mr. Justice Hanington and the very voluminous evidence —not all directly relevant, it must be confessed — I am compelled to agree with the learned judge's conclusions that if capital punishment is necessary in the interests of justice and the security of life, then this is a case where not the slightest reason can exist why this prisoner should not suffer that penalty."

As the justice department prepared its recommendation against commutation in the Collins case, Sheriff Lynds and the petitioners had a final card to play. On Thursday, county coroner Doctor Suther Murray came to examine the prisoner in his cell. According to the *Journal*, Doctor Murray told Sheriff Lynds that while Collins' mind was weak, he would not undertake to say professionally that his condition was such as to relieve him from full responsibility for his actions. He suggested that Doctor Anglin of the Provincial Hospital for Nervous Diseases in Saint John be sent for. The sheriff did not agree. The next day he called in three medical doctors from Hillsborough.

The brief handwritten reports of the men, all addressed "To whom it may concern," were similiar. Though Doctor Murray stopped short of asking for commutation, he said that, having had the opportunity of carefully observing the convicted killer on several occasions, "I am of the opinion that he is and has been, since I have seen him over one year ago, suffering from a certain form of idiocy or weakmindedness caused by self-abuse, and does not realize the enormity of his crime. He is undoubtedly a moral degenerate."

Doctor E.C. Randall, a twenty-five-year veteran of county medical practice, found Collins to be suffering from "congenital insanity and idiocy of a pronounced type and, in my opinion, is thoroughly irresponsible for his actions. He is certainly a person who should not be executed, but detained in some institution fitted to receive and care for that class of people. He has no realization of his position or the enormity of the crime for which he is under sentence."

Doctor John P. Lewis of Hillsborough, after a "thorough examination" and several observations during the past fourteen months, found the prisoner suffering from "congenital insanity and idiocy, and irresponsible for his acts and deeds." He should not be hanged, he said. Doctor Lewis' colleague, Doctor Bliss Marven, who had attended some of the court sessions and visited Collins professionally in his cell, called him "mentally unsound. I should classify him an imbecile. From conversation I learn that he springs from alcoholics, particularly his maternal ancestry. As a medical man I have no hesitation in saying that I do not believe him to be a proper person to be executed."

There were letters from Sheriff Lynds and jailer Willard Porter, witnessed by and sworn before Justice of the Peace Willard O. Wright. Porter said he had Collins in his custody and had been in daily personal communication with him for the past fourteen months, and unhesitatingly declared him to be "of unsound mind and irresponsible for his actions, without any sensibility whatever seemingly of his position, and the fate he is sentenced to. I do not think he is a person who should be executed, but should be imprisoned for life." Porter added that Collins had consistently asserted his innocence of the murder.

Sheriff Lynds, in his declaration, gave his own reading of Collins' condition, saying he had conversed with him a good deal during his incarceration and "I believe him to be a person of unsound mind and irresponsible for his acts." He should not be executed. The sheriff recommended the examining doctors as being very experienced respected physicians within the county. Justice of the Peace Wright added, at the bottom of the sheriff's statement, his own testimonial to the skills of the doctors.

Collins' friends took another step, prevailing upon Premier Robinson, who was in Moncton, to give his endorsement of the doctors' diagnoses. Addressing "to whom it may concern" on the letterhead of his office, the premier referred to the men as "all reputable and reliable. They are all men of good standing in the communities in which they live and recognized as reliable citizens, and are also men who take a high standing in the medical profession."

Premier Robinson also wrote separately to federal Justice Minister Aylesworth, saying Rev. Thomas, chaplain of Dorchester Penitentiary, had asked him to implore mercy for the prisoner. "The Rev. Mr. Thomas has a strong conviction from personal intercourses that the boy might be innocent." The premier pointed out that a number of jurymen, "who are prominent citizens in the county," had voted for acquittal at the second trial. "The further fact, strange as it may seem, that the sheriff who has Collins in custody, will probably resign rather than execute the sentence on the ground that he too does not believe him guilty, causes some doubt to arise; and there certainly should be no doubt in a case of this kind."

Aylesworth replied, as he had earlier to McKeown, that he could not interfere with the decision of the Governor General in Council. McKeown, meanwhile, wanted to know whether a warrant of execution was required from the governor general. "The Criminal Code seems to make no provision for such precept, but it is the opinion of one of our judges that a warrant comes from your department." No such warrant is issued by the government, came the reply. "All arrangements for the execution are necessarily under the charge of the local authorities who are responsible for the administration of criminal justice in the province."

McKeown wrote next to the deputy justice minister, to inform him that Jim Sherren was on his way to Ottawa with the petitions for commutation. "In view of the fact that the evidence was circumstantial wholly, that one jury disagreed, and that every doctor in Albert County certifies that he is irresponsible," McKeown added, "I believe the ends of justice will be fully met by a commutation to life imprisonment."

In his own statement accompanying the petitions, Sherren said there was a widespread feeling in the county that Collins was not responsible for his actions. At the third trial, he said, Collins had not been able to give the testimony that he had given at the second trial. "He was unable to tell us (his counsel) anything or practically anything at all, stating to us that his mind seemed to have failed him utterly and he could recollect nothing. After the death sentence had been passed upon him, I visited him in his cell and he seemed not to understand or comprehend the position in which he was placed. He acted like an imbecile or some person mentally deranged. He had a target which he had made and two or three darts made out of corks and hairpins, and he amused himself with this as a child would. It was impossible to get any reasonable conversation with him."

Sherren suggested that if a commutation be deemed improper, then a medical man of recognized ability in mental diseases ought to be sent to examine Collins' condition. "I would further submit after this be done that Doctor Anglin of Saint John, superintendent of the provincial hospitals for nervous diseases, a recognized expert in those lines, who is within a few hours journey of the place of Collins' confinement, be sent to him."

Sherren had his wish granted partially, for one more player was about to enter the drama. He was Doctor Daniel Phelan. Known in the popular press as a leading "alienist," the fifty-three-year-old surgeon was the medical superintendent of the insane ward at Kingston Pentitentiary in Kingston, Ontario. Just a week before Collins was scheduled to die, Deputy Minister Newcombe sent Doctor Phelan an urgent telegram: "Please come here and see me immediately with a view to going out to Hopewell Cape, N.B., to examine and report upon mental condition of Collins sentenced to be executed next Friday. Wire when you will be here." The decision of the cabinet whether to commute the death sentence would turn on Doctor Phelan's quick assessment of Collins' mental condition.

5.

Tom Collins continued to bide his time in Willard Porter's cell, as the politicians and public servants of the country to which he had come less than two years before were trying to decide whether he should die. Two newspapermen, who went to visit him in the last week, reported that of all people in the village, he seemed the least concerned about his fate.

In his cell in the little stone jail at Hopewell Cape, Collins still maintains the air of cheerfulness, almost indifference, which has characterized him ever since the beginning of the trial. Spending his time in reading, drawing, writing to friends, or amusing himself by throwing a cork and pin dart at a target on the wall, Collins seems to think little of the fact that he has but a few more days to live.

When jailer Porter bore his breakfast to him yesterday morning, the condemned man remarked that he wanted to see no one all day. But when told by Sheriff Lynds that two *Transcript* representatives wished to see him, the prisoner said he would be very glad to see them.

Collins is confined in the centre of the three cells with which the Albert County jail is equipped, and from the small opening cut near the top of the heavy iron-bound oak door which opens into his cell, he can look forth through the jail hallway to the road, and the distant Petitcodiac River. A smiling face and a hand outstretched through the opening in the door met the newspapermen as, accompanied by Sheriff Lynds, they were taken to the cell.

'Glad to see you,' was Collins' greeting. 'Pretty bad weather we're having.'

He spoke as though he was not standing in the shadow of the gallows, and as one who was in his home receiving an ordinary call. His smile was pleasant and he conversed genially as he stood in shirt-sleeves, looking through the opening which for fourteen months had afforded him practically his only view of the outside world. The window by which his cell is lighted is high up, and heavily barred. He was evidently glad to see the visitors and talked freely. His conversation turned quickly to England, and to the life of his old home.

'The Manchester United team is leading the First Division of the Football League,' he said. 'I used to play football in Manchester and we used to have good sport. I played with an industrial school team.'

'What was the best game you ever played in, Tom?' asked one of the men from *The Transcript*.

'We played a game once with a team that had never been beaten and it was great sport. We won the game by a penalty kick a minute before the end.'

He told of being in Glasgow watching the International game at Ibrox Park, on the occasion when a row of seats collapsed, killing many people, and also told of attending games at the Crystal Palace in London.

'Do you smoke, Tom?' asked one of the visitors.

'I like cigarettes,' he replied, and was delighted when some cigars and half a dozen cigarettes were passed through to him.

His cell was stacked high with magazines and reading matter. 'I read all that,' he said, 'and a lot more that I have given away. But I get tired of reading sometimes, and then I draw pictures.'

He was very grateful for the promise of some English newspapers.

The week before the scheduled date of execution, Jim Sherren, who was staying at Ottawa's Russell House, was alarmed by a report in a capital newspaper. He had handed the petitions over to justice department officials on Tuesday, November 5, but the story which appeared the following Friday prompted a concerned letter to Deputy Minister Newcombe. "I understand from the public press," Sherren wrote, "that an Order In Council was made yesterday allowing the law to take its course ... If this be correct, the matter I presume was decided at Wednesday's meeting of the Executive Council. As the petition was only presented the day before and some facts in connection with the case not until late in the afternoon, I am afraid that perhaps all the data referring to Collins' condition may not have been considered."

Sherren pointed out that Collins was a stranger in Canada, with neither friends nor influence. "All efforts which have been made on his behalf have been through the kindness of the people of the County of Albert. The money raised by subscription for his defence was very small and after the first trial my colleague, Hon. H.A. McKeown, now attorney general of New Brunswick, and myself, were compelled to defray the expense out of our own pocket. And certificates as to Collins' condition which have been made by the Albert County doctors were not obtained by influence or by payment of money, but were given by the doctors voluntarily after they had, gratis, made an examination of this unfortunate young man."

Sherren repeated his conviction that Collins was mentally incompetent, perhaps had been during his entire time in Canada. "I take it to be the spirit of the law relating to capital punishment that where a person condemned to death is found mentally irresponsible by medical men qualified to judge, that he should not be executed but incarcerated in some institution fitted to his condition." At the third trial, Sherren said, they had intended to put Collins on the stand again, but the day before the crown case closed, his mind began to wander, and he was unable to recollect anything about the facts he intended giving evidence on. "I have, since the last trial, met some of the jurymen and I may say that had Collins been mentally able to have given his explanation, I feel sure from what the jury have since told me there would have been a disagreement at least."

If the executive council did not deem it wise to grant the commutation on the doctors' certificates alone, he argued, then grant a reprieve and send a commission to inquire into Collins' condition. "I have no hesitation in saying that if this be done, it is my firm opinion that the commission would find him mentally of such a nature that they would decide he was not a person to be executed. If, however, this were declined I would ask a reconsideration of the whole matter, and that some effort be made to ascertain the mental condition of this man before the date of execution."

The deputy minister, the next day, sent a response to the Russell House. He wrote that Sherren was mistaken in supposing that a decision had been made; Collins' fate was still under consideration by the executive council. He assured the Moncton lawyer that his views would be carefully considered. On the same day, he notified Doctor Phelan officially of his assignment in Hopewell Cape. "You will report to me fully at the earliest possible moment," he wired the doctor, "stating your opinion as to the prisoner's mental condition generally, and in particular, but without regarding this as a conclusive test of responsibility or of sufficient capacity, will you be good enough to state your opinion on the question: Is the convict labouring under natural imbecility or disease of the mind to such an extent as to render him incapable of appreciating the fact that he has been convicted and sentenced to death for the murder of Mary Ann McAuley, and that he is presently to suffer the punishment pursuant to the sentence?"

The doctor had five days to get to Albert County, to conduct his examination and to report back to Ottawa. He set out immediately on the *Intercolonial* to the Maritimes, and later would complain of the conditions he found when he arrived in Albert County. "Hopewell Cape is rather backward as to position," he would observe, "and is not accessible by train. It is twenty-two miles from Moncton over a muddy country road. The whole distance I made with horse and buggy on my return trip, as it was the only way I could reach Moncton that day in order to get off my telegram. It was rather tedious, but I was so engrossed in the duties which I was commissioned to perform that I made the best of it." Doctor Phelan's telegram was received by Deputy Minister Newcombe on Wednesday, November 12, less than forty-eight hours before Collins was scheduled to hang. The visit of the "alienist" to Hopewell Cape had been noted by the New Brunswick media but, since they did not know who he was and Sheriff Lynds refused to divulge his identity, they referred to Doctor Phelan in their reports as the "mysterious stranger" who had come to call on Collins.

Wednesday was also the day that the reluctant J.R. Radclive, finally summoned from his Toronto home, arrived at Hopewell Cape. There was no mystery about his identity or his purpose.

6.

Rev. Byron H. Thomas, Protestant chaplain of Dorchester Penitentiary, had taken an interest in the young prisoner jailed at The Cape, after Collins' spiritual adviser left on a trip to Boston. (Ordained in 1888, Rev. Thomas became the penitentiary chaplain that year and would remain until 1911; by 1920, he was still in Dorchester, though no longer serving in the Baptist ministry.) Dorchester and Hopewell were on opposite sides of the Petitcodiac River, but Rev. Thomas made regular ferry crossings to Albert County to talk and pray with Collins. Whether he knew what Doctor Phelan's assessment was is not known, but on the same day that the "alienist" drove to Moncton to report to Ottawa by telegram, Rev. Thomas dispatched his own wire to Sir Wilfrid Laurier.

"As spiritual adviser of Thomas Collins now under sentence of death at Hopewell Cape, I beg to express my unqualified conviction that the condemned man is mentally unsound. In making this statement I am not moved by pity or sympathy, it is a conviction formed by very careful observations during repeated visits to the condemned man's cell. Have had an extensive opportunity of judging, as I have done a good deal of religious work among the insane class. Will be greatly relieved if the cabinet in its wisdom recommends a commutation." The prime minister told his private secretary, E.J. Lemaire, to pass the wire on to the justice department, and to ask whether any word had been received from Doctor Phelan.

One more letter from a New Brunswick cleric urging commutation went to the justice department, this one from Rev. G.B. Trafton of Marysville, a community near Fredericton. Rev. Trafton, pointing out that an Ontario man's death sentence had been reduced on November 6, asked why the same couldn't be granted in Collins' case. "Gentlemen, if you could see him and hear him, notwithstanding all that has been said on either side as touching his case, I believe you could not help being convinced of his irresponsibility. And I ask you in the name of High Heaven if possible to reconsider his case and to commute his sentence to imprisonment for life. This letter is unsolicited."

There was no shortage of clergymen calling on Collins in the days leading up to the date of execution. In the quiet of his prison cell, he had undergone a marked change. "Much of his former cheerfulness has left him," said a reporter who visited the condemned man, "and his demeanor is now serious and thoughtful. He reads the Bible a good deal and appears to be making preparations for the end that soon must come." Just outside the jail walls, and well within the hearing of the condemned man, the carpenters were busy preparing the gallows. Collins was visited by two Salvation Army officers one afternoon, and in the evening Rev. William Lawson, Methodist clergyman of Hillsborough, and Mrs. Isaiah Steeves paid a lengthy visit. Rev. Lawson said the young man was making proper preparations for his last hour, and was gradually reaching a satisfactory spiritual condition. He had not asked him about his guilt or innocence, and there were no reports that a confession was forthcoming. Before leaving, the clergyman and the lady sang several hymns in the cell, and Collins was said to be greatly affected. Some of the hymns were unfamiliar to him, but he was acquainted with one and joined in the singing of it.

Rev. Thomas was expected to remain with the prisoner until the end. It was a gloomy time for the entire community, the preparations for the hanging casting a pall over the village. While there was a strong feeling among many in the county that the ends of justice would be served by imprisonment, it was not a unanimous view, and there were a number to whom a change of sentence would not be welcome news. In fact, an opposing petition was circulated and forty names gathered. "We the electors of Hopewell Cape," it stated in part, "having heard that a petition asking for the commutation of the sentence of Thomas F. Collins has been prepared and circulated throughout this county and in Westmorland

County as well, and that the impression is current that practically all the residents of this place are unified in the prayer of such petition, hereby desire to place ourselves on record as being entirely opposed to any such proceeding."

The petitioners claimed that certain statements in the earlier petition were untrue, that no person ever charged with the crime of murder in New Brunswick had had a fairer chance, or been granted a fairer trial, that it was wrong and mischievous to interfere with the operations of the criminal law, and that some of those who signed the earlier petition did so after being impressed with the thought that the execution of the death penalty would be a stigma on the village. "We on the other hand believe that it would be a stain on the fair name of Hopewell Cape, the shiretown of the county of Albert, if we connive at the miscarriage of justice, or endeavour to assist any officials charged with the unpleasant, but important and honorable duty of carrying out to the letter, the commands of our King and his laws, to shirk or escape the complete requirements of office."

The villagers who signed that petition were not to be disappointed. On Tuesday Doctor Phelan's telegram reporting on his examination of Tom Collins was received by Deputy Justice Minister Newcombe in Ottawa. The cable, sent collect at twelve noon on the wires of the Great North Western Telegraph Company of Canada, was unequivocal and Collins' options had run out.

I find the prisoner Thomas Francis Collins well developed, well nourished, and free from any physical disease or infirmity. His conversation is coherent and intelligent, and his replies to questions do not suggest any particular mental impairment. He has a good memory, can converse intelligently, can argue reasonably, and has no delusions, hallucinations, or illusions. His conduct in relation to those over him has been in agreement with every act of intelligence. He is neither confused in his recollections, nor wanting in words to express himself, and he sleeps and eats well. Whilst he may not be possessed of high mental organization, I do not find that he is labouring under natural imbecility or disease of the mind to such an extent as to render him incapable of appreciating the fact that he has been convicted and sentenced to death for the murder of Mary Ann McAuley, and that he is presently to suffer the punishment in accordance with the sentence. He has full conception of the position in which he is placed and the nature of the sentence passed upon him.

In a letter to the deputy minister two days later, which included an invoice for $99.81, Doctor Phelan said, "the so-called imbecility plea was supposed to have been originated and vigorously circulated by a few sympathetic residents of the district. The plea gained much ground, and adherents to it from all quarters were invoked to support the theory. It was at once apparent that the prisoner had been schooled to play a part or to affect some of the extreme manifestations of the disease, which he failed to carry out successfully under my examination."

As soon as Doctor Phelan's cable was received on Tuesday, November 12, the minister of justice reported to the Governor General in Council that he was unable to see any reasons for interference with the due course of the law. Based on this advice, the Privy Council committee considering the matter, in a report signed by clerk Rudolphe Boudreau, issued a recommendation to Governor General Earl Grey adverse to commutation. The offical business was complete — in Ottawa. At Hopewell Cape, however, Sheriff Lynds was still holding out, refusing to let Collins be taken to the gallows without an authoritative declaration from the federal government.

Shortly after 4:00 p.m. on Thursday afternoon, Attorney General H.A. McKeown sent from Fredericton identical cables over Canadian Pacific telegraph wires to Ottawa, one to Justice Minister Aylesworth, the other to Secretary of State R.W. Scott. They read: "Will you please see that the pleasure of his excellency is communicated to the sheriff of Albert County, New Brunswick, as to carrying out death penalty on Thomas F. Collins, sentenced to be hanged on fifteenth instant. Sheriff declines to act without it." Secretary

285 THE RECTORY MURDER

of State Scott responded immediately, with a wire to Sheriff Lynds stating that the law be allowed to take its course. It was followed by a letter from P. Pelletier, acting under-secretary of state. At 1:20 a.m. Sheriff Lynds cabled his acknowledgement of the decision from Ottawa.

J.R. Radclive would go to work in the morning.

Chapter 13

Thursday, November 14, 1907
Friday, November 15, 1907

1.

Reporter Elmer Ferguson recalled many years later that he had spent the eve of the execution playing cards with the hangman in his room at the Albert Hotel. "Radclive drank a good deal of whiskey to settle his nerves. No one would speak to him except myself, so we became quite chummy. He grew nervous as he ran out of whiskey. The night before the hanging, he and I played cards in the little parlour of the small hotel and, upon retiring, or at least preparing to do so, I warned John to be sure to waken me in time, as I wanted to be on the job for my first assignment of the kind. John said he might forget, suggested I bunk in with him, which I did."

2.

Collins reacted with "absolute composure" to the news that the campaign for commutation had failed, and that the death sentence would be carried out, Ferguson wrote on the day before the scheduled execution.

> The nature of the unofficial report of the government's refusal to interfere with the sentence was imparted to the condemned man by Sheriff Lynds, the prisoner receiving the intelligence that removed his last hope with the same coolness of demeanor that he has shown all through, and giving undoubted evidence that he will be game to the end. Although the doomed prisoner had evidently hoped

for the best, it is not probable that the final decision at Ottawa was a great surprise. He had referred frequently of the matter to visitors, as though he might get a reprieve, but in conversation not long ago he expressed himself to the effect that the petition would probably not accomplish anything. He still stoutly protests his innocence.

Collins told friends that he was resigned to his fate. He reportedly gave Rev. Thomas a long list of relatives in England to be notified of his death. One of his last wishes was that the magazines and other reading matter in his cell be given to the library of the Maritime Penitentiary at Dorchester. "In the last few days," a reporter observed, "a great change has come over the prisoner. He still retains the wonderful composure which characterized him during his trials, but from worldly matters his attention has turned to his spiritual welfare."

During a prayer with Rev. Thomas, he broke down and asked once again that they recite together with the minister the 51st Psalm: "Have mercy upon me, O God, according to thy lovingkindness; according unto the multitude of thy tender mercies blot out my transgressions. Wash me thoroughly from mine iniquity, and cleanse me from my sin. For I acknowledge my transgressions: and my sin is ever before me." Rev. Thomas claimed that the young man had had a wonderful religious training, and could quote many passages from the New Testament; his reported fondness for the words "my sin is ever before me" led some observers to wager that he might make a confession.

3.

Collins had passed a very bad night Wednesday, sleeping only about two hours, and spending a great deal of his time pacing the floor of his cell. He ate nothing when breakfast came the next morning, but drank three cups of tea. Rev. Thomas was in the cell again, and Mrs. Isaiah Steeves — who had also started a subscription list for the fund towards his defence the previous fall — spent a couple of hours with him. During his interview with her, Collins twice broke down. He ate a little stew for dinner and drank a cup of tea for supper, but refused more solid food. He complained of being unable to sleep, saying he felt he needed rest.

Shortly after five o'clock in the afternoon, he asked Sheriff Lynds to summon the reporters for the *Globe* and the *Transcript* to his cell.

Collins was pale and showed the strain under which he was laboring, but smiled cheerfully as he stretched a steady hand through the opening in the cell door to shake hands and seemed very pleased to meet *The Transcript* representative.

'*The Transcript* has been very fair to me all the way through,' he said after a few words of greeting had been exchanged, 'and so has the *St. John Globe*. I want to thank you for this, and I want you to thank through your paper all the friends who have been so kind to me.

'*The Transcript* has been very fair to me hasn't it, Mr. Thomas?' he asked, turning to his spiritual advisor.

'You sent me some books and papers,' he added to the reporter, 'and although I can't reward you, I know that the Lord will.

'I wish to express my thanks for the thoughtful attention of Rev. Mr. Thomas and my dear mother, Mrs. Steeves, and the other friends who have visited me and sent me literature to while away the hours of my confinement. I am ready to die, and shall try to go like a man. I am trusting in my Saviour, who has proven my greatest source of comfort in my trouble, and know that he will never forsake me.

'The people have been very good to me,' Collins said, and his voice trembled. 'Mother is here with me now, and Rev. Mr. Thomas.

'I am not afraid to die, and I will play the man to the end, and I am glad that Radclive is here, so that there will be no bungling. I am trusting in my Maker, who has looked after me through my trouble, and will look after me to the end.'

Collins' voice was steady as he spoke of his impending death, but it trembled as he stretched forth his hand through the cell door opening and said, 'Goodbye.'

That evening he dictated to the chaplain a formal letter of thanks.

To my dear friends:

I thank the editors and staff of the *St. John Globe, St. John Sun* and *Moncton Transcript* for their kind treatment in reference to my case; also to the kind people of Albert and Westmorland counties for their kindness in signing the petition for clemency in my behalf; also to the kind people who wrote private letters in my behalf to the cabinet officials who had the disposition of my case; also my heartfelt thanks to those generous people who contributed to the fund for my counsel, Hon. H.A. McKeown, who with his learned colleague, Mr. James C. Sherren, did all that human aid could do for me, for which the Lord will reward them. I thank also Sheriff Lynds for his great kindness and consideration for me; also Mrs. I.B. Steeves, who has been a mother to me and tried her best to save me; also to the jailer, Mr. Porter, his wife and daughter, Laura; Mr. James Archibald, wife and children; Mr. H.B. Coonan, constable, for their kindly favors; not forgetting all the many friends who visited me in the cell, remembering also those who wrote me letters in my hours of trouble. I earnestly pray that the Lord will reward my spiritual adviser, Rev. B.H. Thomas, and the Rev. H.D. Worden.

With these words I will close my letter of thanks, declaring that I am trusting in Jesus Christ, who died for me and the world for the remission of all sins. Does not the Holy Word say, 'He that believeth in Me hath everlasting life'? I am trusting in him who died for me.

Thomas Francis Collins
Hopewell, Albert Co., November 14, 1907

A story in the *Sun* described the mood of the community on Thursday.

Thomas Francis Collins' last night has arrived and by the time the sun is shining over the shiretown the condemned murderer of Mary Ann McAuley will have paid the penalty of his deed. Resting under the shadow of the dreadful event, the first of its kind in its history, the quiet village has over it a mantle of gloom, and a feeling of depression and awe pervades the entire community. All day long the villagers and strangers passing along the main street have been watching the tall walls of the enclosure now completed, in which the doomed man will be swung into eternity.

The scaffold was finished at six o'clock tonight to the entire satisfaction of hangman Radclive, who speaks highly of the work done by foreman W.E. Calhoun, the builder. The platform stands on four posts and is eight feet square and eleven feet from the ground. In the centre is a double trap door, the two leaves of which fall from the centre on hinges each side. The doors are held in position by cross bars, released by the moving of a lever. Through this opening the condemned man drops almost to the ground, or nearly eleven feet. The rope with the proper amount of slack is fastened to a cross beam six feet above his head.

The trap was tested this evening and found to work satisfactorily.

The prisoner is making preparations for the end and is in a penitent frame of mind.

A pathetic feature of today was the giving away by the condemned man of various trinkets of articles in his possession to members of the jailer's family and others who have befriended him, to all of which he has expressed his gratitude for their kindly acts.

The large pile of magazines which fills one corner of his cell, the prisoner gave to Chaplain Thomas, his spiritual adviser, for use in Dorchester penitentiary.

To Mrs. Steeves he gave the following poem:

My Dear Mother,
A brighter vision of the light,
Oh mother dear, as from thy face,
Will live in works of pure delight
For love of God or love of right.

Today we grieve and say farewell
With trembling lips and silent tear,
And view the spell we know so well
Throughout this long and dreary year.

May peace and rest be thine alone,
For here thy steps are gently led
To raise and cheer in our distress,
As faith without its work is dead.

COLLINS

Collins was deeply moved when being visited for the last time tonight by Constable Coonan, who knew him so well and for whom the condemned man had a strong liking.

Many letters were received by the prisoner today of a deeply religious tone. One came from Rev. H.D. Worden, who is now in Boston.

The prisoner met Radclive for the first time tonight. When Sheriff Lynds asked Collins if he would see Radclive, the prisoner replied that he would rather not. Later, however, he said he would like to see the hangman. When Radclive visited him, accompanied by the sheriff, Collins grasped his hand and told the executioner that he did not blame him.

Rev. Mr. Thomas said late tonight that he confidently expected Collins to confess to the terrible crime. The confession, if one is made, will not be made public until after the execution.

Men were engaged Thursday afternoon digging the grave by the jail, near a small clump of trees. In the evening, the coffin was carried to the waiting room, and coroner Doctor B.A. Marven had already empanelled a jury in readiness for the inquest.

4.

Several times during the night, Collins broke down and wept uncontrollably on the chaplain's shoulder. Mrs. Steeves, who was to stay until after midnight despite Radclive's protestations, was overcome when Collins kissed her a last farewell. "Goodbye, mother" were his final words to her as she left the cell. It took some time for him to recover, but he eventually composed himself and lay down on the cot. Rev. Thomas remained seated beside him; a number of Collins' favourite hymns were read: "How Firm a Foundation," "What a Friend we Have in Jesus," "Jesus is the One," "Nearer my God to Thee," "Just as I am." The chaplain read and explained passages of Scripture: the 121st Psalm, the 21st Psalm and Chapter Three of the Gospel According to St. John. As he recited the 16th verse — " ... that whosoever believeth in him should not perish, but have everlasting life" — Collins whispered over and over the word "whosoever." Then he added, "That means even me."

At ten minutes past three in the morning, he dropped into a quiet sleep, awaking about five minutes after six. A plate of fried eggs was brought in, but he ate very sparingly. He insisted, however, that Rev. Thomas eat something, and the chaplain had a cup of tea. A short solemn Scripture reading was followed by an earnest prayer, then Collins said his last goodbyes. With arms thrown round the chaplain's neck, he said, "Tell Mrs. Steeves, Sheriff Lynds and my other friends that I am trusting in Jesus. Tell them that I will not disappoint them, but will be brave and courageous to the end." Overcome with emotion once again, he kissed the chaplain and bade him farewell.

5.

Half-past six.

It was grey daylight, the sun hanging low in the cool silvery haze of a cloudless November sky, pale and low over the wide brown river below the jail, its water lapping the mud banks in languid ripples like syrup. The air was cold, and the weak light had not begun to melt the early frost from the trampled grass in the square, or from the smooth skin of the dark river alders along the mud banks, or from the grey shingles of the canted roofs floating in the river mist below the courthouse. The dampness spread beneath the upturned collars of the hunched men, who were passing by the rail fence with its tangle of bare rose briers in front of the jail.

John Radclive with his worn black hanging-coat and ravaged face, a ghoul's cruel parody of the county physician, gripped his black bag of efficient instruments in a gloved fist. He went immediately to the gallows, its gimmicked floor and wide plank steps protected from the early frost by high spruce slab walls thrown up against the curiosity of the villagers. Black felt hung on four sides almost to the ground beneath the scaffold. The dawn light inside the enclosure was dim, but sufficient for the hangman to see that all was in order for the day's work. The black cap was draped over the railing, and the leather strap for binding the prisoner's legs was thrown over the crossbeam. The stout one-inch thick manila rope, with its lethal slip-noose, was suspended from the cross-piece like a fat drugged serpent. Satisfied with the preparations, Radclive dismissed the watchman who had been stationed at the gallows through the night. Then he stood alone in thoughtful repose on the scaffold, waiting to be summoned.

At twenty minutes past seven, he was called to the cell. With solemn demeanour, he went down the short passageway, to where Collins and Rev. Thomas waited. The smell of wood-smoke was in the air, but the fire in the small stove had been left to die down some time before. Collins, standing in shirt sleeves with Rev. Thomas at his side, was shivering.

Extending his hand, Radclive said, "Good morning, Mr. Collins."

"Good morning," said Collins, taking the executioner's hand.

Sheriff Lynds, his broad face distorted by a scowl, came in with another man, James A. Simpson of Amherst, deputy sheriff of Cumberland County, Nova Scotia. Lynds had refused consistently to play any role in carrying out the court's sentence on the young man, and he had decided he would not witness the execution either. Besides Deputy Sheriff Joshua B. Babkirk of Elgin, the official party would consist of jailer Willard Porter and constables Joseph Irving, Elmer Smith and Herman Coonan. Sheriff Lynds had also issued passes to Rev. Thomas and Rev. Lawson of Hillsborough; coroner Doctor Bliss A. Marven and Doctor J.T. Lewis of Hillsborough; Elmer Ferguson of the *Transcript;* Rupert Walker, *St. John Telegraph;* W. Hutchinson, *St. John Globe*; F.G. Moore, *St. John Sun;* C.B. Manning, *Moncton Times*; H. McCready, *Moncton Free Speech*. They would all climb to the scaffold to observe the young man's last living moments.

Deputy Sheriff Babkirk asked Collins to turn, so he could manacle his wrists behind his back. The handcuffs jangled, and the cell filled with the steady breathing of the men. Collins' eyes darted from the grave faces to Babkirk's metal cuffs. Just before he was pinioned, he asked Rev. Thomas to place his hand over his own as he walked up to the rope. Radclive whispered briefly in the chaplain's ear, and the minister nodded. Sheriff Lynds turned and went through the cell door to the passageway, and the procession to the gallows began.

With the two clergymen slightly behind him, Collins walked along the narrow wooden tunnel that led to the scaffold. He was dressed in the clothing he had been wearing when he was arrested — a blue serge jacket and a white shirt. His eyes were red-rimmed from weeping and his face pale, but he marched with a firm steady step. Rev. Thomas' hand gripped his. There was a powerful acrid smell of pitch from the green lumber, and grey light slotted through cracks between the rough-edged slab boards. Outside — but for the brushing wind — silence. Collins looked straight ahead until he reached the foot of the steps leading to the place of execution, then he looked up, and without faltering, began to ascend to the scaffold. The heavy planks with their temporary spikes gave lightly and creaked under the weight of the men. On the platform above, Collins gazed as if entranced at the noose and the other homely implements. The hangman came up the steps just behind him, followed by Deputy Sheriff Simpson.

Once on the platform, John Radclive moved purposefully, wasting neither time nor effort. He placed his hand on Collins' arm, and directed him to the precise centre of the trapdoor. The young man stood shuddering on the scaffold, like a newborn calf, drawing short breaths and watching the executioner intently. Then he closed his eyes, shutting out the men and the slab wall and the grey dawn light, as the black hood slid over his face. The musty smell of the cloth came up his nose, and he felt a strap go snugly round his ankles, as Radclive buckled his feet together. There was nothing then, but the breathing in his ears. Something heavy brushed against his nose through the cloth, then he felt the heavy rope settle on his shoulders. The noose twisted slightly, and he could feel then the weight of the knot, adjusted by Radclive, pressing against his left ear; rough hemp fibres pulled against his throat and chin through the thin cotton.

Radclive's small methodical hands gathered the slack, coiled the rope into short loops at Collins' shoulder and bound them with a thread, so they would not become entangled with the falling body. The thread would snap and release the coils, as the body dropped through the trap. Down in the village, above the river, unseen dogs disturbed from their rest suddenly began to bark one after the other, until there was a muffled distant chorus. The men on the platform — the doomed one, the instrument of the King's will, the servants of the fierce retributive Jehovah of the Old Testament, the mute witnesses standing in for the mob the politicians had banned from the ritual, the men of medicine — stood motionless, each thinking his own thoughts. The hangman stepped back. The young man stood in stiff and silent solitude on the trap. An expiration of breath, then Chaplain Thomas, standing to one side, began to recite The Lord's Prayer, speaking the words in slow cadence.

"*Our Father which art in Heaven, hallowed be Thy name.*

"Thy Kingdom come. Thy will be done, in earth as it is in Heaven.

"Give us this day our daily bread.

"And forgive us our debts as we forgive our debtors.

"And lead us not into temptation, but deliver us from evil ..."

It was precisely 7:25 a.m.

The phrase was the signal, and Radclive pushed the wooden lever. With a dull grating sound, the heavy trapdoors fell open on their hinges and slapped the frame beneath with a loud single thump that sent a shudder through the structure. Collins' clenched hooded form shot from sight. The threaded coils of the rope separated, and the length of hemp snapped into a rigid line that trembled momentarily, then slowly began to swing in tiny declining circles. The men on the platform stood motionless, their heads bowed, as the chaplain finished the prayer. The dogs continued to bark in the distance.

Beneath the platform, Doctor Marven and Doctor Lewis pushed through the black curtain and went to the side of the swaying hooded figure. There was the biting smell of voided bowels. The limbs convulsed within their bindings; the torso twisted slightly as its slow orbit at the end of the rope diminished. The doctors waited; the silent men above them waited. Even though the spinal column had been severed in the fall, Collins' heart continued for a time to do its work. Then after seven minutes it, too, failed, and the doctors were able to pronounce Collins' life extinct. They said later that he had died the instant the rope broke his fall, the spinal cord having been dislocated that efficiently. The body had dropped nine-and-a-half feet, stopping with the toes eighteen inches above the sawdust. It was left to hang in the shadows beneath the scaffold for several minutes more. When it was cut down by Radclive, the cadaver was placed in the green pine box waiting like a cradle in the sitting room of the jail.

6.

The reporters, wanting time to digest what they had just seen before phoning their editors, went off by themselves to begin their stories. Elmer Ferguson would write his account of the execution in a notebook balanced on his knee, as he crossed the river to Dorchester to catch the train for Moncton. Rev. Thomas, showing the strain he had been under in staying with Collins for most of the twenty-four hours leading to the hanging, was very emotional as he spoke to the newsmen. "Although Collins made no confession or statement of guilt," he told them, "I believe he died in the possession of a Christian's hope. He had changed greatly of late and manifested a sincere belief in Christ as his Saviour." Mrs. Steeves, who was staying at the home of Sheriff Lynds, was visited by two of the reporters, who thought Collins might have made a last-minute confession of guilt to her. But she was so distraught that she refused to talk to anyone, only sending word that she had no statement whatever to make. She would not respond to a message asking whether Collins had confessed.

(In the days and weeks that followed the execution, there would be published reports of a confession, all based on anonymous sources, but those who had been with Collins at the end would continue to deny it. Jailer Willard Porter would say he knew nothing of a confession; Collins had not admitted the crime to him, nor to anyone in his family, nor to anyone else who had charge of the jail. Furthermore, he did not believe any such admission had ever been made. When she broke her silence some days later, Mrs. Steeves would emphatically deny there had been a confession.

"That's false, absolutely false. He never made any such admission as this, I am positive. If there was anyone in the world to whom he would have confessed, it would have been me. I have said to newspaper reporters and other people time and again that the boy never once admitted the least shadow of guilt. The people who claim to know that he admitted the crime are only seeking notoriety." She had asked Rev.

Thomas about a confession, but Collins had made no admission of any sort either to him, or as far as he knew, to anyone else. "I was with Collins from Thursday forenoon until early on the morning of his execution, and if he was going to make a confession, he certainly would have done so to me. I have been in the cell in company with Mr. Thomas while Collins was at prayer, and there never was any such incident as mentioned while I was there. You can say from me that all those reports about the boy confessing are absolute lies."

Sheriff Lynds would also reject the claims. "There is not one word of truth in this morning's statement that you have read to me." Collins never admitted to any of the attendants that he was guilty, and the rumours to that effect were wholly unfounded; the sheriff believed he would certainly have known of it, if any such thing had happened. "Mr. Thomas did not say that there was no public confession. He said absolutely that there was no confession of any kind. This morning's story is nonsense." For his part, Rev. Thomas would claim that such reports come to him as "a complete surprise." He had made a statement to the representatives of justice at Ottawa — a record of his statement has not survived — and beyond that, he had nothing to say. "I desire very much that the newspapers allow the matter to stand just there. I am still suffering nervously from the effects of my dreadful experience. Let me repeat finally that the executed man complied with all that the Holy Bible required of him."

The editor of the *Albert Journal* would use this last remark as a premise from which to argue that Collins must have confessed; he could not have complied with the teachings of the Bible, if he went to his grave without confessing his sins. "In other words, Collins did not protest his innocence. He did not go out of the world silent as to the crime. He confessed his guilt — admitted the murder, gave the motive, and told where he placed the axe after the victim was dead and the robbery committed. It is well that this fact has become public for it must remove any doubt as to the unfortunate man's guilt, and his guilt was apparently not clear to all. The taking of a human life by the law is an awful thing, but the punishment is one that fits the crime for which it is the penalty. It is to be hoped sincerely that the New Ireland tragedy will now be allowed to be forgotten.")

Though Coroner Marven had his jury ready immediately the body was taken from the rope, he received an urgent professional call that forced postponement of the inquest until later in the day. When it came, the verdict was that "the said Thomas F. Collins came to his death by a process of Law issued from Mr. Justice Hanington's Court and in obedience to the said order of said court on November 15th 1907." There was a brief funeral service, conducted by Rev. Thomas and Rev. Lawson. The coffin was carried to the unmarked plot by the jail and lowered into the shallow grave. The gravel was thrown in on it, and the men went home.

7.

Picture the boy a final time. With his imaginary friend and his bobbing cowlick, he comes through the tall brown grass in the apple orchard on the knoll behind the courthouse. It is late afternoon, and the sun is sliding below the trees behind him. Long shadows tumble across the field. He can hear the hammers of the men working by the jail. He can see the small mound of earth where the hole had been dug yesterday by men with picks and shovels. The boy had watched from a distance then, fascinated by the sight of the men taking turns standing in the hole as the dirt and rocks rattled out. Now a man and a woman stand motionless by the mound; the woman has a large book in one hand pressed against the dark swell of her dress. The hammer sounds echo from the knoll and drift over the wide impassive estuary of the river below.

The boy and his companion amble side-by-side along the path beside the courthouse, then cross to the front of the stone jail. The men are tearing down the building he had, from a distance, watched them build yesterday. There are screeching sounds as they pry the boards and nails loose, and toss the slabs onto a wagon. A high platform on four stout legs is slowly coming apart, and there is a square hole in the centre of it. The men are ferociously mute as they work, not shouting and laughing like those he had often seen carrying boxes and barrels on and off the boats down at the wharf.

The boy thinks all the activity — and the hole in the ground, too — has to do with the Collins who is in the jail, but no one has explained it to him. He had been told simply to keep away from there. He had heard talk about how this Collins had once killed somebody with an axe, and how a man was coming to *hang* this Collins. What could that mean? At first he had imagined — like a picture book scene of fairies and dwarves — a figure dangling from the coat rack by the front door, or from one of the curved hooks behind the kitchen stove, legs kicking the air foolishly.

But the talk he had heard had been solemn, quiet, portentous, suggesting strange adult doings in a world that little boys could only peer in at, divining, curious, but profoundly apart yet. Hanging, he had perceived with a kind of fleeting but pristine comprehension and shock, meant dying. The boy thought he knew what dying was. He had seen the flattened lifeless body of a rabbit slowly appear one spring from beneath a shrinking mound of dirty snow and ice, fascinated by the sun's slow release of clotted fur and grinning, lunging yellow teeth and dulled flat eyes. He had once seen a man in a blur of violent and stupid frustration, swing a long pole across the back of a horse that was refusing to pull a wagonload of gravel. The heavy pole had skidded across the slick harness, skipped over the hames, and smacked the animal with lethal accuracy behind the ears. The horse had dropped instantly, in sudden and dumb astonishment, beneath a clatter of chains and harness buckles. The man with the pole had gaped on the scene with a marvellously vacant incomprehensibility, his mouth wide open and wordless, but the horse hadn't moved again. Then he had had to pull the harness and straps out from under it, ferociously levering and rocking the carcass this way and that, until it lay in the road in naked reproach. Finally he had brought another horse (furiously muttering to himself) to drag the first away, with its limp trailing hooves and blood-flecked leering muzzle leaving behind (for the boy to study and, finally, to scuff) parallel paths in the powder-brown road dust.

The boy chips away ponderously at this new and still astonishing idea of one man wilfully and with determined purpose clubbing the life out of another. What can it mean? And how is this hanging thing part of it? Uncomprehending and fastidiously mute, he and his imaginary friend stand and watch as the men, in their shirtsleeves and suspenders, knock down the great beams above the platform and heave them onto the wagon with the boards. The boy thinks he might go into the jail building and study Collins himself, but the broad stone steps look like a battlement and the massive wooden door with its iron hinges surely doesn't open to a child's hand.

Instead he watches the workmen some more, as they pry out spikes and hoist boards to sweat-stained shoulders and furiously spit brown gobs of stringy liquid to the ground. Then an old yellow cur, with its nose to the ground, drifting like smoke past the half-loaded wagon and beneath what is left of the platform, stops and sniffs at the dirt, before being chased out of there by one of the workmen, who throws a bent nail at it. The dog flinches from the spot, then drifts in a miraculous dream of soundless locomotion on past the end of the jail and around the corner, the boy and his companion following along. He comes to the mound of new earth and sniffs around its perimeter, before losing interest and slipping silently, as if he had never been, into the long grass on the swale where the kids skate in the wintertime, when there's enough ice. The boy and his friend stare at the mound of dirt. The man and woman have gone away, and they are alone. The boy puzzles over the meaning of the hole now filled; then, like the dog, he forgets about it, too, and continues on across the field for home. The sun is behind it now, and the shadows are gone. The boy is hungry, so is his friend, and it will soon be time for supper.

Years later someone finds a large flat stone, and carries it to the mound that has settled almost out of sight in the steadfast shadow of the impassive jail. They stand it up at one end of the slowly withdrawing grave hill, and splash the crude letters "T.C." on it with paint. The stone stands there for many years before it, too, disappears.